Narrative Innovation

and Incoherence

Narrative

Innovation

and Incoherence

Ideology in Defoe,

Goldsmith, Austen,

Eliot, and

Hemingway

Michael M. Boardman

Duke University Press, Durham and London 1992

PR
826
.B6
1992

© 1992 Duke University Press
All rights reserved
Printed in the United States of America
on acid-free paper ∞

Library of Congress Cataloging-in-Publication Data
Boardman, Michael M., 1945–
Narrative innovation and incoherence: ideology in Defoe, Goldsmith, Austen, Eliot,
and Hemingway / Michael M. Boardman.
p.   cm.
Includes bibliographical references and index.
ISBN 0-8223-1239-5 (cloth)
1. English fiction—History and criticism.   2. Hemingway, Ernest, 1899–1961—
Style.   3. Narration (Rhetoric)   4. Fiction—Technique.
I. Title.
PR826.B6   1992   92-3785
823.009′23—dc20   CIP

For Paula

Contents

Preface

My subject in this book is narrative innovation as it comes to reflect fundamental and, sometimes, disturbing changes in an author's worldview over the course of a career. The "ideology" of the title is, therefore, broadly defined, but I choose the term in place of "belief" or "ideas" because I wish to suggest that this process of changing involves a certain felt *urgency*. Having thought "with" an ideology for decades, many authors come at a point of crisis to think "about" it, and that is the moment when a revolution in fictional form—and that outmoded concept, meaning—may occur.

It is customary for an author to thank those who have helped in the writing of a book and to disavow their responsibility for the more egregious errors. My debts to the work of R. S. Crane, to the late Sheldon Sacks and his close friend, Ralph Rader, and to David Richter and James Phelan will be obvious. Walter Anderson read my musings on Austen and contributed many useful suggestions, although I fear that he still thinks I haven't quite gotten *Persuasion* "right." My colleagues at Tulane University were of signal assistance in their admirable and diverse expertise, especially for a project that took up so many authors and years. I particularly thank

Janice Carlisle, Donald Pizer, and Jerry Snare for reading parts of the book. Colin Machlachlan gave the kind of support only someone who seems to write a book a year knows how to give. Of Paula Badeaux's help and support, apart from its wisdom, one might say that its felicity is in the glow of her spirits.

1

An Essay
on Innovation

Rudolf Arnheim tells of the sculptor Jacques Lipchitz gazing at one of Juan Gris's cubist pictures, one "in which the layman discovers little but an agglomeration of building material." Lipchitz exclaims to the artist, "'This is beautiful! Do not touch it any more! It is complete.'" Gris, "flying into a rage," shouts, "'Complete? Don't you see that I have not finished the moustache yet?'" Arnheim makes the "point": "To [Gris] the picture evidently contained the image of a man so clearly that he expected everyone to see it immediately in all its detail" (117–18).

Originality, invention, the "new"—what I call innovation in this book—imply the discovery of a form perfectly expressive of some new way of seeing the world.[1] In the novel, as in painting, the task is to find "the exact equivalent of the objects," although such a prescription raises more questions than it answers. One kind of innovation, then, is "the unsought and unnoticed product of a gifted artist's successful attempt to be honest and truthful" (Arnheim, 117), although this may be the serene view of the matter, and the novelist's insight is as often misperceived as Gris's moustache. Often—innovation not being a single activity or kind of product—only the occasion for a new structure comes upon the writer unsought, and it provokes an almost frantic attempt to break out of tried and reassuring methods of composition into new territory. The innovative "moment" may be anything but tranquil, as Irving Howe, speaking of *Daniel Deronda,* implies: "Toward the end of their careers, great writers are sometimes roused to a new energy by thoughts of risk. Some final stab at an area of human experience they had neglected or at a theme only recently become urgent: this excites their imagination" (Howe, vii). Over several years of thinking about the development of the novel, I noticed that a number of texts, especially those written late in novelists' careers, exhibit this kind of "urgency," a sense of too much to say in too short a time, and I began to wonder whether these final novels might not compose a distinct group.

It is clear, of course, that the accidental fact of a novel being an author's last is not necessarily crucial, although it might be interesting. With many authors, the career begins with innovations that are then refined or even "spent" along the way, only to be reestablished later; in the case of Ernest Hemingway, for example, after the misadventure of *To Have and Have Not.* I eventually came to see that Daniel Defoe, Oliver Goldsmith, Jane Austen, and George Eliot were all infected late in their careers with a similar strong desire to break new ground. Hemingway's crisis was earlier in his life, but it might form a useful contrast, especially since the urgency in his case was forced upon him. It certainly seems to be as fretful a "site" of innovation as any of the others, and it has the added virtue of allowing me to talk about what happens after the "crisis" has passed. I also came to see that the anxiety I found in these books was probably owing to a desire to do something completely new, something that *had* to be done. Might it be possible to construct a "poetics" of urgent innovation, or innovative urgency? Or, since authors, despite numerous attempts to banish them from the text, seem to be an important part of the process, was what I needed more like a "rhetoric" or a "philosophy" of innovation?

Before I could even begin to sort through these projects, however, I had to address some preliminary problems. I needed to see whether I could locate a site of inquiry, at a time when "author" and even "reader" are questionable doctrines. Jan Mukarovsky offers a plausible direction: "Experimental aesthetics, as founded by Fechner, began with the axiom that there exist universally necessary conditions for the existence of beauty, and that to ascertain them it is sufficient to isolate, through a number of experiments, the chance deviations of individual taste. As we know, further development forced experimental aesthetics to respect the changeability of norms and to take into account their bases" (24). Where, after all, does a new literary structure take place? Since the disappearance of the author as a valid consideration in postmodernist criticism and the demotion of the text (in the work of critics who still believe in the existence of texts) to the status of historical repository, where was I to look at innovation, unless I was willing to assume that it is a product of changing readers—always a possibility—or resides in the mind of God?

Second, did I too quickly dismiss the fact that *Roxana, The Vicar of Wakefield, Persuasion,* and *Daniel Deronda* are all "last novels"? In the simple sense, no. Usually a novelist, like a plumber, a painter, or a dealer in junk bonds, is unaware that the present task, which looks like all the others, is really the last. Of the authors I ended up studying, only Jane Austen may have been fighting against time, although Eliot was not in good health in the mid-1870s. Defoe went on to write much more, although nothing that took him past what he discovered in *Roxana. Vicar* is Goldsmith's only novel, and his further attempts at comedy, in drama, did not push his experiment further. Hemingway was barely into the middle of his career when he wrote *To Have and Have Not,* and although it is a kind of *ignis fatuus,* it still lit the path back to his earlier success. The question of a terminal work would not go away (perhaps pointing up how problematic the notion of "last" might be). I noticed, for example, that *Roxana, Persuasion,* and *Deronda* are, of each writer's works, the least discussed in the critical literature and, a more subjective judgment, the most "difficult," spawning a large number of readings and exhibiting a wider span of disagreement. There is something about them that puzzles critics and puts them off. Each, for example, has been called incoherent, a common verdict on Goldsmith's pastoral comedy and Hemingway's "proletarian" novel as well. If critics habitually read these novels through the lens of the earlier careers, whence the distortion—from the works themselves, the careers, or the critics?

What I came to see, to jump ahead, was that these works all invite "misreading" because the early careers of each novelist school readers to expect an angle of vision that was no longer acceptable to the author. When momentous personal change occurs, what often happens is that the way one *sees* changes drastically. Whatever metaphor one selects—framework, perspective, or vision—what changes is the way the outside world is related to consciousness. Urgent innovation comes about because one is suddenly seeing not just with new glasses but with new eyes as well.

When I began to wonder about how new novelistic forms originate, I thought I already possessed a number of explanations, and my debt to the many writers on novelty, especially in regard to the concept of genius, with which it is often allied, can be traced in the Notes.[2] The first explanation is that innovation just happens and there is no way to say how. It is countergeneric and essentially ahistorical, which is why, in T. S. Eliot's view, the truly new work always changes previous ones, modifies the entire map of the literarily "possible," an idea to which I return more than once in this book. Since there can be no science—not even at the level of probability of a poetics—of the accidental, or of the unique (a "truth" some social sciences have been foundering on from the beginning), I was determined to ignore this possibility even if it seemed likely. If Croce is right and all works represent unique intuitions, then the best one can do is to set about compiling an "atomistic" history.[3] Another direction to explore, somewhat uncomfortably close to the unacceptable one, is that new forms usually occur at the beginning of careers and represent the uncharted territory of an accidental discovery that takes already developed materials and subjects them to a new kind of energy. One might, therefore, compose separate anatomies of innovative situations but never explain them. One of the reasons critics like Ian Watt insist upon seeing Defoe's *Robinson Crusoe* as entirely new, even though its formal features recall an older tradition, is that Crusoe is so incomparably more developed than his literary predecessors such as Selkirk, springing wondrously unexpected from Defoe's sixty-year-old mind (Watt 1957). Yet this ignores literary history: to the extent that Defoe's first "novel" is new, it is because he perfected what dozens of pseudohistorians before him had done. About this sort of innovation I have little to add, except to suggest what pressures to innovate might have come to influence a Defoe, writing at the end of a narrative tradition that makes a virtue of lying like the truth.

Another possibility is that new forms evolve. A novelist trudges along, finally arriving at the innovation, which then emerges as a fitting, "logical" culmination to a series of small refinements. This "genetic" model implies a number of assumptions with which I quickly became uncomfortable. First, I had long before concluded that no sum of parts, new or old, enabled me to explain whole structures. As Samuel Johnson reminds us, "Pound St. Paul's church into atoms, and consider any single atom; it is, to be sure, good for nothing: but, put all these atoms together, and you have St. Paul's Church" (Boswell, 1:440). Johnson is talking about "felicity," but his point applies as well to comedies, for example, which are commodious enough as wholes to tolerate a great deal of pain, even to make misery contribute to risibility; and to some tragedies, which may have notoriously laughable but fully functional elements.

An additional problem is that there seems no way to "pin" technique to innovation, to argue that this or that new way of telling a story *had* to come about because of, say, the evolution or invention of a new subject matter. For example, while Samuel Beckett's novels seem entirely new, and it is possible to argue that the particular point of view in a certain novel is appropriate, it is quite another thing to say it couldn't have been done differently. Artists of all sorts frequently devise techniques to enable them to meet one task, only to find their invention inappropriate to the very different requirements of the next one. Indeed, what works brilliantly in one novel frequently serves as a drag on a subsequent one. When I read Norman Mailer's *Executioner's Song*, I was struck with how "right" the lifeless, flat style is as a mirror of Gary Gilmore's life. Then Mailer wrote *Ancient Evenings* and I realized that either he was the benefactor of a happy accident in the earlier novel, and the style became inappropriately habitual, or he mistakenly judged it suitable for a novel requiring a different technique.

Nor does it seem logical to assume that the precise configuration of an innovative structure is in any simple way invariably expressive of a shift in the author's ideology. It does not follow that because George Eliot's last novel is much more strikingly bifurcated than her earlier ones, she at some point between *Middlemarch* and *Daniel Deronda* became a Hegelian, any more than Faulkner's four parts of *The Sound and the Fury* suggest that he was a pre-Chicago Aristotelian.

So far, these two general possibilities have centered on authors. It is worth considering that authors are really the Muses' amanuenses, responding to unseen but powerful "laws" of development that have nothing to do with their own beliefs and intentions. There are a number of possibilities. Defoe's *Roxana* might be the inscription of latent generic laws not activated by the earlier fictions. For the new work to be "born" is for it to be a product of genetics, but also, by definition, to be like what came before—Plato's problem of naming and identity, of recognizing the many that issue from the one. The marked difference-within-similarity of *Roxana,* as compared with the earlier narratives, is that its episodes begin to take on a causal relationship—begin, that is, to resemble a progressive novelistic structure. Perhaps some generic rule involving narrative linkage provides for the eventual emergence of a "tighter" arrangement, prepared for in some mysterious way by stories based on merely additive patterns, such as *Moll Flanders.* Perhaps there is a similar law for subject matter, so that any novelist working her way through the possibilities of romantic comedy, like Jane Austen, must inevitably arrive at a permutation that begins to question the role of marriage as fulfillment, and something like *Persuasion* emerges.

This genetic model differs from my previous one, for it removes the author as an agent, except in the trivial sense of being the proximate cause of the new form. While some of my best friends are authors, this subtraction of the sentient being from the process might have to be endured, and it does seem to fit right in with some current trends in theory. Even so, the important question about the genetic model is not whether it is politically acceptable but rather whether a view of the author as a mere fixture, through which language flows, is tenable logically, historically—I stop short of "really."

This study highlights a number of narrative innovations that do not quite "work." Even so, my emphasis on the disjunctive features of these texts should not be taken to mean that I despair of narrative unity, much less that I accept any sort of radical linguistic determinacy. My assumptions in this regard are shamelessly timid: I do not see the necessity to adopt the all-or-nothing linguistic position of the Derrideans, but I do not think that radical innovations often achieve the kind of unity the New Critics liked to think they perceived. Language "works," but not because it is "grounded," and one therefore does not need to resort to a discredited logocentric model to bring the author back into serious consideration as a site of the creative process. One need only assume, as M. H. Abrams does, that what Jacques Derrida "can be said to reveal"—almost, as it were, against his own skepticism about the stability of language— "is that the communicative efficacy of language rests on no other or better ground than that both writers and readers tacitly accept and apply the regularities and limits of an inherited social and linguistic contract" (312). Like so many of our most recently erected linguistic and poetic "first principles," the infinite unreliability of language, its unmooring from intention and control—and the resultant "death of the author" announced by Barthes—remain theoretical constructs not only unproven but also self-refuting, in theory and in practice. In theory, if we could not make ourselves understood, if our "agency" as authors were a chimera, the principle of indeterminacy would itself befuddle us. In practice, authors speak to readers and are, imperfectly but successfully, understood.

The problem with the full genetic model, then, is that it does not work. If it did, all authors who submit themselves to the laws of genre—which means all authors—would be innovators. They would at least exhibit some sort of development explainable by reference to generic principles; and that is not the case. For example, since some of the principles of modernist story telling have attained almost the status of dogma—impersonality, internality, attenuated closure, complex and multiple time schemes and points of view, relativity—one might expect that one development from such practices would be reactive novels embodying a new sense of the value of, say, the unironic happy ending. Yet there seems to be no such law of genre at work, at least not in "serious" fiction. While plenty of authors rebel at the constraints of modernist fabulation—

Ken Kesey was one, even though he used many familiar techniques—within the career of a writer like Bernard Malamud, it is difficult to see conventions being overturned by strictly generic pressures. One specific feature of Malamud's fiction, the attenuated closure, the muting of expectations, which is fully expressive of his thought (as it is of so many modern novelists), appears again and again. Genre, which has a perplexing relationship with ideology, is habitual, sometimes irresistibly so. Once an author develops a favorite way of representing reality, what principle of story telling demands that it be abandoned for something else?

History, Innovation, Ideology, and Authorship

"Anthropology," Pierre Macherey contends, "is merely an impoverished and inverted theology: in place of the god-man is installed Man." The idea of writer or artist as "a creator belongs to a humanist ideology" in which "man is released from his function in an order external to himself, restored to his so-called powers" (66). Macherey objects, of course, to this "profoundly reactionary" ideology. Yet, in regard to innovation, the idea of "the author" is indispensable—the idea would have to be invented if authors did not exist to be the uncertain repositories of subjectivity—because innovation, unlike the laws of production Macherey wishes to substitute for the uneven workings of volition, is neither predictable nor the expression of some "force" apart from the author.[4] As one of the best writers on innovation—an anthropologist—H. G. Barnett notes, "It is . . . often said that an invention is the expression of a need. This statement can have no meaning when it is applied to the abstraction called culture, for a culture never needed anything" (15). The general problem with theories of innovation that attempt to make it "one thing"—a function of history, for example—is that they must presume the existence of relationships of causality. "But," Albert Rothenberg reminds us, "if creations are truly unheralded and new, they are intrinsically unexpected and therefore unpredictable. More important, if there is real discontinuity in the creator's thought during the creative process, we can never predict the occurrence of creative ideas" (336). Melvin New suggests that "housing authority in an author or a text may not be linguistically feasible or justifiable, but, as Burke warned us two hundred years ago, there are modes of falsehood truer than truth" (10).

One does not have to embrace a materialist viewpoint to believe that novels are in some crucial way products of their authors' time. A historical model of innovation might look something like this: texts always contain within them structures that are homologies of historical conflict; characters and their invented relationships parallel within variation the dialectical process of events and therefore can only be read in the context of those events. This is not to say that "decoding" the historical subtext is somehow automatic or simple; it is never possible to predict *how* a text will embody its engendering historical moment, only that it will do so. The task of the literary historian, therefore, is to reconstruct the context of the imaginative work, since its meaning will always be specific to its time.

My sketch fails to take into account, however, the fact that "history" is hardly a unitary concept in contemporary historicist criticism. Take, for example, the relationship between ideology and history. Do innovations, like the novel itself, come about because they offer a way to say something that must be said at a certain time and cannot be said in any other way? This is something like Michael McKeon's thesis in his recent study of that recurring problem, always waiting to give rise to another book, the rise of the novel. Before he can assume that the novel arose because of a need to express certain compelling ideas about the good and the true, McKeon must define *ideas,* and their necessary intercourse with authors, as portable and unitary: "It is precisely the capacity of intellectual structures [here, roughly equivalent to Marx's notion of the "simple abstraction"] to be abstracted from the dense undergrowth of thought that permits them to enter into the ongoing process of antagonistic and mutually defining interrelation" (212). Here, however, it seems to me that McKeon has notions of what ideas are, and how they are "used" by authors, that do not have much explanatory force. Indeed, the question is precisely whether authors *do* use ideas or are instead used by them—*that* old question. The problem with seeing ideas as somehow controlling is that no matter how simple, when they are abstracted from the context in which they arose, they cease to be ideas. Ideas *are* the undergrowth of thought. Their function in the system of thought that gives them their meaning disappears when they are abstracted. Indeed, it is impossible, in one important way, to take any idea out of its context; it simply becomes a different idea if subjected to the force of a different set of assumptions. The "ongoing process" is, therefore, not one in which mutual definition takes place, but simply, often destructively, a clashing of warring imperatives, employing the same terms but seldom modifying anything.

Much intellectual exertion is devoted to finding this or that new explanation for historical events and for history itself. Most master narratives, as they have come to be called recently, do not outlive their indicters, but so powerful is the impulse to construct them that few critics can resist. Indeed, part of the equipment of interpretation seems to be the willingness to invent new subsuming explanations, even in the work of "anti-interpretative" theorists like Gilles Deleuze and Félix Guattari, Derrida, and Louis Althusser, as Fredric Jameson has pointed out. Jameson, indeed, for all his sharp discrimination among interpretative assumptions and strategies—and here I suppose there is no real contradiction— immediately places himself in the vanguard of those who offer a new, if not a "key" to, history. Historical events, for Jameson, "can recover their original urgency for us only if they are retold within the unity of a single great collective story . . . sharing a single fundamental theme," which is the great Marxist struggle to find and establish freedom (1981:19).

Whether or not one shares in Jameson's "collective story," it is clear that reconstructing—imperfectly, as best one can—moments of innovative urgency is the only way to experience something akin to their immediacy. Central to the attempt to *explain* these moments of crisis is some ascription of causality, although Marxist theorists like Louis Althusser, participating in a general questioning of the logic of history, reject precisely the kind of connection I am trying to make between individual ideological crisis and formal innovation. The choice, given even the most tentative accession to the existence of causality, is not between varieties of causation— material, expressive, or structural, in Althusser's view (in Jameson

1981:23–25)—but rather between events as subject to laws and events as purposeful (and/but) chaotic. Perhaps it is time, for example, to assume that what "explains" Defoe's extraordinary narratives, if anything does, is available only through the closest attention to the incredibly complex, mutable phenomenon of *a person writing*, even if such specificity might temporarily disrupt some of our attempts at historical generalization. David Saunders and Ian Hunter recently suggested a rigorous definition of authorship in the early eighteenth century, involving "a contingent and unpredictable series of crosscutting intersections between the technological, economic, and cultural forces unleashed by the 'literatory,' the legal forms created to regulate these forces, and the literate techniques of the Protestant ethos which were disseminated and transformed by them" (509). Even the notion of the "writing I" requires more precise situation: "the subject form is not something promised by history or required by language; it is something brought into being and maintained as a definite mode of conduct by certain ethical institutions peculiar to the history of the West. The subject is a manner in which individuals possess the attributes of particular kinds of personhood" (503). The consequences of such a contingent view of authorship, and for me the site of innovation, have been nicely summarized by John Richetti: "In practice rather than from the enthusiastic generalizing heights of theory, Defoe's vantage point on social experience is internal, partial and pragmatic, an insider's perspective, sometimes subversive and manipulative, sometimes deeply and confusingly implicated" (54).

While every critical practice inevitably leaves out more than it addresses, a full-bore historicist methodology embraces one very forbidding fallacy, the *post hoc, ergo propter hoc*. Historicism assumes that authors are invariably creatures of the social moment and that the most important thing about their fictions is how they reveal history behind the veil of fabulation. While both of these assumptions have strong evidence to back them, as witness the many recent readings that "reinsert" works back into their historical niche, there is no necessary relationship between the existence of a scene of historical conflict and the process, intensely personal and idiosyncratic, that results in a fictional text. Michael Sprinker offers a solution (to which I return in my final chapter) in his recent proposal to unite neo-Aristotelian poetics with Macherey's materialist theory of history as structural causality. Sprinker argues that the achievement "for poetics" would be functional status as "an autonomous discipline within the global science of history" (206). The problem is that novels are especially tricky in this respect, since they so often contain specific structures that only *seem* to demand historical explication. Even so, wherever the site of innovation is, it clearly is not in the author's current events, for one obvious reason. Novels have plots, and plots come not from history but from the faculty of invention. Of course, if by plot one thinks merely of sequences of events, then there is a superficial resemblance between novels and history. A more complex notion of plot, involving ideology, is necessary, however, to understand narrative innovation. Such permutations and the attitudes that engender them are more powerful explanations of innovation than anything found in the novelist's current events, or even in the historical "forces" at work. Michael McKeon is right, then, to insist upon "the inescapable historicity of form" (6), but how one defines "history" makes all the difference. I do not think the *specific* complexity of a Defoe can be explained by reference to seventeenth-century problems of knowledge and conduct. Historicism ignores one troubling but recurring practice of authors, their tendency to make ironic, reverse, or even deconstruct history, as McKeon might have noted from the Bakhtin passage he quotes: "For any and every straightforward genre, any and every direct discourse—epic, tragic, lyric, philosophical—may and indeed must itself become the object of representation, the object of a parodic travestying 'mimicry'" (12).

Innovations do not, of course, come about in a vacuum. My thesis throughout this volume is that explanations for such complex phenomena must presuppose and explore the parallel biographical complexity that, in part, engenders them. This complexity, never fully demonstrable or even knowable, arises because, as Saunders and Hunter have suggested, authors share with other beings the fact that they are not single entities but are composed instead of a multiplicity of responsive capabilities. Defoe was, among other things, a businessman, a government agent, a commercial author—as well as a charitable author who desired his readers' well-being—a popular thinker who knew his Hobbes and Locke, a father, a lover, an occasional bankrupt, a convict, and a reader of Bunyan, among many other "roles" and "identities." Which Defoe wrote when and for what purpose?

Another possibility that must be considered is that the new novel is always in a relationship of hostile competition with other novels, even with ones yet unwritten. The authorial task is always to achieve the truly new, to break with influence and strike out alone, with all the many consequences detailed by Harold Bloom (1973). The logic of such an explanation seems unassailable. Authors prize originality unless they are writing only for money, and even that goal does not necessarily discourage innovation. Yet I wonder if most novelists would accede to such a description of their efforts to create new structures. Such a work of "fiction based on scholarship," as Geoffrey Hartman put it (91), seems more like the hypothesis of someone who studies—probably poetry, at that— rather than creates novels, for it puts uppermost that which makes the author a solitary, tormented character in his or her own drama rather than a more or less stodgy worker, a sort of shoemaker trebly vexed with sore fingers, recalcitrant leather, and grumpy customers. Among other things, novelists are makers, and as such they are often more interested in getting their novels written than they are in shedding influence, even if they are aware of it. Critics always construct "plausible" authors—I fabricate my own in the pages that follow—so that they can endow them with behavior that makes their own theories more convincing. One of my imaginary authors, who bears some resemblance to a real novelist I met in Chicago not long ago, finds my notions of what novelists "do" surprising. For example, I have always preferred to believe that most novelists are engaged in "imagining a world." This novelist, however, looked very skeptical and said, "Oh, no, I always write about myself. I don't know anything else."

There is no one way that new novels are written. The first law of innovation is that there are no laws of innovation or of creation in general: every situation is different. Like other people trying to get their work done, however, novelists sometimes build on what they have done before, refining to produce one brilliant plot after another. Indeed, this is what most readers want their favorite storytellers to do. A glance at my shelf of Ross MacDonald mysteries fills me with regret that there will be no more of them. The one time MacDonald tried a kind of "Freudian plot," substituting unconscious motivation for his usual carefully worked out structure of transgressions buried in the past, I was disappointed at the attempted innovation. Some novelists never have a reason to strike out anew. They find an expressive form and repeat it again and again, satisfied that their talents are well employed. Such writers are not complacent or inferior; they have just not found themselves subject to innovative pressure. As Barnett reminds us, "Within conventional limits individual deviation is inevitable; for excursions beyond those limits special conditions are necessary" (21). It would be unwarranted to assume that there is a privileged breed of authors who by virtue of their superior capabilities create the new. One does not have to share Paul Feyerabend's view of creativity as a "dangerous myth" to appreciate the "tremendous problems" caused by setting the author and other "creators" off from the rest of the world. Nor does one have to accept his denial that individuals can be seen as having "ideas and a will of their own" to accept that authors are not "separated from the rest of nature" (708–9). The impulse toward innovation may come unbidden, even unwelcome; it may be actively sought out; but it comes for some reason, although not always one that is recoverable. With all the authors I have chosen to study, however—and none of them is thought of primarily as a creator of new structures—the revolutionary moment occurred when the previously developed compositional methods were found to be inadequate. This, at least, is the definition of Howe's "urgency" at which I arrived, although it is still too general a formulation to explain much.

While this sense of the failure or incompleteness of earlier efforts at mimesis is not the site of innovation—the emerging structure, on paper as signs but really only a "something" in potential, is the site—it is the situation. Even so, the variety of innovation I study here is only one of many. I am not particularly interested, for example, in something that has been created specifically to be new. What the novels I focus on share is a sense of the inadequacy of the old ways of telling a story. Some conviction almost too important for fiction came along to demand attention, either before the first word was written or, like a disturbing intrusion, in the midst. The new structure emerged when the carefully wrought subjects and techniques of the earlier novels seemed suddenly outmoded—at the worst based on falsifying premises, at the best, elegant play. The new structure is characterized by a dominant tone, often strident, that must coexist uneasily on the same pages with traces of the older ways of dealing with fictional reality— sometimes superseded parts of the original intention, sometimes inadvertent reminders of the past. In *Roxana*, it is a kind of oppressiveness, the weight of his heroine's sinful conduct bearing down Defoe's efforts to turn Roxana into a tragic heroine; in *The Vicar of Wakefield*, a wistfulness that yields to moral and political insistence, only to yield in turn, with jarring contrast, to comic playfulness with the imposition of a happy ending; in *Persuasion*, a deep sadness, even amidst Anne's final happiness, that "cancels" the vestiges of the old comic action; in *Daniel Deronda*, a bitterness that should be erased by Deronda's success but is instead only made bitterer by it; and in *To Have and Have Not*, brutal, unforgiving accusation, tragedy as social attack. Something went wrong, in life and art, so that the new structure issued from almost a new person.

Innovation and Personality

What is the connection between author and innovation? When one sets out to remake oneself, to abandon all those forms that have led to disappointment and pain in the past, it is usually not enough just to find a way to do better what hasn't worked before. In fact, that is usually just what won't work. Some authors are able to revise their thoughts and behavior without necessarily overturning the entire basis of their lives. They discard one part of the past but, after intensive self-questioning, reaffirm their fundamental soundness. Others, however, see, just as the drug addict, the racist, the alcoholic, or the misogynist must finally see to get "well," that their behavior has been part of a burdensome structure that has turned every decision, every interaction with others, into an invitation to calamity. The whole personality, or at least as much of it as can be changed with conscious effort, must be revised. Such a person begins to see that even what he or she has always thought of as past successes were only partial, were really fatally flawed expressions of the same alienation even when they seemed most amiable. At the moment of such painful insight, there is nothing to do except begin all over again, with the most frowning distrust of the ways of the past.

The novels I discuss are artistic equivalents of such moments, although, with the possible exception of *To Have and Have Not,* in which the sublimity of the innovation is clouded by the feelings of animosity that produced it, they are not products of self-hatred.[5] Not only does each begin anew the quest for the signifying structure the author thought already found through diligent and repeated effort, each also cancels the past, denies its claim to adequacy in the present "crisis." Like any quest for a new way to deal with the world, the novelist's search for a new structure has nothing of the certainty, even comfort, of successive experimentation; nothing of the gradual, confident march toward a perceived goal. It is like an attempt to juggle while bent over by a heavy burden. The new structure, especially when it comes at the end of a career, will always emphasize its own struggles to be new, for it will always carry with it uneasily assimilated traces of the old.

Then too, the more certain the novelist's path toward success and the more distinctive the body of accomplishment, the more disturbing the new structure will be, especially since it springs from a *conviction* of necessity. For this reason, all of the books I study here leave traces of their unquiet genesis on readers. None is entirely coherent, but that consideration pales in importance next to the expressive attempt to remake representation. Like the damaged or defeated personality, the novel of ideological or personal urgency makes fitful starts toward repair and, even if it approaches success, reveals its struggle to be whole. It is innovation that represents, artistically, a kind of therapy of violence, a shattering of old molds and now-uncomfortable conventions to break through to something that will achieve the impossible: finally to get it said right.

The personal genesis of urgent innovation has generic consequences. Maria Corti has pointed out a situation in contemporary Italian literature in which the "genres are in crisis because the codifications that regulated the thematic-formal relation are broken." Yet this is always the spectacle in the kind of innovation I am identifying. Since "genre offers an initial physiognomy and conditions the sign quality" of all the other narrative elements, the author who "chooses a literary genre" while in the midst of a crisis superimposes the outlines of the disturbance on the new example of the genre (123). The result is often that the new work "skews" the generic principles in such a way as to transform their very ideological basis. Defoe took the imitation of a true memoir, perfected in works such as *Robinson Crusoe, Moll Flanders,* and *Colonel Jack,* and turned it into the progressive action plot. Goldsmith became dissatisfied with the political implications of his own comic innovation and abandoned it for direct didacticism, only, in turn, to abandon the ideological integrity of his political insights when he arrived at closure. Austen explored the map of dynamic, powerfully progressive comic fiction but ended up writing a static action that challenges the basis of romantic fulfillment. Eliot developed the potential of a harmonious, multiple plot of social realism, but turned finally to a kind of disharmonious duality. Hemingway created existential tragedy and then, out of frustration and anger with part of his readership, wrote a social tragedy that, while abusing his talents, also taught him how *not* to subordinate social elements, permitting him then to perfect a new social representation in *For Whom the Bell Tolls.*

These five authors demonstrate Clayton Koelb's thesis that "since the New Critical revolution . . . narrative theory has tended to shy away from attempts to examine the narrative imagination," believing, "quite understandably, that poetic invention is necessarily a function of the individual writer's personality, education, and working habits . . . so context-bound as to be different for every writer and possibly every text" (509–10). In the following pages I argue that there is a way to talk about the site of innovation, and that the fact of innovative uniqueness is its greatest interest. Yet Koelb and the New Critics he refers to were right to distrust attempts to formulate or systematize discussion about narrative invention. Especially in regard to the kind of innovation I am concerned with, there is never any way of predicting the new structure. Since generic warping and deflection may occur for a large number of reasons, the kind of personal crisis that sometimes leads to innovation can never be predicted. Nor are there any rules about what will happen under the force and pressure of the author's need to create something new to satisfy the perceived deficiency. Urgent innovation is always sui generis, a powerful refutation to those who believe that any but the most trivial of human events is capable of being understood in the abstract, much less predicted, by the use of a theoretical model. At the same time, innovation cannot be understood as a unique event, apart from its history. Novelistic actions provide no more than "places" for ideas, which remain commonplaces, their meaning only a potentiality, until they become expressive in the novelistic plot.

Innovation is, then, only one example of activities that need to be investigated in the overdue reinstatement of individual volition as a serious subject of inquiry.

This brief introduction begs at least two very important questions. First, what necessary connection might there be between a shift in authorial belief and a shift in novelistic structure? The problem, of course, extends out from literary studies, since it is not farfetched to argue that all verbal structures exhibit a drastic tension between intention and performance, and even more widely, that all works of art question the question of meaning. Even a consciously "artless" diary, intended only for the eyes of the composer, will exhibit a tendency toward artfulness. To write is to posture, to wish to be thought meaningful.

If the spectacle of urgent innovation teaches us anything, it is that questions like that of meaning may not be answered abstractly, apart from the booming, buzzing confusion of the individual act of narrativity. Accordingly, I leave the demonstration of the possible connections between story and significance to be examined in the individual cases that follow.

Second, I am assuming that my reader is aware, as I am, that any attempt to assign meaning to an act of innovation is itself an act of imposition. My histories of these sites are inevitably colored by my assumptions about such matters as intention, structure, and belief. Others will come along to argue about my interpretations of these moments of innovation; I only wish to suggest that they should be prominent features on the critical map.

2

Defoe's *Roxana*

Structure and Belief

Defoe's last major fiction is the first of a long line of British narratives that have come to be known as *actions*. To be precise, I should say that *Roxana* became an action in the writing, but that qualification will make sense only later. The action involves the representation of a dynamic instability, the complication of that situation, and its aesthetically satisfying resolution. While other prominent narrative forms have also come to be called novels, actions represent one of the most prominent and diverse lines of British and American fiction. Since R. S. Crane refined the model, from Aristotle's *Poetics,* it has been adopted by many critics and has made possible a high degree of clarity and rigor in treating a great number and variety of realistic fictions, both dramatic and narrative. Indeed, the model is now so well known that I suspect a definition of it is unnecessary.[1]

It is no accident that all of the works I treat at length in this book are examples of the form, or begin as actions only to reach for features of other forms, courting incoherence.[2] The action, by virtue of its use of the materials of fiction to create a causal, anticipatory experience for the reader, presents a complex ideological problem to writers, especially when they accept the challenge of designing new forms to express new insights. Novelistic structure and belief are always in an uneasy dialectical relationship. New beliefs sometimes cause new forms, and new forms may themselves provoke new beliefs, an assertion that may defy credulity but which I hope to demonstrate. The task of creating an action is always difficult; other forms, like the episodic picaresque, have less stringent requirements for their "arrangement" and require less ideological consistency. Since the action requires represented value—in all but the most trivial examples of the form—the author cannot avoid ideology, although the necessary relationship between the action and belief, which I seem to be taking for granted, is not at all resolved. For example, narrative is often just as much an experiment in ideas as it is in form: writers sometimes "work their way" toward belief, trying out represented ideas, rejecting some, embracing others, in a manner that casts doubt on any notion of *fictional* ideology as determined. One might expect that some ideas implied by the characters and events taking form would be disturbing, would even provoke attempts at self-suppression. Then too, since no one can gather in all the implications of a realistic story, some potentially threatening beliefs might remain as covert implications of the overt structure.

Even those familiar with the form and its explanatory history seldom agree about how ideas function in progressive, probabilistic fiction, much less how they might generate new structures. This study, unlike others in the same critical tradition, takes as its particular province the expressive problems, inherent in the site of innovation, that result in failures of coherence, formal and ideological.[3]

Pseudofactual Form and Limitation

From *Crusoe* to *Moll* to *Colonel Jack,* Defoe's great fictional narratives do not seem to present us with the same set of problems that later actions do. The stories strike many readers as much more like uncertainly remembered confessions than the creations of any wily fabricator—which, of course, is just what Defoe wanted. Readers of each generation, encountering Defoe anew, come to their own radically different terms with the difficult simplicity, the tangled implications of situation and detail, of his first-personal stories, for these imitations or refinements of true stories are all structurally ambiguous. Unlike a tightly plotted, carefully subordinated novel, the pseudomemoir seems to issue a blanket invitation to readers to expatiate. Defoe's narratives are semantic "places" or "occasions"; not one even approaches ideological coherence, until *Roxana*. There are moments, such as Crusoe stuffing his nonexistent pockets or Moll's mundane musing about being tempted to child murder, that have beckoned every commentator to revelries of explication. Defoe is like a particularly tolerant and accommodating host: he lets each reader have his or her own way with his stories, as the critical histories of each will attest.

Such heavily traveled "crossings" are one reason so many continue to rediscover Defoe's importance. Since interpretative certainty, or even stability, has not been a critical virtue for some time, the implicit invitation Defoe's works extend to multiply not only "readings" but even interpretative strategies is cause for celebration. The more Defoe's narratives mean, the better they are. With this view I have no real quarrel, since even in Babylon linguistic confusion finally found its exegetes. Even so, a distinction is in order here: even if all texts, by virtue of their being constructed from words, are or can be made to seem inherently duplicitous, the possibility still remains that some, for structural or rhetorical reasons, are more duplicitous than others. It is by now a kind of unexamined dogma that all texts, especially fictional texts, "mean" in a nearly infinite variety of ways, although the evidence for plurisignificance is usually drawn from the multiplicity of interpretations, not from—how could it be?—the experience of reading. It is slightly odd, then, that an examination of the interpretative history of the canon indicates that some texts generate a larger number of sharply contrasting readings than others. One explanation is that some texts inspire a greater number of incompatible critical frameworks than others, and only seem to be problematic; but another is that some texts, for generic or idiosyncratic reasons, are simply less stable than others.

Defoe's works present one such interesting case, and one historical consequence of his textual instability is innovation. He was an author almost obsessed with the necessity that narrative convey ideology, but the pseudofactual form he refined closes off represented belief. In *Roxana* he discovered a narrative structure of sufficient rhetorical stability to allow him to mold his reader's beliefs, just by virtue of their comprehending the plot. His development from pseudomemoir to novel was dictated by the impenetrability of his earlier stories. To begin with Defoe, then, is to begin with a paradigm: frequently, I shall argue, some perceived deficiency of the forms an author has pioneered leads to an innovation that provides a solution—while often creating new problems.

The considerations that would have encouraged authors on both sides of the Channel to write truthlike stories have been fairly well documented (see Stewart; Showalter). Defoe's choice, in *Robinson Crusoe,* of an ideologically unstable narrative form encourages idiosyncratic response. His stories, and the prefaces to them he probably composed, are full of theories economic and political, reflections of positions taken elsewhere, unconstrained by the fictional persona. Critics take these ideas very seriously. Elsewhere I argue that it is a mistake to substitute these often trite homilies for the complex experience of the "recollected" life itself.[4] However, it is also a mistake to assume that Defoe had no moral purpose when he wrote the lives of Crusoe, Moll, and the others. Outside his fiction, Defoe often displayed a serious desire to point his readers toward worldly happiness and the salvation of their souls. Like the dissenting diarists he used as one model for his confessional narratives, Defoe often saw the hand of God in matters most mundane (Starr). So, while Ian Bell is right to emphasize Defoe's qualities as a thoroughly professional writer, it is equally right to emphasize that he wished to be a beneficent one as well (1985, chap. 1). The question is not his intention, which he shared with almost every eighteenth-century author, but how his choice of narrative structures affected his aims.

A meld of commercial and moral concerns may be traced through most of Defoe's writings. Even in *Roxana,* which seems to totter precariously on the edge of titillation, the preface performs an act of generic schizophrenia, inviting the story to be read as scandal chronicle yet insisting upon its capacity to provoke "Noble Inferences" (2). Defoe was not self-deluded or mendacious. If his stories do not teach as he wanted them to, isn't one explanation that he inadvertently chose a *kind* of story that insists upon remaining stubbornly antimythic? His choice of narrative form makes the systematic inculcation of morality impossible. While it has been repeatedly demonstrated that no single narrative tradition "explains" Defoe's works (Richetti 1987), the narrative strategies he took over and adapted to his own unique ends almost all spring from the factual or pseudofactual tradition. Criminal confession, spiritual autobiography, scandal chronicle, travel adventure—these are a few of the genres of factuality. They depend on referentiality, or at least the illusion of it, established by a narrative method in which causality and pattern are absent, or skewed, or confused, in which the random and contingent nature of the world is reflected in the subject and technique of the story.

Examples abound in Defoe's works. Crusoe yearns for the sound of another human being but declines to attack the cannibals, to take a prisoner as a companion, because of the killing that might be involved. Yet when the time comes to fire, his moral reservations disappear. He even composes a bloodthirsty tabulation of how each "savage" is killed. Moll refuses to recognize her own moral degeneration in her horrifying urge to kill a little girl, but rather reasons that parents shouldn't let their children go wandering about the city alone. These moments leave the reader unguided, pondering, but with nowhere to "arrive." Defoe's narratives are not coherent ideological structures, which is why it now seems almost inevitable that someone as resistant to didacticism as Virginia Woolf found in Defoe a kindred worker. While she did not share Defoe's desire to achieve an illusion of factuality, she was as dedicated a "realist" as Defoe, intent upon capturing the dismaying, sometimes exhilarating, incoherence of consciousness. Perhaps it shouldn't surprise us, as it seems not to have surprised Woolf, if the moral intention of a narrative more tellingly reveals itself when we look closely at the way the entire enterprise of a story is conducted rather than at what its morally unmoored characters say in the story's ferment. This disjunction between what the story says and what the story's form says is as true of Defoe as it is of Woolf.

Defoe's attraction to the pseudomemoir surely had something to do with his expectation that a true-seeming story would be granted more credibility than a "romance," for, as Johnson put it later in the century, the "mind revolts from evident falsehood, and fiction loses its force when it departs from the resemblance of reality" (76), a caveat Defoe took even more literally than Johnson did. Defoe's task was to make sure that the hand of the artist was hidden, that only the sophisticated reader—for whom he did not write anyway—will see the work as a fabrication, and not as "remembered."

One wonders how long Defoe could remain content with a narrative strategy once he became aware of its liabilities, which effectively cancel coherent ideological intention. While narrative structures, like skyscrapers, entail a degree of instability—and not just because of the instability of language itself—the genre of pseudomemoir is one that, properly executed, closes off opportunities for authorial moralizing. One small irony of Defoe's career is that he was strongly influenced by certain French pseudomemoirists, like Courtilz, whose work Defoe took to be "true History." It is a kind of palimpsest: Defoe's reading the memoirs of the Count de Rochefort, taking the account as true, and then writing an even more entertaining example of the same genre, a fascinating fiction "epitomizing" the effects of a real memoir—unaware that his models were as fictional as his own refinement of them. While this explosion of the illusion of intentionality is amusing, it remains to be seen how tolerable it would be for an author who took seriously his moral intention. Why should Defoe be any less sensitive than Fielding and Richardson to the ideological liabilities of narrative innovations? If their near obsession with the relationship between fictional form and moral efficacy led them to even more direct didacticism in their later fictions, *Grandison* and *Amelia*, why shouldn't the same impulse have made Defoe uneasy in the presence of an ideological ambiguity much more pronounced than anything found in *Pamela* or *Joseph Andrews* (Rader 1973)?

What interests me at this point, then, are the ways in which the choice of a form—in Defoe's case, the imitation of a true story—perhaps for reasons originally distinct from an author's larger ethical intentions, leads on to at least an implicit recognition that the form has moral liabilities that must be avoided, eliminated, or surmounted by a new form. This lands us at the doorway of the innovation that came to be the novel: Defoe's *Roxana*.[5]

In viewing Defoe's last major fiction as an innovative "solution" to ethical and formal problems created by the generic liabilities of the pseudofactual mode, I continue my concern with Defoe's development as a storyteller. In his final major narrative, Defoe's innovation is more than just in the tale's structure, although that too was new to English prose fiction. The nature of the story itself changes, as the previously inert thematic elements so many critics have tried to make into "centers" of Defoe's fiction become functional. Of course, Defoe's seven earlier works are not a seamless web indistinguishable in their structures and effects. Some are clearly intended to be read as if they were literally true, such as *A Journal of the Plague Year* and *The Memoirs of a Cavalier.* Others, such as *Moll Flanders* and *Colonel Jack,* maximize or even exaggerate the pleasures available much more sparingly in real memoirs, but with care taken not to attract attention to the process of "epitomizing." While these differences are far from trivial, any two Defoe narratives written before *Roxana* may easily seem much more similar to each other than either would to *Roxana.*

What is new about *Roxana* is precisely that Defoe's ideas become functions in the telling of the story instead of remaining merely present, or, in James Phelan's term, mere "dimensions" (292–99). The new structure is more demanding, more restrictive, than the pseudofactual form it supplants.[6] If there has never been much question that Defoe was trying to use his stories to teach his readers, how these tales taught in the 1720s and how they might teach a reader today are more difficult questions. The problem, which is easily sensed and identified but not so easily solved, is that Defoe's choice of the pseudofactual mode *precludes,* because of the mode's insistence on authorial silence, the functionalization of ethical content. Defoe's ideas are there but there is no way to "read" them, except by begging the question. For example, we may find echoes of Defoe's fictionally presented beliefs in his expository works. What, then, do we do with them? May we risk assuming that an idea does not significantly change its meaning once it becomes part of a fiction? Let us isolate one element of the work: character. In the sense of a fictive being we can believe might exist, a character interacts with ethical content to reveal the "madeness" of the narrative and the presence of a designing author. Many of the ideas in *Roxana* fully justify a thematic approach which would in the earlier narratives lead only to multiplying incommensurable readings.[7] Instead of their usual status as floating, tantalizing invitations to speculation, the ideas Defoe employs to create Roxana's character invite generalization from the story-telling context; that is, consideration as aspects of the book's universality and, as a result, of Defoe's specific intention and meaning. Defoe's earlier comprehensive intention was to compose a narrative that mirrored the shape and effects of a true story; but that intention is (partially, imperfectly?) hidden in works like *Moll Flanders*. The reader responds to the illusion, but not to the intention behind it. Now, Defoe's ideology, finding a new form, becomes expressive. This distinction, then, between ideas that are simply "there" and ideas that are put to the service of a dynamic plot, enables us to see the nature of Defoe's innovation in *Roxana*. In the earlier pseudo-memoirs, it is technically impossible to identify ideas as either "dimensions" or "functions" (see Phelan).

If the illusion is to remain undetected, an imitation of a true story must not reveal traces of its synthetic genesis, although elements may have expressive or rhetorical functions so long as they are "attributable" to the narrator. Ideational elements do not function in true stories as they do in recognizable fictions—as subordinate to the task of creating an imagined world. For example, in *The Conquest of America*, Tzvetan Todorov suggests that Columbus undertook his voyages of exploration "primarily" to amass a sufficient fortune to mount a new Crusade on Jerusalem. Todorov's emphasis of that motive rather than the love of gold itself, or the desire for new adventure, or the spread of the Holy Word, is not a functional act of story telling but an interpretation either to accept or dismiss. Now we may see why so many critics sense that *Roxana* is a new kind of story: it is positively recognizable as a story made and not remembered, as discourse.

To assert that the subordination of ideology (among other elements) in *Roxana* keys us to its genesis as invention, and not pseudohistory, is only to say that it is an early novel. One paradox of the variety of forms that came to be known as the novel, given what the form owes to the factual and pseudofactual traditions of narrative, is that its realism is designed to be "read through." It is contingent, an exercise in "what if?" The psychological demands upon the reader of the action's formal structures proclaim them as things wrought unapologetically as purposeful fictions, stories that insist upon reordering the world, even if we resist the imposition and wish to substitute our own versions. Even more recent writers, such as Truman Capote, John Hersey, and Norman Mailer, who "embellish" true stories out of a distrust of or boredom with overt fictions, still want their distinctive narrative voices to echo in the hollows of lives like Gary Gilmore's. Shunning the artful fiction, they still wish to be recognized as artful. For this reason, although their "nonfiction novels" resemble Defoe's narratives, they belong to a different narrative class.

The Defoe of *Robinson Crusoe* and *A Journal of the Plague Year* has no ambition to signify novelistically or to have his pseudo-memoirs classed as "art." In the flux of his true-seeming stories, intentions are concealed and unrecognizable, questions the non-form refuses by virtue of its opacity; all of the postmodernist qualities beautifully caught, by the way, in Coetzee's recent retelling of the Crusoe/Roxana/Defoe stories, *Foe*. It is a virtue of his pseudomemoirs that they are almost infinitely conformable to what each reader thinks life is. Moll, Jack, H. F., and the Cavalier are in their widely accommodating ideological spaces like the speakers of naïve memoirs Defoe intends them to resemble, and Defoe is the original "readerly" writer. While the pseudomemoir may be a trick, it is a wondrously skillful one. To see just how difficult Defoe's task is, it is only necessary to try to write a "novel" today that succeeds not only in seeming like a true story (the easier task) but also in fixing the attention of readers dull and acute, naïve and sagacious, superficial and penetrating. It is as if Defoe found in the older factual literature and its imitations a principle of ambiguity that is itself stable: narrate in such a manner that nothing is predictable and nothing, once it happens, is at all unbelievable. More is involved, of course. Episodes seem carefully balanced to suggest the absence of causality. Moll is kidnapped by gypsies who simply lose interest in her and deposit her at Colchester. She marries one brother only to be seduced, in the same house, by the other—a nicely complicatable situation which Defoe allows to drop. No conjugal disaster ensues because the younger brother has the good grace to die. Later, Moll is convicted and condemned to death. Finally, the reader, thirsting for a moral to pluck out, for the age's beloved poetic justice, anticipates a pathetic lesson, the reverse eighteen years in advance of the moral of Pamela's story. Yet Moll's promised demise on the gallows is a chimera, like any other fate we might venture to predict for her. She escapes the gallows and is transported to America. It is a fortunate calamity that reunites her with her family and makes possible an old age of calm repentance, so that Defoe may write the end to his string of episodes. The chorus is mute. There is no wailing. If there is a moral to her story, it is the inadvertent, extraneous one of the unpredictability of life and stories.

One reason the novel became such an important form is that it allows authors, especially those writing in the eighteenth and nineteenth centuries, to design narrative versions of the drama's "structures of anticipation," in which readers' expectations that a character deserves happiness or punishment may be created by specific morally charged situations. In those situations—which authors may satisfy or frustrate, depending upon their ideological intentions—the reader participates, for the sake of the experience itself, in the interdependency of ideology and character. A character's decision, or even a failure to decide, leads on to a particular outcome, not in some kind of lockstep progression but in the most probable manner the writer is capable of devising. The strategy of such structures of desire is unashamedly subversive. Novelists like Richardson and Fielding learned to pin ideology to the developing story, to induce in the reader an attitude of receptivity, a strategy later novelists employed again and again. Even in 1740 a reader might not have actively valued female chastity, but to "consume" *Pamela* is to consume Richardson's desires for her.

One does not have to cherish Derrida to react uneasily to such an intention. Johnson warned his readers about the "comedy of romance," which in the eighteenth century replaced the "wild strain of imagination" of earlier romance with probable "scenes of the universal drama." The danger of this new fiction, in Johnson's view, is that it readily seduces the moral imagination. Take "an adventurer . . . levelled with the rest of the world . . . as may be the lot of any other man," and the result is that "young spectators fix their eyes upon him with closer attention, and hope by observing his behaviour and success to regulate their own practices" (*Rambler*, no. 4). If one suspects that—in contrast to his dismissal of dramatic illusion in the "Preface to Shakespeare"—Johnson overestimated the power of literary illusion, it is arguable that the intention he located is at the heart of the traditional novel. Strong empathy with a character leads to identification with that character's moral struggles and to at least a temporary identification with the moral principles that constitute the field on which those struggles are played out.

Johnson was looking back on his recent past, specifically the 1740s. He did not have Defoe's fictions in mind, and, although he praised the "merit" of a "man, who, bred a tradesman, had written so variously and so well" (Boswell, 3:267–68), he might have found the pretensions of Defoe's narratives to didactic efficacy dubious. Moll, after all, is a moral cipher, as I argue at length elsewhere, and her story only multiplies the reader's inability to decide what she is, what she deserves, and why she ends (does she "end"?) as she does (Boardman 1983, esp. chap. 4). This is why her story is Defoe's most typical and, for what the form is designed to be, his best. Without attempting to fix the degree of unknowability Defoe's stories usually imply, is it not likely that Moll's very inscrutability would make Defoe uncomfortable? What is the sum of a series of question marks? Moll is captivating precisely because she is, as a probable being, a character in the making, consistently and fascinatingly underdetermined. Ian Bell points out that Defoe, in 1723, slandered *Robinson Crusoe, Moll Flanders,* and *Colonel Jack* as each a "romantic Tale . . . adventures." Bell goes on to suggest that the "unerring way in which Defoe disparages his own creations here is delightful. It shows the victory of the committed professional writer over the anxious Puritan" (33). This is too attractive a thesis to ignore. Even so, it is interesting that in 1723 Defoe published none of the narratives for which we most remember him. Perhaps the irony Bell finds is not best seen as the exhilaration of the professional writer at the success of "commercial" novels, but rather as the uneasy recognition that his stories leave unsettled crucial questions involving money, sex, and crime. It is just as plausible that Defoe, realizing the liabilities of the pseudofactual form he perfected, would attempt to avoid them in his next fiction. As Bell himself said earlier, the "use of the first-person narrators allows Defoe the space to be unattached to the ideas offered" (27). Precisely—but for the writer-for-bread who is also a moral polemicist, is that detachment comforting or threatening, empowering or debilitating?

Jack and the Captain and Crusoe all render superfluous our attempts to surround them with the trappings of a genre—much less to "interpret" them, to discover an embedded communal significance—even with almost three centuries of knowledge of the possibilities of novelistic form to back us up. Despite the genre each story superficially seems to suggest, Defoe's fictions, until *Roxana*, trace the pattern of only two closely related narrative forms, both perfected by Defoe: the imitated true story and the epitome of the true story. Of course, in order not to seem to be a new species of writing—which, to Defoe, they probably were—each narrative poses as a more familiar form. Moll is the heroine of her own criminal memoir, the Captain tells his version of military history, and Singleton narrates a travel adventure. Roxana seems to have jumped from the pages of a scandal chronicle, a generic identification constantly reinforced by her refusal to name names. These are only poses, however, part of the paraphernalia of verisimilitude.

Where, then, did Defoe's innovation come from? Anything like a full answer to the question presupposes access to Defoe's consciousness as he wrote; or, at the very least, much more in the way of biographical materials than exist for Defoe from which to construct an explanation. Even so, *Roxana* may itself be read, formally and biographically, as its own explanation. Like the other writers I consider, Defoe discovered a new form in the blank spaces of his earlier works, principally in the gap between the pseudofactual form and didactic purpose. Defoe solved his problem by sticking with the realistic story and refining its possibilities for representing values, ones perhaps always held but never represented coherently until *Roxana*. Unlike Goldsmith, he did not abandon realism for the more direct means available in the parable, but, like Goldsmith, found a new form for personal, rhetorical reasons. Defoe's task was to represent moral issues with some degree of moral determinacy.

As we shall see, however, the novel, along with its potential for representing intended, conscious belief, has a subversive, even disreputable side, although, despite the confidence with which some critics pursue "absent causes," such causes are much slipperier than formal intentions. Richardson, for example, cannot avoid revealing his own fascination with forbidden sexuality in the very act of writing a novel about chastity. All stories have a tendency to unearth a hidden ideology the author may not have examined. If too many novels written by men, for example, seem to embody sexist clichés, might it be because the novel draws them forth from an author who, having contemplated other moral issues, has not examined *that* one? It's one of the things he thinks *with* rather than *about*. In the pressure of assigning causality in the novel's world, authors may have their attention so fixed upon their overt meaning that they allow the commonplaces of the marketplace, or the forbidden asides of the unconscious, to slip in. As we shall see with Defoe, the novel has its underside of unintended belief, not accidentally but as a result of the demands of the action to represent whole a world of ethical consequence. Whether we should attend to a novel's "present" or its "absent" ideology—indeed, what the ethics or politics of "reading for omissions" might be—are questions I reserve for the final chapter.

Roxana *and the Subordination of Belief*

One of the many paradoxes involving Defoe's fictions is that while they seem to be naïve and artless "found" memoirs, they are in fact all synthetic constructs. Nor is the problem solved by noting the "madeness" of his texts: their teleology remains that of the true story, or, more frequently, the covertly "dressed-up" true story, no matter what we know them in fact to be. *Roxana* complicates the problem by beginning as the other stories do and then metamorphosing into a synthetic structure. For some this may be a distinction without a difference; for them, these books are all novels because we know them to be novels. The resubordination of elements in *Roxana,* however, resulting in a text the reader experiences as positively fictional, is in fact nothing less than a revolution in fictional form.

It is difficult to believe that Defoe could have failed to recognize the opportunities the new form afforded. Here is a way of ordering fictional experience so as to suggest that the world does not work randomly, a new, strongly causal mimesis without the value chaos of the old. Everywhere else in Defoe's fiction, the relationship between ideological elements and any necessary plot progression is haphazard. Only in *Roxana* do we see all the elements of the fictional synthesis combine to make something like a functional whole. Defoe came close to achieving the radical transfer of dramatic structure to prose fiction—that this was in his mind I do not suggest—that constituted the morphological rejuvenation of narrative in the eighteenth century (see Sacks 1972:197; Brown). To take one pattern familiar to all readers of the "great tradition" (from which Defoe, of course, is specifically excluded): the sequence of act, reflection, consequence, and rendered fate found in so many variations in novels from Richardson until now but barely even hinted at in Defoe until *Roxana.* In *Clarissa,* for example, the entire plot, with all its complex twistings, is generated by Clarissa's refusal to relinquish the integrity that defines her as a person. Her identity is crucially dependent upon resisting, on the one hand, any attempts by her family to force her to marry against her will, and, on the other, the temptations to disobedience and flight her family's cruelty would make so irresistible to ordinary mortals. Each situation in which she finds herself moving in one direction or the other—and she never moves very far until the crucial garden scene that seals her fate—causes an orgy of self-examination, which itself results in a renewed commitment to preserve her integrity. While this iterative pattern could hypothetically continue forever, it is accompanied in the book by another, which has little to do with her volition—and therefore her identity—but is itself caused by everything Clarissa is: Lovelace's almost demonic obsession to "have" her, to subdue her pride by mastering her body. In this sense, Clarissa's fate turns on the conflict between Lovelace's hunger for domination and her own insistence upon persevering in her resolves or perishing in the attempt. The completeness of the tragic action depends as well on an initially hidden potentiality in Lovelace's character; his obsession can be just as damning. The resources for representing ideology in such a narrative pattern are obvious. Since the very values that define Clarissa and Lovelace were chosen not only to be productive of plausible, consistent characters but also to ground the conflict on serious issues, Clarissa and her tormentor accomplish the ubiquitous aim of the eighteenth-century novelist: they both entertain and instruct.

At this point we might ask why, when Defoe began to perceive the moral inefficacy of the pseudofactual form, he did not turn to older and more established forms, proven vehicles for the inculcation of morality. Certainly they were available to an author as steeped in homiletic lore as Defoe. Much commoner than the verisimilar fictions that gave rise to Defoe's innovation are works like *Utopia,* John Bunyan's fables, or even Defoe's own earlier political allegories that employ the strategy of parable. Even after the verisimilar novel in England was established, many writers, like Johnson, continued to devise fictions whose "messages" are unburdened by mimetic indirection. Goldsmith turned from a career of formal didacticism to the complexities of comic realism, in *Vicar,* only to abandon the new enterprise in mid-book in order to return to the old way of story telling, just to be sure that readers could not miss his meaning. Then too, among those narrative forms with some resemblance to the classical genres, Defoe had available the resources of satire. In fact, he earlier composed a long narrative satire, the *Consolidator,* and his *Shortest Way with the Dissenters* is a fine example of opaque imitation or covert, unstable irony, with a clear political message once (if) the deadpan mask has been penetrated (Boardman 1977). Defoe, however, chose another path: he refined the virtues of realistic fiction and discovered the unique role of value in the action form.

First of all, it is clear to every reader who picks up *Robinson Crusoe* that realism is a mode that once discovered cannot be casually abandoned. It is the very quirkiness of existence that Defoe's original manner of story telling is so appropriately designed to capture. Realism, however, is not a form but a method. If Defoe was to find a way to communicate through his fiction, in a way that would not result in mere homilies hanging on the story like so many plums to be picked, then he needed to find a role of subordination for values different from that of the parable and the satire. Whatever other virtues those two forms may possess, parables and satires, at least in Defoe's time, usually remind readers of shared, accepted values that the reader is expected simply to have ignored or forgotten. What Defoe discovered in the progress of his last major fiction was the key to a new world of narrative meaning. The action form does not just *employ* values in the telling of a story. In the telling, values become something like experience. What Roxana's story means is virtually equivalent to what is told and how it is told. Finally, and much more a revelation to Defoe: the action form results in new, nonhomiletic meaning precisely because its meaning/experience is not communicable in the commonplaces of religion, economics, or sociology. Defoe discovered in narrative what the great Greek and Elizabethan dramatists knew in their bones: the universal is the merely, splendidly probable.

That the action form represented for Defoe a radical departure from his usual method seems equally obvious, although its implications for Defoe's communicative intentions may not be. Crusoe and Moll Flanders are often faced with choices. Sometimes those choices are free; sometimes external forces impinge on choice. Whatever each character chooses, the apparatus of the story's telling expresses no standard of judgment to which the reader may turn. As Carol Kay perceptively notes in *Political Constructions,* "no critical account can make every page seem necessary and harmoniously integrated into overarching structures of plot and character development which teach an implied author's values" (63). The reader never knows, that is, until the outcome, whether a choice is for better or worse. Sometimes, especially with Crusoe, the rhetoric accompanying the choice is prescient with the narrator's hindsight. Even then, however, Crusoe's retrospective judgments of his actions are not always reliable. His life is full of "ill hours," but many of them turn out middling well. Or, to put it differently, since no standard of judging exists within the story, the reader is thrown back upon deciding (Rader 1973; Boardman 1983).

This floating ethical content is, as I have suggested, an advantage in the imitated true story because true stories are always similarly ambiguous in regard to values. Is it good or bad that

Crusoe goes away to sea? The question seems trivial. Readers faced with such moments in most of Defoe's stories can only wonder what the consequences of the act will be. Novels put the question entirely differently. While never "settling" the issues, the action induces in the reader a dialectic of attraction and repulsion, hope and fear. When Clarissa flees the garden with Lovelace, the reader knows in advance the likely consequences of her act. Everything the novelist has done has made probable the connection between flight and Clarissa's destruction. In its acquiescence in causality the novel implies a purposeful universe and an ideological final cause in art, at least until such structures become "ironized"—first, and only partially, by a Fielding intent on bebunking the notion of "virtue rewarded," and then by almost every formal innovator since Joseph Conrad.

The relationship between anticipatory knowledge and moral questions makes possible a highly charged fictional experience. If the novelist believes strongly enough in one or another kind of moral causality, the very experience of the fiction conveys a powerful message, without direct preaching. To read such a fiction is to be exposed to the ethical constructs underlying its events. Readers are, of course, always free to reject both beliefs and their expressive structure, to learn not to "follow the text." For the accepting reader, however, the skillful novelist may imbue even highly idiosyncratic beliefs with rhetorical power. One need only think of Austen's ability to convince us of the power of gratitude as an integral part of love in *Pride and Prejudice,* or of Wharton swaying her readers to active admiration of elegance and social beauty in *The House of Mirth,* or of Hemingway impressing us with the stern beauty of the bullfight in *The Sun Also Rises* to see the potential power of the action's representation of value at least to anticipate skepticism, if not to counter it.

It is, however, not just the generic innovation of *Roxana* that is the source of the power of this "first self-conscious novel" (Durant, 168). As I shall suggest about all these books—and about urgent innovation in general—some shift in belief always informs the innovation itself. A new book resulted in part because Defoe needed a new expressive form, but the urgency of the ideas made the innovative form necessary. Even if we believe that there are no new ideas, they are a revelation to the author, whose innovation expresses them with such force and conviction that they seem new. Form enables ideology and is produced by it. Critics for decades have recognized the ideological power of Defoe's last major fiction. Recently, Ian Bell argued persuasively that "Roxana evokes much more clearly" than earlier works the "psychological consequences of amoral survival in a world of unforgiving economic circumstances" (2). It is indeed this representation of acts having consequences that forms the heart of the novel's discourse. Bell sees Defoe's innovation as even more startlingly radical: "By dramatically confirming [Roxana's] severity, the book undermines our whole category of reading, and retrospectively transforms the book from its sporadic mimetic, ironic and even comic modes to tragedy" (184). Like Robert D. Hume and myself, Bell places the novel in a more traditional category, indicating Defoe's development toward generic stability. More recently, Clive Probyn, in a penetrating study of the eighteenth-century English novel, has contended that *Roxana* represents with "electrifying clarity" themes that are merely "muddled" in *Moll Flanders:* "It is in this novel that Defoe separates, almost perfectly, the muddle of Moll's (and his own) imposition of an external, socially conditioned, and utterly conventional social morality upon an inner, self-wrought, and rigorously feminist perspective on the question of personal identity" (41). While I suggest later that the book's feminism is largely delusive, Probyn's response to Defoe's successful linking of idea and action testifies to the innovative nature of the book. Even so, I have yet to make explicit the importance of this step to the history of the novel and to Defoe's own intentions. It is no less than a revolution of fictional form, although, as I have indicated, one without converts or even many admirers until the twentieth century. What the new action form does—and we should not forget that *Roxana,* compared with *Pamela* or *Joseph Andrews,* is an imperfect example—is to combine in one narrative experience the pleasures of realistic narrative with the moral efficacy of the parable. For the first time in English fiction, a realistic story was given a structure that would permit thematic coherence.

To understand Defoe's innovation thoroughly, it will be necessary to see not only how action and ideology become one but also to explain another notable feature of the book: its almost "hot-house" intensity. As disturbing as the book has been to readers since the eighteenth century, one wonders if it was not also profoundly unsettling to its creator. At the very least, it may be interesting to explore the possibility that Defoe stopped writing prose fiction in 1724 as much because of his discovery of its revelatory power as because *Roxana* resulted in only one edition.

Structural Causality

For a book that enacts the connection between sin and misery, representing for the first time in realistic prose fiction the age's favorite commonplace, poetic justice, Defoe's last effort shows only ambiguous signs early on of knowing where it is going. Roxana seems to know that the conclusion of her story will somehow involve her doom, and that of her maid and friend, Amy, too. Two early foreshadowings make clear that Defoe intends for Roxana's sin to be judged in the event. She tells us that it was "but a bad Coin" which Amy "was paid in at last, as will appear in its Place"; then we learn that Roxana "ill requited her at last" (16, 26). A different sort of reference occurs when she is in the midst of her affair with the Prince. Lamenting that she is "a Whore," she observes that repeated wickedness makes the conscience "sleep fast, not to be awaken'd while the Tide of Pleasure continues to flow, or till something dark and dreadful brings us to ourselves again" (69). This kind of foreboding does not commit Roxana to the specific kind of fate the earlier references to Amy do, which makes one wonder if, in Defoe's mind, the fates of mistress and maid were originally to have been differentiated instead of merged. Nevertheless, it is clear that foreshadowing, even of a specific nature, does not constitute the establishment of a causal structure linking sin and retribution. Defoe could, as he often did, simply explain away such anticipatory comments when he arrives at the end of the story. Or the "doom" can be perfunctory. Indeed, if one looks only at the book's last paragraph—"I was brought so low again, that my Repentance seem'd to be only the Consequence of my misery, as my Misery was of my Crime"—instead of the entire complex action that leads up to that truncated but appropriate conclusion, it is easy to conclude that Defoe has ignored all his preparatory work to manufacture another summary closure.

Defoe's narratives usually have a standard of verisimilitude in which it is a violation for a story to signal its own synthetic nature. So, with *Roxana*, he finds himself in something of a bind: his own ideology of divine retribution, never more than casually active in any of his narratives, now requires that he show Roxana suffering for her willful sin. This he could have done with ease, and just as casually as he allowed his earlier sinners to escape. Somewhere in the process of writing his last great narrative, however, he discovered that the best way to "point a moral" is to design a causal structure. Then, every reader, by virtue of recognizing in anticipation the prospective doom that must by necessity be entailed on Roxana's transgressions, will experience the thematic message on every page, not just as an afterthought. Defoe's verisimilitude is only accidentally at the service of his earlier moral intentions (with the possible exception of *A Journal of the Plague Year*, in which the sickened city serves as a continuing metaphor of personal alienation from God). With the innovative relation between structure and belief developed in *Roxana*, the ethically neutral, "free-floating" verisimilitude of the earlier narratives is replaced by a thoroughly ideological verisimilitude.

As I have argued elsewhere, it is strictly proper to speak of this progressive structure only in regard to the last section of the novel, from the chronological shift to the conclusion (1983:139–43). Yet, even long before that, the mutterings of doom make for a very strange narrative structure, one that harkens forward without at the same time enabling the reader to ascertain the precise connection between Roxana's actions and her fate. The work has a kind of inevitability, which is what critics are responding to when they argue that it is a coherent tragic action. Yet that inevitability, as manifested in our ability to predict the *quality* (as opposed to the fact, which she predicts herself) of Roxana's moral downfall, does not extend to the parts, to the extended episodes, like the one involving the Prince. Nor is there, until the shift, a standard of unity, involving the sin and retribution pairing, that connects episode to episode.

It is too easy to conclude that Defoe was in over his head, that the poetics of the new form were too much for him, that he didn't know how to incorporate the presence of an implied author, or how to use the strategy if he did know. More interesting, I think, than Defoe's possible success is that he was struggling with multiple innovations, two distinct sets of problems. Not only was he trying to write the first thematically purposeful action plot in English prose fiction, he had to satisfy the additional demands of the action's tragic pattern. Some of his difficulties came from one set of problems, some from the other. At times the tragic plot runs into problems with the overall ideology of the action plot. For example, for Defoe's general purposes, Roxana must not sincerely repent her sins. When Roxana puts her maid to bed with her own "husband," it is a sign that she has sunk lower than Moll ever does. While Roxana recognizes her own complicity, she cannot ask for forgiveness, even later, when Amy murders her daughter. Throughout the book Roxana has "only such a Repentance as a Criminal has at the Place of Execution, who is sorry, not that he has committed the Crime . . . but sorry *that he is to be Hang'd for it*" (129).

The most untragic story of all is the one that represents deserved misfortune. So one problem is how to suggest that Roxana is sinned against as well as sinning. Defoe fails to elevate her above the tawdriness of her deeds, and in that regard fails to create moving tragedy—but, viewed differently, Roxana's failure to achieve tragic stature is an indication of Defoe's deep ambivalence toward his heroine. The other difficulty is more serious. Whether the action is to be tragic or merely retributive, if the causal connection between Roxana's sin and her fate is to be thematically efficacious, Defoe has to find somewhere to locate the moral consciousness that will do the judging. If his earlier fiction taught him anything, it should have been that verisimilitude can get along without evaluation, as writers like Flaubert were to demonstrate in later years. Since we must, for the sake of the "moral," witness a character who cannot repent, Defoe's problem is where to place the retrospective, Olympian consciousness that must judge Roxana. By virtue of one of her ideological functions, the need for her to relate her own story, Roxana is closed off from performing another. Her passage to self-revelation, requisite to the tragic action, is occluded by the demands of the moral action. Unlike Moll, who narrates her life from a point of serenity, Roxana must remain unregenerate as she closes her story. Perhaps the story needs a vantage point, someone to say, "No, Roxana turned out all right at the end; it was what preyed on Roxana, what foul dust floated in the wake of her dreams." F. Scott Fitzgerald's solution to the problem of aesthetic distance in narrative was only possible, however, with the advent of a tradition of decentering the first-person narrator. Nick's uneasy mixture of admiration and disdain is a perfect blend to tell the story of Gatsby's fragile, deluded dream. Roxana must tell her own story for her self-condemnation to exert its full force because the spectacle Defoe wishes to exhibit is the horrible price in anguish a sinner must pay for her sin.

Of course, much can be accomplished by juxtaposition, by showing rather than telling, and that is just what Defoe had to rely on. It is here, in his attempts not only to reveal the tragedy through the consciousness of the very person who is experiencing it but also to have that narrator somehow convey the complex ideology that gives the story its moral seriousness, that we may conjecture what specific beliefs compelled Defoe to make his leap into the precincts of the novel.

The Novel as Exigence

Both Defoe and Roxana flee from past deeds, Defoe from the twin embarrassments of standing in the pillory and having to declare himself bankrupt, Roxana from her life as a paid mistress. Both creator and character are often deeply concerned with secrecy, Defoe as a spy and later as a double agent in print, Roxana as the fearful keeper, from her husband and even from her own daughter, of her dark secrets. Both learn to live in the presence of those they distrust, fear, even hate. Defoe complained to Charles De La Faye in 1718 that he was "Posted among Papists, Jacobites, and Enraged High Tories, a Generation who I Profess My Very Soul abhorrs. . . . Nay I often Venture to Let things pass which are a little shocking that I may not Render my Self Suspected" (Healey, 454). Roxana is under such severe self-imposed restraint not to reveal herself to her daughter, "so dangerous a Person," that, "for want of Vent, I thought I shou'd have burst" (284). Defoe's personal concerns contribute to the material action, and his own proximity to the vital situation of pursuit and flight assuredly lends *Roxana* much of its power, the effect one often feels when in the presence of a fictional illusion that is so gripping that one tends—even without evidence—to suspect its counterpart in the life of the author. It resembles, in the novel, the sort of lyric intensity one detects in a poem like "Prufrock," in which the representation of experience, obviously imagined in a character not meant to be confused with the author, nevertheless possesses a power inexplicable apart from our conception of it as issuing from the author's own pains and pleasures. Hemingway's explanation, that the author knows what to leave out in order to make us feel it all the more strongly by its absence, is another part of the effect. In stories like "Big Two-Hearted River," the sense of lyric intensity comes from our intuitive belief that Hemingway did indeed drop from that train in Seney, Michigan; did walk out on the bridge and see trout finning below him in the river; did need, at some point in his life, like Nick, to escape from something very disturbing to a simpler life. This conviction that the story is situated, both geographically and psychically, can be confirmed by anyone who has stood on the Soo Line railway bridge in Seney—over the Fox, not the Big Two-Hearted River—and subsequently read the story with a new kind of pleasure and immediacy.

A psychoanalytic critic might argue that this sense of identification arises because that is precisely what is happening: the character is living out the author's hidden conflicts—distanced, made into art, but personal nevertheless. While there is much of Defoe in Roxana, there are also many conflicting indications that Defoe conceived of Roxana as decidedly an "other." No simple autobiographical explanation for her relationship with her creator will suffice. For one thing, the two "models" on whom Defoe supposedly based Roxana—Mary Butler and Mademoiselle Bardou—were hardly people he could admire (Moore, 249–50). More important, as we shall shortly see, a hidden point of view in the novel suggests an even more fundamental alienation from his great moral reprobate, as well as the covert urgency that fueled the innovation.

Much of the novelistic complexity of Roxana's character is owing to just this duality, this mixture of attraction and repulsion in Defoe. Yet even if Roxana's terrible guilt-sickness, paralleling an analogous situation in Defoe's life, makes the novel all that much more interesting for us, it is still far from anything like a reliable indicator of the novel's or Defoe's meaning. The reason is, again, the nature of the book's innovation. In *Moll Flanders* or *Robinson Crusoe,* one often encounters ideas Defoe expressed elsewhere and one may be confident that Defoe is repeating himself in the fictional narrative. Even so, those ideas are never functionally expressive, never thematically activated. Such a subordination of personal belief to the demands of the action did not occur until *Roxana.* Here, however, one encounters another problematic feature of the action: its subject matter, the material "given" of the plot, may or may not reflect deep personal conviction. That Defoe chose to tell a story about a courtesan indicates very little about his personal beliefs. Only in the precise arrangement of fictional elements, the way ideas interact to create the action plot, can one discern the workings of beliefs that in all probability were Defoe's. This ideational functionality is, of course, Defoe's innovation in prose fiction, but it does not result in a form that is ideologically "transparent"—quite the contrary.

Often the most surprising discoveries about an action are the implications of relationships between overt beliefs. In the novels of Jane Austen one expects the fully functional thematization of Austen's views, although, as I argue in the next chapter, one may occasionally be surprised by what she features. It is clear that the sad fate of Charlotte Lucas plays up a contrast to Elizabeth's fate that the affective structure of *Pride and Prejudice* demands. It is equally clear that most experienced readers of Austen's fiction would not know what to do with a substructure that is not thematically operant, and this is just another indication that the one hundred years between Defoe and Austen was a century of narrative experimentation, especially in regard to the incorporation of values into mimetic fictions. One difficulty with the plots of actions, however, is that they tend to subordinate thematic issues in functionally different ways that may nevertheless easily be confused. For example, what might be termed the overt plot—the story the author intends to tell, the mimetic subject "chosen" from the welter of possibilities presented by experience or imagination, this "problem" of artful making—demands for its moral seriousness the representation of beliefs that are *not* usually "invented." It would be possible for Defoe to tell the story of a woman whose life as a paid mistress carries with it either no moral message at all or such a confused one that no reader can reliably decipher it. As I have argued, the status of ideological elements in most of his narratives is ambiguous. Even so, as soon as Defoe sees that he is committed to representing an action that *by definition* is moral— that is, an exemplification of the wages of sin—he cannot avoid endowing Roxana's life story with significance.

Moral Action, Tragic Action

Two aspects of Defoe's innovation in *Roxana* impinge upon each other. On the one hand, Defoe's entire career as protonovelist points toward creating a morally expressive action. In this sense, his story of a young woman who "wanted neither Wit, Beauty, or Money" (7) and who will exemplify in her downward path the anguish that is sin's punishment here on earth—the overt plot of *Roxana*—is a likely if not inevitable development from a career of inventing truthlike stories in which transgression does *not* necessarily entail damnation. All his energies, earlier thwarted by the very form he essayed, point toward the thematization of realistic action. Despite the rhetoric of repentance throughout the book, the plot's standard of inclusion dictates that the reader see early on that not only will Roxana not repent but also that her wrongdoing will not be "forgiven" by the implied author. She will be judged, and the plot of the novel is the realistic arrangement, in both poetic and rhetorical senses, of that judgment. Or, viewed in terms of Crocean poetics, Defoe finds a structure to convey whole his morally defined mimetic intuition.

Roxana's story presents Defoe with a series of branching alternatives. He might allow it to tend toward the punitive. Some scenes in the novel seem designed to elicit from the reader the disgust and condemnation appropriate to such an action; for example, the one in which Roxana encourages her own lover to sleep with her maid Amy, and watches the proceedings. This is, even today, a startling scene, one in which the narrator sees with horrible clarity the need and yet the danger of her turning her maid into a whore to "balance" her own sin. The novel's entire concluding sequence, in which Roxana gradually comes to acquiesce in the murder of her daughter, also seems to be an invitation to the severest kind of disapprobation. Indeed, many readers find Roxana fully deserving of her fate. At the same time, Defoe's attraction to her almost gives her tragic stature. Her sin is balanced by her suffering, and she does not whine or shrink from a full recognition of her guilt. Then too, from the beginning she is a victim of necessity, although she continues to sin after she is wealthy. The progress of her fortunes—from well-being to poverty, and then a rise toward stupendous material success, capped by the threat of exposure from her daughter and the likely loss of her fortune and even her liberty if her husband finds out about her shady past— suggests the tragic and not the punitive action. Whether the story calls forth tragic catharsis or satisfaction in justice done, Defoe finally finds a way to join individual acts, their consequences in Roxana's character, and the subsequent instability of action that results from that character attempting to make her way in a hostile world. While the plot suggests inevitability—a causal universe— Roxana's individual acts, viewed in isolation, are neutral in regard to values. The inevitability is one of form, and not material. Roxana's sins are punished because Defoe not only represents the sinner's finding her retribution right here on earth (even if quite the contrary is the fate of most villains), but also his own authorial, judging presence.

Roxana recognizes sin and commits it anyway. This awareness gives her a paradoxical stature, like Macbeth's. Unlike Moll, she sees herself clearly, and the retrospective narrator can judge her erring self, in an early version of what Dickens later discovered in the possibilities of the older Pip judging the younger. Because she "sinn'd with open Eyes," she "thereby had a double Guilt" upon her (43). She induces her new "husband" to commit adultery with her maid, and the pattern of sin and guilt is played out in the rest of the novel. One suspects that initially Defoe intended no more than to have Roxana's sins be punished by some objectification of divine Providence at the end of the story. It is this commonplace of Augustan England—poetic justice—that is behind the overt plot. In working his way toward this structure, Defoe is forced to specify, far more than in any of his other fictions, the precise moral and situational causes of his heroine's downfall. Since, above all, this is a story of personal sin and retribution—not, that is, a story about a malignant or uncaring cosmos waiting to punish overweening pride—Roxana may not "accidentally" fall into misery; she brings it upon herself in her interaction with other characters who, though perhaps, like Amy, are sinners themselves, fail to exculpate Roxana.

In this chiasmus of intentions, Roxana's tragedy departs from the purely punitive, for something in the character he has created attracts Defoe. Earlier forced into secrecy and hiding himself, knowing what it is to pretend to be what one is not, perhaps he feels a kinship with Roxana's desperate refusal to be known. Perhaps she allows him to play out, in a harmless fictional plot, fantasies too disreputable even for conscious thought; the intense voyeurism of some scenes stand out as sharply as they do in *Pamela*. At any rate, Defoe's great sinner, through her clear sight and self-understanding, becomes finally a character whose fall is affecting. Defoe represents not only the painful consequences of sin but also the pain itself. Roxana gains sympathy, becomes worthy of the tragic action Defoe designs for her, even while Defoe's unstinting judgment causes the reader to withhold full pity. The action form has, as one of its potential powers (one George Eliot developed to the fullest), the ability to represent mixed states of being, characters who attract the reader to the unrolling of their destinies even though they may be deficiently "heroic." Roxana's unsimplifiable character is the threshold of the modern world.

Defoe's ambivalence toward his creation, his use of her as example and as complex mimetic character—someone to care about, not just to use, as Bunyan and Johnson (skillfully, of course) used their didactic figures—creates the novel's second system of implication, the tragic one. It is easy enough to show Roxana sinning and suffering for it. Once she becomes something more than a mere carrier of the notion of poetic justice, develops into a "possible person," she moves toward the tragic. At this point, when the elements of plot coalesce around the Dutch Merchant, Defoe needs to find a way to represent the tragic fate so that it entails more than mere retribution. In specifying the causes and conditions of Roxana's fate, the way in which Defoe arranges for Roxana "to pay for Moll's holiday" (Flynn 1990:87), a covert ideology surfaces, unexamined but just as "present." As I argue throughout this volume, innovations in form frequently call forth representations of belief that "trail along" behind overt ideology, as if the story somehow creates part of its own authorial image. It is one thing to imagine a character whole, to endow her with beliefs that enact the author's ideas of what such a person might believe in such-and-such a situation. This is realism and, from the point of view of the psychological genesis of fictional plots, at least the conscious part of it, the surest measure of authorial intention. A standard of appropriateness, absent in the earlier pseudofactual narratives, makes the novel a powerful representation of ideology as well as reality. Characters can express authorial belief as a function of their plausibility. In any action that requires the representation of a change of state, character, or belief, the plot must be arranged causally. Static characters require that their creators decide how they should plausibly *be*. When the task is to specify *why* someone emerges from a long sequence of events either rewarded by fate or doomed to destruction, the representational task assumes political, even religious, consequences. This was, of course, Thomas Hardy's great difficulty. In Michael Henchard he constructed a convincing tragic figure who brings his troubles upon himself. A little intoxication, a little frustration with the way of the world, sell the wife, and later reap the consequences. At some point, however, Hardy changed his mind about the source of misery and turned to tragic actions that call for social causality, in the stories of Tess and Jude. In so doing, he parted company with many of his readers and created a significant problem for himself: How can Tess and Jude be tragic when the source of their troubles is largely outside themselves? Tragedy is a philosophical genre, whether in the novel, the drama, or on television. It requires that authors, real and implied, take stands, as Defoe found out.

This description of Hardy's difficulties is a useful oversimplification. The action form, unlike other literary forms, is a hybrid born of a realism that is neutral in regard to specific values and yet dependent for its very existence on the desire to give voice to belief. Defoe's difficulties begin not with the overt action but with his attempts to motivate Roxana's downfall. One part of the plot Defoe sees clearly is the role Roxana's gender will play. The first step on her road to perdition is, as so often is the case in Moll's story, involvement with a man who fails to provide for her. To this extent, and in other regards, the conscious, overt ideology of this book is as thoroughly feminist as Defoe's views of women—and they seem to have been relatively liberated—allow. Unlike Moll, Roxana is even given the opportunity to lecture the reader on the fate of women who trust men. First, of course, is her wonderful speech, "Never, Ladies, marry a Fool," on the theme of her first husband (8). While this passage is nearly comic, the consequences of Roxana's being left penniless are not: she yields up her virtue. By the time she meets the Dutch Merchant, who plays such an important part in the tragic sequence that concludes the novel, she is ready to lecture at length on the right and ability of women to manage their own fortunes and the dangers of trusting men: "The very Nature of the Marriage-Contract was . . . nothing but giving up Liberty, Estate, Authority, and every-thing, to the Man, and the Woman was indeed, a meer Woman ever after, that is to say, a Slave" (148).

It is no easy task to maintain one's admiration for Defoe's, or Roxana's, liberated views after Roxana herself confesses that this argument is a sham and that her real reason for rejecting the Dutch Merchant is that she has "a mortal Aversion to marrying him, or indeed, any-body else," because she still thinks herself "young, and handsome enough to please a Man of Quality," perhaps even the Prince again (161). In other words, behind Roxana's feminist views is an unrepentant sinner—and certainly in Defoe's view, liberation purchased at the price of one's soul is no freedom at all. Indeed, she alienates the Dutch Merchant so that he leaves her, deeply sad-dened by her refusal to marry him so as to satisfy the conventional hopes their sexual liaison has given him. She goes on to the high life of crime, the revelation of which later, when she is back with him again, so terrifies her because he would see all her protesta-tions of independence as so much Satan's rhetoric to justify her continued sinning. At that later point in the novel, the reasons for holding on to her own fortune, expressed in her oft-quoted manifesto, are reintegrated as causal elements, a terrible threat to her security, even her freedom. If the Dutch Merchant finds out about her lewdness, Roxana will indeed be in danger of losing "Liberty, Estate, Authority, and every-thing." Here, before the instability actually begins, her new feminism is old lust writ large, although until she becomes practiced in sin, it is, as is usual in Defoe, lust provoked by necessity.

Innovative structures frequently present us with such moments. The overt ideology of the developing plot, its authorized, respectable beliefs functioning as subordinated elements in the "official" plot, crosses paths with a second set of beliefs, unmeditated and unbidden, but arising because of the powerful demand that the progressive plot be motivated. Innovation draws forth confession. In this case, the need to generate a compelling sequence of events leading to Roxana's downfall provokes an overdetermined set of beliefs about female sexuality. The precise elements Defoe employs to specify Roxana's fate, to cause it and to define it, are economic ones, which affect men as well as women, as they do in his earlier books. Colonel Jack finds himself forced to criminality out of necessity, as does Moll. Yet the requirements of the new progressive structure force Defoe to give Roxana strong, continuing reasons for prolonging her career long after the pinch of necessity ceases to bruise. She must persist in what is viewed in the religious and social terms of the book's causal plot as her immoral life if the tragic outcome of her story is to be probable and emotionally convincing. As she puts it herself, late in her long career: "*Why am I a Whore now?*" (202). While Defoe does not provide Roxana with the "forbidden" answer to that question—an admission of her relish for the sexual act—the way he has her ponder her compulsion indicates that indeed Roxana, unlike Moll, is a "whore" because she wants to be. This is a moment of relatively "free" choice for Defoe. The plot of the novel requires that he establish the economic and social conditions, and Roxana's understanding of them, that form the basis for her ruin at the hands of her husband in this male-dominated society: marriage for women "was a dear Way of purchasing their Ease; for very often when the Trouble was taken off of their Hands, so was their Money too" (153). This passage occurs, of course, in the context of her famous feminist manifesto. Defoe has, therefore, all he needs to make psychologically convincing the entire sequence that ends with Roxana's startling acquiescence in the murder of her daughter; and his causal structure, while based on the economics of gender, is "respectable" because Roxana sins out of necessity. What she most fears, after she marries the Dutch Merchant, is the revelation that she has not been truthful about her motives and that she has, unlike him, shamefully neglected her children. Yet Roxana's fate, and the final turn of the plot, rests on another kind of fear.

After she and the Dutch Merchant part, Roxana is neither poor nor threatened with economic bondage through marriage. So why is she still a whore? "I cou'd not without blushing, as wicked as I was, answer that I lov'd it for the sake of the Vice, and that I delighted in being a Whore, *as such;* I say, I cou'd not say this, even to myself, *and all alone,* nor indeed, wou'd it have been true; I was never able in Justice, and with Truth, to say I was so wicked as that" (202). The answer, which she finds inadequate, is "Necessity . . . excess of Avarice . . . excess of vanity . . . Pride." These are the "Baits" and "Chains" by which she is "too fast held for any Reasoning" that she is "then Mistress of"—a nice, unconscious pun (202). As is so often the case with Roxana, her clear sight allows her a glimpse of her own motives, even though she cannot bring herself to admit them. So the question continues to rattle around in her brain, *"What am I a Whore for now?"* (203). The problem is complicated, of course, by the fact that Roxana's sin is crucial to the moral action. The fundamental proposition of the book is that here the sins of other characters, like Moll, will now be judged.

The overt choices of ideational elements signal an author whose innovation is to be put to the service of a freeing ideology. Roxana may be a rogue, may be designed as a warning to all readers, but she also has a past that justifies her, if not to herself, at least to many readers. Her first husband, the "fool," leaves her so destitute that her virtue is not proof against the kindness of the jeweller, her landlord. She yields to him much more from gratitude than from passion. The reader is clearly meant to believe that Roxana's moral lapses are simultaneously reprehensible and perfectly understandable. She will not be the effective moral exemplum she is designed to be if her failings are not somehow softened. This is why, as a fully realized part of Defoe's positive intention, Roxana is given sufficient latitude to escape the kind of opprobrium a punitive action would require. The reader is not to despise but rather to condemn her out of compassion.

A Second Ideology

If this is the comprehensive, humane, perhaps even the conscious intention that informs most of the choices Defoe initially makes in constructing his action, it is not the entire story. As preconditions for the causal action that ends the book, and as Defoe is called upon more and more to represent the precise situations of sin and the plausible reasons for Roxana's moral doom, a second ideology, in partial conflict with that of the overt action, begins to be apparent. First of all, other than her brewer husband and, less important, her "old lewd Favorite" later on, all the men in the book are exemplary figures, except in their understandable eagerness to sleep with Roxana. Even men who manage to avoid being captivated by Roxana's charms, like her brother-in-law, are represented as high-minded and charitable, ready to commit disinterested acts of benevolence. It is clear that, with a few exceptions, Roxana passes through life meeting only the best of the male sex and is, for Defoe and the reader, defined morally by contrast with them. For the sake of the overt action and its didactic freight, so far so good. The reader needs to know that in comparison with the Dutch Merchant, who always scrupulously guards the well-being of his children, no matter what the circumstances of their birth, Roxana is careless of her offspring, at least until late in her career. This sharp moral contrast serves the action well: among her other sins Roxana is an unfit mother. Since her failings are functions of the overt plot, however, they are largely ambiguous as indicators of authorial belief. Defoe needs to contrast Roxana with someone who will have a great deal to say about her fate, and her future husband is a logical choice: she will fear his good nature, fear that he will despise her if he finds out how criminally neglectful of her own children she has been. Put another way, this contrast is not a particularly gender-bound one, except in the sense that some readers, then and now, might consider uncaring behavior toward a person's own children more monstrous in a woman than in a man. The fact that Defoe chose to tell this story about a female sinner makes this contrast with a man almost inevitable.

Even so, it is this one cliché, formally functional and ethically neutral as a part of the *overt plot,* that opens the book up for inspection and reveals its covert ideology. It is most clearly represented at moments when Defoe's formal choices are more or less unconstrained by the demands of his own plot. No choice, of course, is ever undictated, ever really free, if only because writers usually choose to represent what they know best. Then too, all sorts of pressures to represent one kind of narrative causality rather than something else may come forth from unseen, unseeable corners of the psyche, those recesses of fear and secret desire that writers share with the rest of humanity. Even so, even if one wants to grant that "choice" in such matters is a mere chimera, some narrative choices are freer than others. It is these less constrained elements that allow the writer, depending upon the end in view, either to echo the clichés of the age or to construct a new and perhaps exemplary image of the writing self.

For Defoe, it begins to be apparent, Roxana's sin is clearly a feminine transgression. Perhaps even more surprising, however, is that the retribution Defoe has in store for her is somehow "appropriate" to female crime. Defoe conceives of Roxana, no matter how much he has come to admire her, as an example of specifically feminine lewdness. The plot enacts, usually against the overt rhetoric of women's independence and capability, a number of anti-feminine commonplaces. Its causal structure ascribes virtue and rational disinterest to men, promotes a view of female carnality as an involuntary coup of the weak will, and punishes Roxana's womanly transgression with the pain of lost fortune. Thus it is appropriate that female lust forfeit its whore-begotten lucre, and the later continuation of the novel (not by Defoe) appropriately works out Roxana's punishment by her husband. The plot of the action requires that the author create his or her own presence for the story's sake. Defoe has finally done so, and, whatever he thought he believed about women, a disguised set of stereotyping beliefs has been called forth by the urgent requirements of the new form.

That Defoe, and readers, find much to like in Roxana just makes these indirectly expressed beliefs that much worse. The affective resources of the action are directed at attracting us to a character who is defined in precisely the terms that should make us despise the degree to which she partakes of the "general character of women." In this way, the action becomes a treacherous resource, a way to represent ideology, but not always the ideology the author intends to promulgate. Johnson was right in saying that the action can teach against the reader's will; but it can also teach us things the author thinks hidden. For example, it is necessary for the sake of the plot that Roxana accumulate a debt of sensual sin scandalous enough to make plausible her extreme reluctance to have it revealed to the Dutch Merchant. For this reason she is allied with a series of men. All that is absolutely necessary is that they be her lovers. Defoe is free to specify whatever particular traits he wishes for them, just so long as it is clear that Roxana sins willfully. Even so, one after another, her men are represented as morally superior to Roxana in ways that are themselves, especially in Defoe's time, matters of gender. Indeed, Roxana frequently sins against the direct urgings, or at least the examples, of these male paragons.

In this book it is the women who are consistently the inferior parents. This is the case even very early in the book, when Defoe most probably did not know exactly how it was going to end. When Roxana's husband leaves her and, as she says, the "Misery of my own Circumstances hardned my Heart against my own Flesh and Blood" (19), it is Amy who reports to Roxana the details of how her children, whom Roxana is forced to farm out to relatives, are received. At the first place Amy takes them, she pushes them into the house and makes a quick exit. The children's aunt receives them bitterly: "what does she send her Bratts to me for?" (20). Her inhumanity is quickly and sharply countered by her husband, however, who arrives a short time later and immediately views sympathetically the plight of the unfortunates, who include among them the daughter, Susan, who many years later will become her mother's nemesis. Unlike his wife, whose "Heart was harden'd against all pity"—like Roxana—this man, who is not even "nearly related to the Children," says at once that "something must be done" (22). His argument against his wife's almost savage lack of charity is based on scripture and on a simple good heart. Roxana herself summarizes: "It would take up too long a Part of this Story to give a particular Account with what a charitable Tenderness this good Person, who was but Uncle-in-Law to them, manag'd that Affair . . . but 'tis enough to say he acted more like a Father to them, than an Uncle-in-Law, tho' all along much against his Wife's Consent, who was of a Disposition not so tender and compassionate as her Husband" (24–25). The retrospective point of view brings out Roxana's duplicity, her clear vision glancing back with the knowledge of later sorrow. The lesson, however, is not just that Roxana, in ignoring ties of consanguinity, lays up a store of damnation. It is also that men—these men, at least—do not commit such horrors.

If what I have been saying about the free-floating nature of ethical elements in most of Defoe's works before *Roxana* is at all accurate, perhaps I ought to be less willing at this point to draw conclusions about Defoe's beliefs. It might be argued that since this section comes early in the book, long before the disparate elements of the story fall into a coherent novelistic arrangement, it is not possible to say whether Defoe really believed that women as a group are naturally less caring of children than men, although clearly we are meant to believe that Roxana is capable of neglecting her own, in part as an element in the general portrait of a fallen woman, in part so that her final catastrophe is plausible. Yet, once a storyteller begins to think functionally, as Defoe has in this novel, unassimilated, or what I have called "optional," elements stand out in a way they never do in Defoe's pseudofactual works. Having begun to think of Roxana's character as part of something larger, as something to specify for the overall plot, different standards of construction now prevail. If Defoe is faced with an episode like this one—which, while requiring that he move the action forward by ridding Roxana of her children and while providing another moral contrast, still leaves the *means* of those ends largely indifferent— and he nevertheless sets up the moral contrasts in terms of gender, he has tipped his hand. The action requires the author to think functionally, but it lies in ambush, so to speak, for the appearance

of an unexamined belief. The form is therefore a rich but treacherous repository of authorial belief, conscious and otherwise. It is
no accident that such a causal structure, especially in its overtly
moral nineteenth-century examples, has become a favorite subject
of the deconstructionists.

In the act of slicing off this or that section of reality to endow
with causality, no author can foresee all of the possible implications
of his or her selection. While some "omissions" may seem more
heinous than others—racial and sexual ones are currently most
particularly objectionable, as they should be—the politics of absence will always change from age to age. I have more to say about
this question in the final chapter, but it may just be that critiques of
absence, more than any other form of adversarial criticism, are
doomed to very short periods of relevance.

Even so, it is not possible to ignore Defoe's hidden bias, which
is most striking when he is thinking functionally in *Roxana*. Here,
however, the issue is trickier, since, as with many later novelists,
other thematic functions may be so distinct from gender issues—in
the mind of the author, at least—that what seem to be sexist
elements creep in by "overlap." For example, it is necessary that
Roxana's last husband, the Dutch Merchant, be represented as
likely to abhor the precise nature of Roxana's past transgressions.
He is a good father, an honest man, and unwilling to continue an
illicit sexual union when Roxana first rejects his proposal of marriage. Between her two liaisons with him, her life as a highly paid
courtesan is just what would fill him with loathing if he ever found
out—and she knows it, which is why she later goes along with Amy
in ridding them both of Susan's threat. Nothing in these necessities
of plot tips the slightest hint that Defoe thinks the Dutch Merchant is morally superior by virtue of being a man; he is morally
superior to Roxana so that he can fulfill a narrative function that
also requires him to be male. In addition, of course, this concluding
action, in which the Dutch Merchant acts as a fearful catalyst, is
the tightest part of the book, where narrative functions are often
most stringently prescribed by the exigencies of plot.

Yet it is at those interstices of the book in which male characters
seem overdetermined, given their particular function, that Defoe's
concealed sexual bias becomes most apparent. The Prince, for

example, initially is just another exciting, albeit more exotic, lover for Roxana. He has had many sexual partners and knows how to hide his acts from the public eye and, most of the time, from his saintly wife. He is a sophisticated and attractive moral step downward, in the direction of the "old lewd Favorite" Roxana ends up accommodating for money later on. Even so, he also plays his part, as do most of Roxana's men, in the larger overt action, which has as its means to a moral conclusion a consistent comparison of preferable moral alternatives with Roxana's disreputable practices. The Prince is, under that scheme, a responsible father to their illegitimate child, and his "reformation" after his wife's death causes him to view his life with Roxana and his other mistresses with loathing and removes him from her arms.

It becomes clear that Defoe represents all of Roxana's lovers, and a number of men she meets only casually or in business, as *more* superior to Roxana than they need to be for the sake of either the general moral action or the more tightly constructed tragic conclusion. For better or worse, this is the way the action form operates: requiring that beliefs be specified for the sake of the plot, it invites thematization at every turn, even where the demands of the action would settle for less specification. This first action in English prose fiction, in its expressive choices, allows Defoe to speak through his plot. To speak, of course, is always an act of exclusion, to choose to say this rather than something else. What Carol Houlihan Flynn says of Defoe's "cranky, late work," *Conjugal Lewdness,* applies as well to *Roxana:* "Defoe ends up entangled in the argument he tries to make" (38).

It is now possible to explain one puzzling feature of the book: the sexual tawdriness it shares with another pioneering action, Samuel Richardson's *Pamela.* Even readers sympathetic to Roxana's need to provide for herself are often shocked by the early scene in which she puts her maid and alter ego, Amy, to bed with the jeweller and then watches the sexual show. Roxana is shocked by her own actions, and her explanation is part of the novel's overt, conventional plot. "Had I look'd upon myself as a Wife, you cannot suppose I would have been willing to have let my Husband lye with my Maid, much less, before my Face, for I stood-by all the while;

but as I thought myself a Whore, I cannot say but that it was something design'd in my Thoughts, that my Maid should be a Whore too, and should not reproach me with it" (47). While it is another step toward the moral doom Roxana is to suffer, the description of Roxana's act is startling by virtue of its very explicitness and the indirect but unmistakable language of sexuality in which it is narrated.

> I sat her down, pull'd off her Stockings and Shooes, and all her Cloaths, Piece by Piece, and led her to the Bed to him: *Here,* says I, *try what you can do with your Maid* Amy: She pull'd back a little, would not let me pull off her Cloaths at first, but it was hot Weather, and she had not many Cloaths on, and particularly, no Stays on; and at last, when she see I was in earnest, she let me do what I wou'd; so I fairly stript her, and then I threw open the Bed, and thrust her in.

"This is enough," Roxana summarizes, "to convince any-body that I did not think him my Husband, and that I had cast off all Principle, and all Modesty, and had effectually stifled Conscience" (46). That conventional, formulaic self-condemnation is part of the moral action, as is Roxana's psychologically compelling explanation that she wanted Amy to "be a Whore too," but these explanations miss what is also going on, titillation. That recognition Roxana skillfully avoids. The jeweller's only role is cheerfully to accept the gift of Amy's innocence. It is Amy and Roxana who are the centers of our attention. Amy barely struggles, she has few garments on, it is hot. Roxana is herself excited by her part in undressing Amy: she strips, she throws, she thrusts. It is as if the language suggests Roxana's verging on a voyeuristic orgasm—and Defoe has Roxana describe the disrobing twice. The scene is far more sexually charged than seems required by anything in the overt plot. In fact, it runs the risk of alienating the reticent or religious reader from Roxana almost before her story gets under way. As another surfacing of the submerged plot—the representation of the dangers of feminine lust—however, its language of sexual excitement undermines the language of self-reproach Roxana goes on to employ. While it is risky to suggest that Defoe himself took covert pleasure in his representation of Roxana's sexual escapades, the moral plot is here countered by the tendency of mimesis to create its own unofficial interests.

In writing a kind of protoaction, Defoe ascribed causality of character to a train of events. In doing so, he revealed that he was at least highly interested in the idea of a woman who likes physical love. Why need we go further? Must we assume that because Defoe doomed Roxana for her sensual sins that he feared female sexuality? I don't think the conclusion follows, especially since one of the functions of a novel for an author is the opportunity to "try out" a belief. In his version of the living/writing Defoe, J. M. Coetzee represents his character, "Foe," as fearful of Roxana's sexuality. Foe reacts with alarm when Susan/Roxana assumes the superior position as they make love. It is an interesting idea to explore in a novel about a fictional Defoe, but I do not think it automatically means that Coetzee tosses and turns at night worrying about whether women will get on top.

Here, as in the other innovations to be studied, the new form serves as a reply that raises more questions than it answers. An attempt at reparation, it opens new theaters of conflict with the reader and with the writing self. The urgent innovation is like a new personality—a gesture toward putting the past in its place so it may be superseded, abolished, forgotten. Even a genuinely new form like *Roxana* often turns back on the author the suppressed ideology of earlier efforts. It is, however, more dangerous to extract ideology from stories than most commentators seem to realize. Indeed, the assurance with which I have identified a "hidden" ideology in *Roxana* is undermined by my awareness of the always vexing problematic of the relationship between narrative form and belief, a question I return to in the concluding chapter.

In the next chapter I offer two very different examples of innovative comic form split apart by conflicting ideologies. In the works of Goldsmith and Austen, innovative structures refuse to encompass everything they provoke and reject the older ways of writing and reading comedy, only to fail to substitute alternatives.

3

Comic Fiction and
Ideological Instability
Goldsmith and Austen

Charlotte's Way

Jane Austen claimed to her nephew, James Edward Austen-Leigh, that her intention in her fiction was "to create, not to reproduce" (*Memoir*, 375). Freed, if she was, from the need to be true to the psychological complexity of real people, did she find the task of invention just as constricting in a different way? The very terms of the comic actions she chose to write forced her to think hard about matters central to happiness, her own as well as her characters', since her fiction was always intended to be serious. One remembers the painful moment in *Pride and Prejudice* when Lizzy Bennet exclaims to her best friend: "Engaged to Mr. Collins! my dear Charlotte,—impossible!" Charlotte, having "regained her composure," explains that since she is "not romantic," her expectations in marriage encompass "only a comfortable home." Given Collins's situation, her "chance of happiness with him is as fair, as most people can boast on entering the marriage state" (113). Austen's world may hold the tragic, but it does not usually linger over it.

The outcome of Charlotte's acceptance of the ludicrous Collins is probably a lesson in the despair born of cynicism, one she chooses not to share with her friend, or Austen with the reader. However, in a famous passage, Austen gives Charlotte's reasons: "Without thinking highly either of men or of matrimony, marriage had always been her object; it was the only honourable provision for well-educated young women of small fortune, and however uncertain of giving happiness, must be their pleasantest preservative from want" (111). A reasonable view of this line of the plot is that Austen needed Charlotte's sad decision, her exile to the back parlor and vain hopes for entertainment from her poultry, only to contrast as a kind of "alternate fate" with Lizzy's marriage of sensibilities. Even so, it is a mistake to assume from such a striking opposition of fates that Austen held Charlotte's Way in unqualified scorn. Indeed, Charlotte's very language, if not her sentiments, are almost Johnsonian, and the bestowal of such diction may indicate that Austen took her views seriously, even if they only make Lizzy laugh. "Happiness in marriage," Charlotte rejoins, "is entirely a matter of chance. If the dispositions of the parties are ever so well known to each other, or ever so similar before-hand, it does not advance their felicity in the least. They always contrive to grow sufficiently unlike afterwards to have their share of vexation; and it is better to know as little as possible of the defects of the person with whom you are to pass your life" (19). Even with its comic undertones—"share of vexation"—the reader cannot view Charlotte's decision as mere stupid avarice. The distance between her eloquent self-defense and her future spouse's doltish utterances is the linguistic measure of the unhappiness she embraces. Yet any attempt to convict her of cynicism makes one wonder what else she could have done. Charlotte, in short, is not just a plot function but an ideological alternative that Austen took with sad seriousness (see Phelan, 294–95).

Even so, the comic plot that contains Charlotte's views encourages the reader to repudiate Charlotte's Way. Perhaps comedy always doubles back upon itself in this fashion, raising unanswerable questions about the relationship between merit and fate in the very presentation of deserving and undeserving characters. Austen certainly didn't decipher the code of conduct in relation to marriage, in real life or in art. Writing to her niece, Fanny, who was trying to decide how to respond to the attentions of a young man, Austen advised her "not to think of accepting him unless you really do like him. Anything is to be preferred or endured rather than marrying without Affection" (Chapman, 410). That "anything"—spinster-hood, for example, one alternative to Charlotte's "only honourable provision"—implies female choice, no matter how bleak, how so-cially "forced," a meaning that "spinster" must evoke. Later in life, however, Austen was less certain. She wrote, again to Fanny, who did not marry after all, "Single Women have a dreadful propensity for being poor—which is one very strong argument in favour of Matrimony . . . you will in the course of the next two or three years, meet with somebody more generally unexceptionable than anyone you have yet known" (Chapman, 483). Here, in the guise of playful advice, which she might offer but would never take herself, is Charlotte's Way.

Austen was as aware as anyone of the role marriage may play in the general drama of the vanity of human wishes. The comic forms she took as her own, however, required her to present at least the il-lusion of better and worse ways of going about marrying—al-though marriage is only the particular metaphor for moral choice she chose to elucidate—since comedy makes a steady diet of admi-ration for some characters, those who "do right," and at least mild disapproval for those who go astray. Even so, serious comedy does not solve the problem of merit, it only makes it unavoidable. In her refusal to write a comic "virtue rewarded" lies Austen's great com-plexity. Yet the tension between the abeyance of ideology and the requirements of "lightness" and "brightness" in comedy remains throughout Austen's work as a generic legacy. What might have happened if her own comic forms had increasingly reminded her, in their demands that deserving characters be rewarded, of these unanswerable questions about merit and fate? Put another way, if one invests one's artistic faith in the serious representation of comic fulfillment, only to find the reward the form requires—no matter how whimsically you contrive to bestow it on an Emma or a Fanny—conflicting with the way the world treats merit, won't comedy itself begin to look suspect? Even were it one of the steadfast properties of narrative to be ideologically impenetrable, or even confused, my point would still hold. Austen might very well have started searching for a new kind of story, even if she alone perceived the disturbing implications of her earlier ones.

Defoe's task was to find an ideologically effective narrative structure. Subsequent experiments—in Richardson, Fielding, Goldsmith, and Burney, among many others—centered on the latent thematic potential of the new progressive narrative structure, the novel. As its fundamental, defining operation, the action creates expectations of a probable fate for a character. Many of the constructional difficulties in the action arise because of the unquestioned necessity that fiction be didactic as well as entertaining. The spectacle one encounters at every turn in early English fiction is the explosion of ideology, the inundation of story by a torrent of didactic material. Pert Pamela yields place to the majestic Clarissa—surely an improvement, except in the length that Richardson thought established her moral grandeur—only to be supplanted by the deadly perfection of Grandison, a lamentable adherence if ever there was one to Johnson's stricture that fiction should show only the "most perfect idea of virtue."[1]

Neither Richardson nor Fielding ever completely abandoned the realistic action for the more direct moralizing of the parable, although it does seem, in *Grandison* and even at times in *Amelia*, that the scintillation of the earlier novels was somehow misplaced. One certainly can argue that Richardson and Fielding, unlike Defoe and the other authors I am studying, spent their innovations at the beginning of their novelistic careers, only to refine and even vitiate them in passions of exemplary activity later. The didactic pressures on the innovation of comic forms near the rise of the novel may perhaps be seen most clearly in the single novel Goldsmith wrote. His popular success with *The Vicar of Wakefield* masked his confusion about how ideas might function in realistic comic fiction. His difficulties in turn opened up the later ones of Jane Austen, who devoted her career first to solving the problems she inherited from earlier comic fiction and then, dissatisfied with the implications of what she had wrought, to attempting to find an alternative to the traditional action of romantic fulfillment. Both novelists had to find ways to respond to the action's requirement that the author decide what part virtue plays in the world; and both, Goldsmith obviously, Austen less so, wrote novels that are only partially adequate representations of the issues. However, in their idiosyncratic, unique responses to the pressures of belief, one may clearly see, as with Defoe, the terrain of the new and, hypothetically, the terms of success within its boundaries.

Goldsmith, Social Pathos, and New Comedy

Not much has been written about *The Vicar of Wakefield* in the past decade, which is puzzling given the book's incontestable status as problematic classic. In part, the silence may be owing to Robert Hopkins's now decades-old interpretation of the work, which "settled" the question of Goldsmith's intention for many readers by making it both unified and pervasively ironic, although Hopkins still had strong opposition (Hopkins; Ferguson). Indeed, many readers still refuse to see the Vicar in anything but a benevolent light, as one of the most prominent of those creations of the later eighteenth-century "amiable humorists," as Tave called them (1960). Despite Hopkins's contention that irony, of a rather ungentle sort, unifies *Vicar*, my years of teaching it convince me that most readers continue to take the Vicar as a basically good but comically flawed character, and their responses are not to be dismissed. More important for my argument here, many readers perceive a shift near the middle of the book, a novelistic sea change. As with most innovations, it is possible to argue persuasively on one side or the other, that the book is coherently comic or the result of mixed intentions. David H. Richter has succinctly detailed the formal problems and the resulting critical disagreements. Goldsmith begins the book with the intention of creating a gentle, comic portrait of an admirable but flawed hero, shows him enduring a series of hardly life-threatening misfortunes, and ends the story with his restoration to serene stability. Formally a descendent of Fielding's *Joseph Andrews*, even in its emphasis on the comic fortunes of a group of people rather than an individual, it enlists the intimacy of the first-person point of view as the best way both to reveal and to judge the Vicar's comic faults. Along the way, however, Goldsmith realizes that he is having difficulty conveying through the consciousness of his narrator the precise judgments necessary for a comic action, especially subtle ethical distinctions and the comic reassurance needed as the family experiences progressively greater misfortunes.

These more serious threats lead us to Goldsmith's innovation and his problems with it. With the Vicar's quest to regain his daughter, the story leaves behind strategies of comic mimesis to adopt the more direct address of the parable, the subject shifting to the precarious position of impoverished, principled virtue in a vicious society. When Goldsmith comes to the end, he therefore faces two sets of closural choices. He may satisfy the earlier comic expectations involving reward, or the Vicar's seemingly irreversible downward plunge may end in his pathetic demise. Goldsmith, with some awkward tightrope work, manages a comic ending. In so doing he sacrifices completeness—the reader's sense of all the significant issues raised by the story being resolved—to closure, the mere sense of an ending (Richter, 171–76).

Unless one is enamored of the ironic interpretation, this analysis seems difficult to resist. It not only explains the fragmentation many readers encounter in the novel, it also precisely pinpoints the critical disagreements surrounding the text almost since its publication. Richter's analysis leaves us only one question: *Why* were the "two halves of *The Vicar* . . . written to diverse ends" (Richter, 172)? The answer lies, it seems to me, in the conflict between the ideas implied by the comic action Goldsmith originally intended to execute and other ideas his social conscience would not permit him to abandon, not even at the price of destroying his comic invention. The story, as originally conceived, demands one set of beliefs for its successful completion. The author, surveying the British Isles from Dublin to Margate, demands another, and the dictates of Goldsmith's pressing social conscience win out, at least briefly.

While Defoe's task was to invent a communicative structure out of the silences of the pseudofactual mode, Goldsmith had available many examples of the new form, the action. He had something else, too, a highly developed tradition of the nonrealistic prose fable, as practiced superbly by his friend Samuel Johnson in *Rasselas* a short time before Goldsmith began *Vicar*. With these two distinct sets of formal requirements beckoning to him, Goldsmith found himself with a choice perhaps unique in the history of prose fiction. He could follow Fielding or Johnson, or find a way to adapt the "comic epic poem in prose" to the work of the apologue, the parable. He possessed, according to Boswell, very definite ideas about how the fable, at least in its "beastly" variety, should be written. Some years after he wrote *Vicar,* "Goldsmith said, that he thought he could write a good fable," a form which he insisted required "simplicity" but also a knack for establishing the illusion of fidelity. The problem was that "in most fables the animals introduced seldom talk in character. . . . The skill . . . consists in making [fish] talk like little fishes." During this disquisition on fabular verisimilitude, Johnson's generously endowed flanks were quivering with amusement, which prompted Goldsmith to assert, "Why, Dr. Johnson, this is not so easy as you seem to think; for if you were to make little fishes talk, they would talk like WHALES" (Boswell, 2:231). Goldsmith may not have had the problem of imagining appropriate fishly talk in *Vicar,* but he did have to find a way to convey, through his narrator, information the Vicar cannot be aware he possesses, a sufficiently difficult act of ventriloquism.

Why did Goldsmith even bother? Since he seems to have been committed, by the end of the novel at least, to a coherent set of beliefs, why didn't he emulate Johnson's complex offering of the *dulce et utile* and write a coherent moral fable like *Rasselas?* Of course, Goldsmith was not Johnson; he lacked his friend's confidence, born of years of presenting reasoned opinions directly to the public. Johnson, who ought to have known, contended that "Goldsmith had no settled notions upon any subject; so he talked always at random" (Boswell, 3:252). Johnson much earlier noted that, when talking, Goldsmith "goes on without knowing how he is to get off" (Boswell, 2:196). Now, while it is probable that Goldsmith, like Johnson himself, did not write as he spoke in casual conversation, here is testimony to the personal origin of two striking features of *Vicar,* its ideological confusion and its change of direction. At the same time, we should not forget that both Boswell and Burke vouched for the general opinion that, in his works, Goldsmith "touched nothing he did not adorn." Boswell actually believed that Goldy's inspired idiocy in conversation had "been greatly exaggerated" (Boswell, 1:412). What emerges from the composite portrait is a man of brilliance whose convictions and rhetorical sense are often less than sure.

On the other hand, it is a mistake to overemphasize Johnson's moral certainty, despite the image of him in conversation that one imbibes from Boswell's *Life*. Based on the evidence of his prayers and meditations, his perplexity about the ways of God was genuine and unremitting. Even so, about many issues, such as the sources of happiness and misery, or the possible relationship between moral uprightness and good fortune, Johnson thought long and thought hard. When he sat down to write *Rasselas* in 1759, the ideas came pouring out. This exposition of the impossibility of permanent happiness is neither shallow nor simplistic, but it is sure. Johnson knew what he wanted to say, and how, and did both quite well indeed. He dealt with many of these same ideas ten years earlier in *The Vanity of Human Wishes*, and while working on the *Dictionary* was obliged (to eat) to elucidate complex moral ideas in *The Rambler*, a twice-weekly task that would tend to hone one's rhetorical facility.

It is easy to forget that most of Goldsmith's *original* works, especially the ones on which his reputation mainly rests, were written after he completed *Vicar*. In 1760 and 1761 he owned neither Johnson's experience nor his certainty. He had published nothing with his own name on the title page. It is not unreasonable to conclude that he never arrived at Johnson's confidence with ideas. In the decade that followed *Vicar*, Goldsmith endured the gratuity of somewhat contradictory conclusions, contributed by Johnson, to both *The Traveller* and *The Deserted Village*. It is no insult to Goldsmith to assert that Johnson needed no such help.

Johnson never subjected himself to the special demands of a mimetic work—with the possible exception of his play *Irene*—a realistic and self-contained world subordinating ideology to the workings of a probable plot. He never faced the exigencies of wedding verisimilar story and idea. This is not to underrate the difficulty or originality of *Rasselas* or Johnson's other works, but only to suggest that his attempts at prose fiction were not new in the way that *Vicar* was. Whatever Goldsmith's limitations as a systematic thinker, the ideological demands his novel placed on him were enormous. *The Vicar of Wakefield* may be most interesting precisely because it shows how the structure of the early comic novel may be warped by radically incommensurable beliefs struggling to achieve expression.

In addition, Goldsmith's ideological task was complicated by his difficulties with point of view. Unlike Johnson, whose serene and distanced narrator in *Rasselas* fully meets his need, Goldsmith had to find a way to design his tale so that the narrator himself could reveal his own fate while immersed in its working out. For the comedy to work, the Vicar must disclose not only his misfortunes and his reactions to them but also, covertly and indirectly, the promised means for their removal. It is the classic difficulty faced by anyone writing a first-person progressive action, comic or otherwise, as authors as diverse as Mark Twain, Joyce Cary, and Hemingway discovered. The ironic tone of the opening chapters of *Vicar* and the clear pattern of happiness interrupted by misfortune which in turn yields to happiness again go far toward establishing a pervasive comic power. Goldsmith's treatment is not, of course, without awkwardness, especially in the handling of Burchell. For example, at one point he reveals to the Vicar that he *is* the Sir William he has seemed to be telling a story about. The Vicar seems at first to ignore the inadvertent disclosure, only shortly later to show that he has heard Burchell's words but not understood their meaning.[2] Mostly, however, Goldsmith's solutions to the novel's early formal demands are more than adequate.

It is only when the threats to the Primrose family become potentially irreversible that Goldsmith's task seems too difficult. Almost every critic of the novel's structure has noticed that something happens to the comic tone when the Vicar is forced to endure a painful burning, commitment to debtor's prison, a son condemned to death, and the death of one daughter and the kidnapping of the other. It is not that these barriers have some inherent quality unsuiting them for comedy, since even death can be comically reversed without violating probability. The problem is rather that Goldsmith loses control of his chief formal innovation in the novel, the dual voice that allows the Vicar to be genial dunce and comic hero in short succession. Even so, since this is a formal problem as capable of solution as others in the novel, it may be more accurate to suggest that Goldsmith somehow lost his reason for perpetuating the comic voice and tone that give the early chapters their vivacity and constitute his chief innovation.

That he limited his revision of the novel to stylistic matters is puzzling, especially given how long the book sat in the publisher's hands, although Goldsmith's explanation to Boswell—"had I made it ever so perfect or correct, I should not have had a shilling more"—is not to be despised (Goldsmith 1966:8). The reason he did not "renovate" his novel is that as he wrote he gradually came to realize, I think, that the first half, which charms so many more readers than the second, Job-like half, distorted his political convictions. While it may be going too far to suggest that, like Defoe, Goldsmith subsequently refrained from attempting another novelistic action because of what he learned about its demands on his own resources of belief, the ideological premises of the comic section of the book conflict sharply with the assumptions of the second part. The shift in structure is a symptom of a change of mind: Goldsmith ended up at odds with his own representation of reality.

The barriers that Goldsmith incorporated as elements of his comic action fall into the two common types: those existing outside the Primrose family and those that are fundamental parts of their character and familial life. Entire comic actions may be based on one or the other. Ordinarily both are present, and an author's emphasis on external or internal barriers may or may not be thematically purposeful; it is impossible to say in advance because the complexity of ideological questions is always owing to the demands of the scene in which they are enacted. In *Joseph Andrews,* no thematic statement is implied by the relative *proportions* of happiness Joseph and Fanny gain, because they have remained true to each other and because they have overcome the wiles of a base world; nor is it clear what they owe to their own goodness and what to help from Adams. Fielding's brand of realism so melds personal and social responsibility that the two are impossible to disentangle, and that is part of Fielding's thematic point. In *Tom Jones,* final fulfillment results through happy accident: neither Tom's reformation, his new prudential resolves, nor any particular success virtue has in defeating evil contributes to the end. That scrupulously avoided connection between active virtue and reward is the very ideological basis of the formal whole (see Wess).

In *Vicar,* the internal barriers to happiness are all initially innocent, and, with the exception of Olivia's loss of chastity, which is scarcely redeemed by the final revelation of the unshammed marriage, they remain so. The mother is foolish and vain, as are the daughters. The sons have little knowledge of the world. The Vicar himself is a failed patriarch. The scene in which he tips over the facial wash his daughters are slyly preparing shows his most serious liability, his indirection—although, in the reading, it seems harmless enough. In public situations with Thornhill, however, the morally neutral idiosyncrasy becomes dangerous. The Vicar's limited wisdom does not allow him sufficient prescience to consistently make the distinction. While he may safely eliminate by subterfuge a harmful cosmetic, the family's acquaintance with Squire Thornhill, begun in the previous chapter, promises threats against which indirection will only invite insult and degradation.

In the sylvan setting of the Primroses' backyard, the first meeting with the Squire seems only vaguely disturbing, and only to the Vicar and the reader, since Goldsmith uses his innovative point of view to align the reader with Primrose. Unlike his wife and daughters, however, the Vicar has already learned from the innkeeper that the Squire is a man "particularly remarkable for his attachment to the fair sex" and that "scarce a farmer's daughter within ten miles round but what had found him successful and faithless" (27). Everything about the first meeting starts to seem slightly ominous. The Squire and his companions are pursuing a stag and are about to dispatch it. He approaches the Primroses with a "careless superior air" and insists upon formally kissing the two daughters, although, for once, they initially resist the affront until Thornhill lets them know that he owns everything within their ken. This implied threat, or promise, as the mother later takes it, gets him his kisses. He prevails upon the girls for a song, but here Primrose puts his foot down—for a perfect stranger, making such a request is presumptuous, and granting it indecorus. As in the wash scene to come, the Vicar attempts to convey indirectly, and only by a cautionary wink aimed at his daughters, the disapproval he should direct at them and the Squire. The Vicar's wink is "counteracted by one from their mother," and the Squire gets his song, too—a love song from Dryden, of all things, with its associations of Restoration licentiousness. By the end of the Squire's flirtations with the Primrose daughters, "an age could not have made them better acquainted," a wonderfully ironic commentary, not just on the social aberrance of the moment and the times but also on the Squire's emptiness and social disqualification to be "known" except on his own terms, illicitly, by inferiors (36).

Like Miss Elizabeth Bennet's mother on first hearing of Mr. Bingley's prospective residence at Netherfield Park, Mrs. Primrose's first and last thought is, what a wonderful thing for my girls. Her own jubilant phrase, "what a fortunate hit," is again ironically revealing, since the acquaintance will result in the near destruction of the family. The Vicar is not fooled. The way he puts it after the Squire departs and he finally gets around to his patriarchal duty—"Disproportioned friendships ever terminate in disgust"—is both on and off target. The problem with the Squire is not so much inequality of rank as a shriveled heart. The Vicar, of course, sees immediately that his neighbor is more interested in conquest than in marriage, but the real problem is the fist of property and wealth hidden inside the velvet glove of the sexual charade. As the Vicar says, "notwithstanding all his ease . . . he seemed perfectly sensible of the distance between us" (37–38). Unlike Austen's Bingley, whose "lively and unreserved" manners at the ball indicate his true character as a man of "amiable qualities," ready to make friends without reminding anyone of his "four or five thousand a year" (*Pride and Prejudice,* 2), Thornhill makes friends with young ladies by reminding them and their mothers of what a prize he would be. Of course, he never intends to be won.

Thornhill, then, is a true villain, a kind of unrepenting Squire B. who, like Richardson's character, bends the country's laws in his attempts to force the wills of his social inferiors. He changes the entire course of the novel. Until Thornhill enters, nothing prevents Goldsmith from continuing the pattern of gentle domestic comedy with which he began the novel and which perhaps has its height of pure good feeling in chapter 4. The family so far deserves nothing but the mildest visitations of domestic inquietude. The loss of their money was not avoidable, as the Vicar rightly observes, by any "prudence of ours" (26). It is an unpleasant economic accident, beneath the notice of a religious man, and certainly nothing on which to base a philosophy. Goldsmith's course seems clear. He must find ways to entangle the felicity of the family, perhaps by the wiles of a less vengeful Thornhill, until the complications may be untied and felicity restored. Even the assumptions for such an action are already present. The heading to chapter 3 is "A migration. The fortunate circumstances of our lives are generally found at last to be of our own procuring." The second half of this summary probably refers to Burchell's story of Sir William, his other identity. It is also a suitable motto for a serious comic action, arguing for the kind of personal responsibility expressed by two of the lines Goldsmith accepted from Johnson for the conclusion of *The Traveller:* "Still to ourselves in every place consign'd / Our own felicity we make or find." Goldsmith chose not to do so, but he could easily have proceeded by showing us the Primrose family learning greater sophistication, discretion, and decorum. In short, *The Vicar of Wakefield* might have been a comic action based on a family's gradual working their way toward a gentle but thorough education in the ways of the world, a series of episodes in the same vein as the doubled scenes of trickery at the fair. Nothing in the material action or its probable development, as we first glimpse it, demands the horrors the Squire inflicts upon the family. Goldsmith needed a parlor or even a bedroom villain, a new Squire B. capable of renouncing his rakedom, not a sideshow monster.

Something other than the implied demands of the story as begun, however, something outside the story, requires just such serious complication, threats that almost remove the novel from the precincts of the comic. Goldsmith believed strongly in the potential joys of a "little neighbourhood, consisting of farmers, who tilled their own grounds, and were equal strangers to opulence and poverty" (31). Yet that ideal expresses little more than a slim possibility in a general scene of bereavement. In this belief that protracted life is protracted woe, a belief he had every personal reason to justify to himself, he agreed with Johnson. It was the source of human unhappiness about which they disagreed. During his acquaintance with Johnson, Goldsmith tried out many different opinions, and certainly Boswell did not record all of them. Are the poor miserable because of the casual malice of the wealthy? Or because of the greed of landowners in enclosing once-public lands?

Or is it the rage of gain, the need to get and spend? Are only the aristocracy to blame, or should the Crown accept its share for not confining their rapacity? To all these probings of the sources of human unhappiness Johnson fairly consistently answered that the liability is in the very fabric of human existence. To be human is to be unhappy, and the Vicar echoes Imlac when he laments "that much has been given man to enjoy, yet still more to suffer" (160). Goldsmith was not satisfied with that answer, any more than Blake would be, although in *Vicar* it is given strong voice in Primrose's prison sermon that looks to a better world after death, repeating sentiments Goldsmith voiced in *Citizen of the World* (Letter xxxv). He wanted to identify something that could be addressed as a cause and cured. His answer in *Vicar* comes to be embodied in the Squire. Power without heart is the source of a substantial quantity of misery. One good villain, adept at having his way and with the law behind him, will thrive at the expense of any goodness Providence puts in his way.

I do not think that Goldsmith originally intended Thornhill to be as thoroughgoing a rascal as he ends up being. He initially provides a kind of distasteful romantic complication, as indicated by the emphasis (before we even see him) on his reputation for philandering and, in his first scene with the family, by his concentration on the daughters. He might have been an early Wickham, with his own uncle a beneficent, covert rival who unmasks himself in the end to set things right. Perhaps the Squire's vague threat reminded Goldsmith of the extralegal power of the upper classes and gave him the notion of using Thornhill as a source of serious misfortune. Once Goldsmith recognizes how he might use the Squire as more than just a romantic unpleasantry, the book's second ideology begins to take over: virtue vexed metamorphoses into virtue besieged. Among the many other problems such a shift entails is what to do with Burchell. As long as his nephew is only an unpleasant "thorn" in the Primroses' side, a social nuisance, Burchell's blinking at the younger man's failings can easily be made believable, just as is Darcy's tolerance of Wickham's campaign of misinformation. But Goldsmith ends up with a villainous nephew whose actions are inexplicably tolerated. For the realistic comic action Goldsmith initiated, this contradiction is a liability; for the apologue about the abuse of power the novel becomes, it is a structural belief.

The two sets of formal demands and their corresponding ideologies force Goldsmith to face just those problems David Richter so cogently traced. Goldsmith's comic action implies in its movement toward final equilibrium that humans have something to do with their own happiness. Thornhill's successful persecution implies the opposite. The role of Burchell, consequently, in his ineptitude and almost willful ignorance of the evil his nephew inflicts upon the Primrose family, is equivalent to the king's benign neglect of the poor in their victimization by the squirearchy.

These homologies are never as neat as my formulations of them imply; but even so, the formal fragmentation of *Vicar* arises because Goldsmith found himself powerfully drawn to representing the social causes of ineradicable human pain. He did not accidentally shift his emphasis because he did not know how to manage a comic action, but, rather, he essayed a form ill-suited to his pressing ideology. Like Austen, who turned away from experiments in complicating the seriousness of comic fiction, Goldsmith found the realistic comic action generically deficient. He wanted threats to the Vicar and his family that would cause real distress in the reader, not the analogy of distress that is part of the well-made comedy, and he wanted them not because he was part of the onset of literary "sentimentality." He wanted an action that reflected the world as he saw it, just as he wanted fish that talk like fish. Desiring to engage the outrage of his reader against social abuses, Goldsmith fell back on a more familiar and more direct manner of ideological representation. Did it not create more confusion than it resolves, the shift to apologue would achieve perhaps the greatest of neoclassical virtues, clarity.

To suggest that Goldsmith's little romance is really a disquisition on human misery may seem at best perverse, in large part, perhaps, because the basic comic tone of the story, powerfully established in the novel's first half, exerts its influence later, even in the absence of specific reassurance (Friedman). If Goldsmith's domestic comedy begins to resemble Job's story, the misery still leads the Vicar to a moral superiority, as expressed in his prison sermon, that is itself serene. The advice he offers his fellow prisoners, to look to God for reward, only confirms the helplessness of the downtrodden. The sermon is the sentimental climax of a sentimental novel, but the novel's social ideology is anything but soft-headed. Even in the hurried and mechanical working out of the comic instability—to which Goldsmith returns at the end— evidence of his pressing beliefs surfaces. For the restoration of the family's fortune and reputation occurs as a result of the same kind of coincidence Goldsmith might have learned from Fielding, whose anger at an indifferent, hurtful society was not that far from Goldsmith's. Fielding knew what he believed before he began *Tom Jones*. If Johnson's opinion can be trusted, "Goldsmith had no settled notions upon any subject" (Boswell, 917). Nevertheless, in writing *Vicar*, he "discovered" a social ideology strong enough to turn him from his formal path.

John Bender (1987) has assembled evidence of Goldsmith's views in the early 1760s; how, that is, "a writer ordinarily described as something of a backward-looking traditionalist" could "find himself on the side of reform" (173). As early as "The Revolution in Low Life" (1762), Goldsmith attacks the accumulation of wealth that (as Bender summarizes) "in the country" permits "magnates" to "abrogate ancient rights and push small farmers—the virtuous 'middle order of mankind'—off the land" (174). In *The Traveller*, Goldsmith laments how "each wanton judge new penal statues draw, / Laws grind the poor, and rich men rule the law." Bender is right to conclude that the "ironies that mid-twentieth-century critics have found in *The Vicar* . . . are generated not by flaws in the character of Dr. Primrose but by contradictions that mark reformist thought during the 1760's" (178).

What I want to add is that once Goldsmith's problem of political expression became complicated by the dynamics of narrative expression, the "case" ceased to be exemplary of mid-century politics and became unique. The very barriers Goldsmith needed for the light, domestic comedy to succeed must have begun to seem too frivolous to command attention. Perhaps he associated comic magnitude with the subject matter itself rather than with the seriousness of its treatment. This is a fundamental misunderstanding of the possible moral effects of comic fiction. *The Vicar of Wakefield* would be an even more radical innovation than it is if Goldsmith had realized that fully ample comic distress, and social consciousness, may arise from domestic as well as from more "serious" sources. In a sense, Goldsmith takes his form too seriously and his own ideas not seriously enough when he ends the novel with the clichés of marriage and restoration of fortune. When Johnson remarked of Goldsmith, in 1763, that he "has been loose in his principles, but he is coming right" (1:408), it is possible that he was taking satisfaction in Goldsmith's abandonment of the very political views that give *Vicar* its moral cogency.

Austen and the Boundaries of the Comic Action

Goldsmith attempted a new kind of comic structure and found its requirements incompatible with his beliefs. Jane Austen's last novel represents a break with the precedents of her own painfully accumulated mastery, but it too shows traces of a mixed intention expressive of a new direction in the subordination of elements. Susan Morgan analyzes the question of whether *Persuasion* is a "departure from the rest of the novels," but concludes that the notion is "wrong for many reasons."[3] One general problem with understanding innovation is evident here. Subjects and techniques may resemble elements in earlier novels but may be subjected to a new narrative "grammar" in the innovative structure. The specific thoughts of a character, for example, are responses to structure; but structure is also an ideological function. It is possible to separate belief from plot, but at the cost of understanding both.[4] Urgent innovations in particular require investigations of their ideological genesis. Austen employed elements recognizable from earlier works when she turned to *Persuasion*, but the new structure emerged from an ideology that transformed their function.

Like the others I am studying, *Persuasion* is not a completely successful innovation. It is, however, a "real development" (Molan, 147). While it may be the case, as Morgan has suggested, that every element in the novel has its precedent elsewhere in Austen, *Persuasion* is nevertheless a striking departure from her previous plots in its subordination of those elements. Employing many elements and strategies that seem to spring from the earlier pages, *Persuasion* manages to call into question the concept of the comic action. Austen's artistic interests shifted away from representing comic barriers and toward the "process by which Anne's happiness is secured" (Molan, 151). Even this useful formulation falls short, since Anne's love for Wentworth is never in question, his love for her is soon apparent, and their reunion by the end of the book is inevitable and experienced as such on every page of the book once we have heard Anne sigh, at the end of chapter 3, "a few months more, and *he*, perhaps, may be walking here." It is not that the ending of the novel departs comic conventions, but that it is drastically overdetermined.

Persuasion is many things, among them another reply to Richardson, in that virtue and reward have no necessary connection; it is a liberation from the moral ideology of comedy Austen inherited from Fielding and Burney, and indirectly from Johnson; it is Austen's personal statement of romantic skepticism, while it is at the same time the most romantic of her novels; and it is a thoroughgoing innovation in the use of her wonted materials. Austen, "subject to those changes which often make the final period of a writer's career the most interesting of all" (Woolf, 146), created a new kind of work. *Persuasion* makes a virtue of misery and employs a structural irony to subordinate comic elements to a noncomic purpose.

Just what *Persuasion* really *is*, formally, has been much debated. Critics have seen it variously as perfectly coherent and as seriously fragmented.[5] I argue that *Persuasion* exhibits the same radical duality of structure that all the other innovations I am concerned with do: they are capable of being read as coherent novels but always contain a second, "disrupting motive." Just as with *Roxana*, the corpus of work Austen completed before the innovation often encourages critics to read *Persuasion* in the light of the earlier formal structures and represented values. Like *Roxana*, *Persuasion* cannot be satisfactorily explained as the natural outcome of successive experiments, because it too emerged from its author's reaction to the implications of her own work. Austen's last novel is, like Defoe's, a kind of "refutation" of her other stories, even though it ends happily and seems to employ many of the comic strategies she used in earlier works.

The best attempts to explain the formal structure of *Persuasion* are the essays by R. S. Crane (1967), Sheldon Sacks (1976), and

Walter Anderson.[6] Crane sees the book as coherent, "one continuous story" involving a "simple series of events"—Anne's and Wentworth's love for each other and their reunion—that nevertheless requires a "fairly large cast of characters." He analyzes the novel as serious comedy, the ending of which moves and delights us not only because the heroine and hero are so successfully portrayed as attractive, morally superior beings, but also because they come together again in a "fuller knowledge" of each other's worth than they possessed eight years before (Crane, 283–84, 288). Since so much of the novel's business involves the "doings and movements of the subordinate characters," Crane turns to James's distinction between elements that are part of the "subject" and those that are part of the "treatment." This is a useful distinction, but in the case of *Persuasion* it is misleading. Even so, Crane's essay is invaluable in its pinpointing of critical questions, such as the unusually large number of characters in the novel, that beg for answers.

Sacks and Anderson, both familiar with Crane's work (and with each other's), argue persuasively that Austen was doing something new in her last novel. Anderson argues that *Persuasion* is the first representation of consciousness for its own sake in English fiction: "In *Persuasion,* Austen, transcending a plot tradition she herself had done most to perfect, anticipated the goals of stream-of-consciousness novels in which the impingement of external events becomes but the occasion for reflection and feeling, evoking the representation of a sensibility for the sake of a mood or a personal vision of life." Anderson suggests that the external plot of the novel—which is a vestige of Austen's older method of story telling—gets in the way of this lyric exploration of consciousness. The novel is fragmented because Austen "did not yet fully possess the technical resources to sustain with perfect economy the passive plot involving Anne's internal suffering."

Sacks views *Persuasion* as a precursor of Virginia Woolf's novels of "lyric revelation," but still fundamentally a coherent comic action that not only contains but makes fully functional a lengthy static section preceding the Lyme Regis episode. For Sacks, even though nothing that happens before Lyme Regis actually moves Anne closer to happiness, the lyric section still serves as comic reassurance in the midst of Anne's seemingly fixed pain. I believe

Sacks would have agreed with Anderson that *Persuasion* is a new form, not "the last of Austen's great achievements, but, more properly . . . a new beginning, reaching one hundred years into the future."

All three critics provide invaluable insights into the innovative nature of *Persuasion*. What is missing—no matter what we think the novel "really is"—may be some sense of why Austen tried something new. Indeed, one might argue that no formal analysis can be complete without some hypothesis about the "bioformal" genesis of a novel's structure, the authorial *why* behind formal choices. Even Sacks does not suggest how Austen might have gotten from *Mansfield Park* and *Emma* to *Persuasion*, although he understood both that "new forms of narrative tend to emerge" when the old ones cease to answer to a writer's needs and that a new form is "likely" to be "a development of principles always latent in the construction of older forms" (Sacks 1976:S108–9). Sacks is more interested in how a single static section of the novel indicates the surprising ways in which comic fiction might develop and still remain within the precincts of the comic. Everywhere Anderson's essay implies that the passive or lyric elements in *Persuasion* act as a kind of informing principle of the novel. Why Austen chose to include elements of a "passive plot" in her last novel is not, I hasten to add, a problem Sacks and Anderson try to solve. Innovations tend to complicate the question of causality, since the *how* is often part of the *why*. Given Austen's career-long insistence upon subordinating all significant elements of a fiction to a coherent purpose, it seems unlikely that she intended the static section as anything but a functional substructure in a larger whole. Sacks and Anderson are, then, both probably correct that the lyric elements of the novel are there for a larger reason, even if Austen did not finish revising the novel (see n. 8, below).

Morgan has provided an interesting explanation for what Anderson sees as unassimilated elements. She contends about Mrs. Smith, for example, that the "irrelevance of her information to the plot or to Anne's happiness is exactly its point" (Morgan, 178). Anne's long delay, and final omission, in conveying her newly discovered information about Mr. Elliot to Lady Russell is thematically expressive of both his unimportance to her fate and her own prior percipience in recognizing the unsoundness of his character. This seems a persuasive argument, but it ignores two considerations. Why invent an entire subplot involving Mr. Elliot and Mrs. Smith, turning on a mere illusion of complication, only to score a relatively minor thematic point? Austen is not usually so uneconomical. Then too, imperfectly assimilated elements may always be explained by treating them as signifying omissions. The answer is too simple, too self-confirming.

A redefinition of Austen's accomplishment as neither coherently comic nor incoherently lyrical may be useful. If I am right about the nature of urgent innovation, it will not be possible to construct such a definition until we understand what in her earlier work made her try, as Woolf said, "to do something which she [had] never yet attempted" (Woolf, 147).

Comic Actions, Merit, and Exertion

While each of Austen's novels is itself a variation in comic form, until *Persuasion* each makes fictive use of a similar causal relationship among merit, happiness, and exertion. Take a superior being and present her with the possibility of marrying her moral and intellectual equal; what needs to happen between meeting and marriage? Actions never present their "questions" in this lifeless manner; everything is dramatized. These are realistic characters, not ideological counters. Nevertheless, each of the novels does a little more than just "try out" the values actively employed in bringing the pair of lovers together and securing their future. The novels vary greatly in how they establish final fulfillment: Lizzy "earns" Darcy by virtue of recognizing and correcting her own failed perceptions, an act of self-evaluation that confirms her worth; Elinor's lover rematerializes because he is, miraculously, no longer engaged; Fanny's beloved cousin, smitten with Mary Crawford, at the very last falls in love with her—in part, it seems, because she has finally attained marriageable age; Emma's Knightley, more of an uncle than a lover to his younger friend, suddenly reveals his love, proposes, and is accepted.

These are oversimplifications of complex resolutions. There is much more to each of these novels than the seeming seriousness or lightness, leisure or hurry, of their endings, although endings may be as ideologically revealing in "fixed" structures like comedy as in seemingly amorphous ones like many modern novels. Each of Austen's heroines navigates a very different course to fulfillment. Each novel, except *Persuasion*, implies a belief in the possibility of affecting, if not controlling, one's own fate. This is the case even with *Mansfield Park*, in which the fortuity of the ending seems complete, a free gift of the comic deity; upon closer examination, however, it proves to be just as firmly based on feminine exertion as the others. What all the novels imply is a set of beliefs Austen eventually rejected as "unreal"—or at least came to look upon, wistfully, as naïve.

Inheriting the constraints of the "moral action" as she did, how could Austen *not* base these novels about marriage on the serious question of how merit and ethically correct behavior are treated by the world? Here one approaches an implied ideology for comedy, one that Goldsmith found he could not patiently abide. For, as in Fielding, even if the comic writer manages to convey the insular nature of his comic world surrounded by the larger world of misery, some rationale for moral exertion on that island must be presented if the comedy is to have its moment of didacticism. A philosophy of even jovial despair, of the vanity of assertion in the void, leaves nothing for the reader to learn but an empty stoicism. Tom may be rewarded by the arbitrary arrangement of his author, but Fielding still manages to recommend the practice of goodness. In the twentieth century, reasons for characters' persisting in their own brand of "the good" are harder to find, but they are nonetheless still available. Cary, in *The Horse's Mouth*, for example, creates a comic action around Gully Jimson's need to get his paintings painted, at no matter what cost, even death. Ken Kesey bases a powerful tragic action on the nobility, even the necessity, of self-sacrifice. Even a seemingly nihilist novel like the recent *Less Than Zero* affirms in its bleak closure that leaving Los Angeles is better for the narrator than staying to endure a certain death of the spirit.

For most of her career, Austen seems to have placed her aesthetic faith in the representation of right conduct that will, one way or another, be rewarded. Of course, the causality of her plots is never simple, since she persistently questions the distinction between action and passivity. The kind of goodness all of her heroines possess is a result of acuity of perception rather than, say, Tom Jones's instinctive benevolence. It is their clear sight that leads to happiness. Even a relative dullard like Edward Ferrars appreciates Elinor's mind, and her thinking is a kind of doing. The sudden fulfillment of heroines such as Elinor and Emma comes about not by accident but because their exertions fit them for reward, even if their virtue is only passive. Of course, no Austen heroine does nothing at all to achieve her happiness, even Anne, although she comes close. By representing clear sight as winning out, even in situations of extreme constraint, like the one Fanny must endure, Austen implies that merit and success are *somehow* connected, at least in the marriage dance. In her hands marriage seems to have been invented for the realistic representation of beings in morally determined action, but it is easy to underestimate how difficult it is to design such a variety of plots and still maintain ideological consistency. Each plot presents a different set of demands for representing the complex interaction of contrasting values. Even so, almost always managing to do the unexpected, her surprises are still at the service of uniting a deserving heroine with her lover and making it seem as if the young woman has a great deal to do with her own success.

There are exceptions to her practice, however, especially in works written late in her career as she moved away from the glittering example of *Pride and Prejudice* and toward the radical experiments of *Mansfield Park* and *Emma*. It may be that *Pride and Prejudice* is closer to some perfection of readerly comic satisfaction than Austen's other works, simply because the fullest pleasure is derived from the happiness of a heroine obliged to do a great deal of "the right thing" to secure her happiness. If some of Austen's heroines are rewarded by accident—and even Lizzy's fate rests in part on fortuity—she is still careful to connect their merit and their fate. The very insistence on reward seems to imply that even if the heroine is shut off by circumstances from exerting herself in her own cause, some way will be found for her to succeed. In Austen's hands, comedy is a generous form, and she withholds her benison of "tolerable comfort" only from those "greatly in fault" (*Mansfield*

Park, 420). To follow the triumph of *Pride and Prejudice* with the story of Elinor and Marianne, Austen had to look at the world through the eyes of youth. It is almost as if, fresh from Lizzy's supreme efforts in remolding her perceptions of Fitzwilliam Darcy, in choking down her humiliation at being the sister of a degraded fool and the daughter of an empty-headed harridan and a sardonic nincompoop, in scorning the classist scorn of Lady Catherine, Austen decided it was time for a more whimsical treatment of marriage.

Lizzy's actively earned fulfillment is only part of a larger Austenean comic world in which the pain of lost love is always temporary and relatively brief, and the heroine always in the way of reward—because she deserves it. Indeed, even in the two novels that seem to diverge from this pattern, *Mansfield Park* and *Emma,* the exceptions only prove the rule. Emma is Austen's only fully realized heroine with serious deficiencies of character, and her meddling is saved from having serious consequences only because it is spectacularly unsuccessful. Unlike Lizzy, whose problems with Darcy come about from an error in judgment, Emma plays with lives, although with the best of intentions. Austen saves Emma for reward—appropriately, with the man who most clearly sees her errors—because even here on the threshold of *Persuasion* she cannot bring herself to separate even less than moral perfection from fulfillment.

Emma may be Austen's most endearing novel, along with the brighter and more youthful *Pride and Prejudice,* simply because the heroine is not quite a paragon. Choosing to follow on this line of innovation, she might have anticipated what Dickens tried in *Great Expectations.* Even so, Austen's growing attraction toward potentially noncomic subjects is evident in *Emma,* and, to the extent that a radical shift in subject *may* signal a generic shift, the novel is important for what Austen would do later in *Persuasion.* For example, there are no significant external barriers to Emma's marrying Knightley. Mr. Woodhouse is never the kind of bar to a happy union that Mr. and Mrs. Bennet are, or even that the Elliots would be, if Anne were still persuadable. Mr. Woodhouse is eccentric, and Emma cherishes him, but she is ready to marry when she falls in love with Knightley. Even Knightley's estate, hardly modest but not comparable to Emma's thirty thousand pounds, is no objection.

Austen's interest in character, its errors and amendments, is never shown to better advantage than in *Emma*. Emma's mortification over her treatment of Miss Bates, followed by new self-knowledge, brings her a step closer to being worthy of Knightley. As is often the case in Shakespearean comedy, a series of recognitions and reconciliations leads on to fulfillment. Unlike the rest of Austen's heroines, however, Emma remains more than a little laughable even after the exhaustion of her comic difficulties. Emma decides, looking back, that she must have "been entirely under a delusion, totally ignorant of her own heart" in her brief attraction to Frank Churchill. Indeed, she concludes, "she had never really cared for Frank Churchill at all!" (402). In the antepenultimate chapter she shows herself ludicrously, harmlessly, of course, still impressed with her ability to arrange the lives of others. She will not "acknowledge that it was with any view of making a match" for the Westons' new daughter with one of her nephews that made her conclude "that a daughter would suit both father and mother best" (444). Even here, Austen is so greatly attracted to the representation of good sense that she only hints at Emma's continued tendencies toward meddling. In other regards Emma is as reformed by her mortification as Lizzy is by hers. When Knightley tells her that Harriet has accepted Robert Martin, he expects her to be distressed, but Emma surprises him. Her insensitive treatment of Miss Bates—the unpleasant "truth" revealed to her by, of course, Knightley—results in Emma's being "agitated, mortified, grieved" (369). Even so, if Emma's moral journey is as long as that of any of Austen's heroines, it is not in the direction of Anne Elliot, and *Emma* is no trial run for *Persuasion*, except in the limited sense that Austen is no longer as concerned with comic barriers as she is with character.

Mansfield Park, which seems most completely to separate both merit and exertion from reward, really does nothing of the sort. Instead, it may be seen as a "reaction" to the ideology of amendment implied by *Emma*. Having written her way from Lizzy and Elinor to Fanny, Austen now seems ready to reward an obedient innocent for doing nothing at all for herself except grow old enough to marry. Yet Austen's frailest, most inactive heroine seems to develop a kind of passive power, so that, next to Anne Elliot, she seems formidable. Austen's experiment involves a simple proposition: what might be made of a heroine without obvious wit or vivacity, in a dependent position, surrounded by a mostly unappreciative household? It is not a matter of hidden merit, for Fanny is a heroine with a diminutive portfolio. Her lover, too, is a man of generally impeccable morals but lacking the verve of a Darcy or a Knightley. Edmund's virtues are all on the side of quiet domesticity. A country clergyman-to-be, he takes his prospective orders seriously; his distaste for frivolity almost matches Fanny's.

She, by virtue of her innocence and passivity—the latter forced upon her—is shut off from those resources of entertaining the reader that all of Austen's other heroines possess, except, of course, Anne, who is silent not from timidity but from misery. *Mansfield Park* could have been Austen's stodgiest novel, especially since she bestowed all of the wit and scintillation on the characters she most disapproved of, Henry and Mary. They seem to belong front and center in a "hypothetical" novel a longer-lived Austen might have written about 1826, a serious exploration of morally flawed beauty and intelligence. Even so, while there is no denying the oddity of Austen's choice of Fanny as her moral and perceptual center, the novel is really all of a piece with the rest of her work before *Persuasion*. In addition to finding a way to make interesting a moral perfection bordering on priggishness, Austen must represent the passivity of a female dependent in a male-dominated household in which most of the other women are either stupid or mean-spirited. The potential harkens forward to Anne Elliot: Austen might have written a borderline sentimental novel of virtue oppressed, allowing the reader to wallow in the pleasures of dolor before rescuing Fanny, and us, at the last moment. Austen chose instead to develop the much more radical idea of a transfiguring passivity. The novel is an objective fantasy—Fanny in the den of the slave owner—that mixes no sentimentality with its feminism.

Except, of course, that Fanny's power comes from her goodness: through a gentle but steadfast adherence to principles seemingly absorbed from the atmosphere, she manages to remake the entire family in her own image. She purges the household of the immoral Mary and Henry and enacts the Cinderella story, marrying her prince. If the ideology of the book is revolutionary, it is also a bit coy and, as a reflection of actual female power, a bit misleading: the more powerless, the more powerful. Even her name, in its variable, uncanny intertextuality with Fielding's heroine, with the creator of Evelina (another passive paragon), and, perhaps, with a glance at Austen's niece, suggests the reach of feminine patience. While the Fannys of the world do not often "rule," it is a pleasure to see them do so, although one wonders if the pleasure is not primarily for Austen's male readers. For the female reader, Fanny may seem most of the time to be auditioning for a new production of "Charlotte's Way," in a supporting role at that. Aunt Norris tries to set Fanny aside, to make her a mere domestic, but Fanny turns the tables. Here she differs from Charlotte, who is condemned to endure Lady Catherine. Through Fanny's goodness, all good things come—even, finally, a fire on a winter day. This novel seems to express a deep belief in the power of feminine inaction, or at least an understanding of the attractions of such a spectacle. Having explored thoroughly all the ways good fortune might issue from moral exertion, Austen now examines how happiness might issue convincingly from a static, mostly private virtue.

It is no accident that *Mansfield Park* begins with a reference to the existence of more pretty women who "deserve" men of large fortune than there are such men in the world. Like the other novels, this one is pinned to the proposition that merit ought to bring reward. Here, however, the question "rewarded with what?" becomes problematic in a way that it is not in the other novels, even *Persuasion*. If Austen goes about as far as she can toward freeing the fortunate conclusion from any dependence upon Fanny's exertions, she also begins to call into question the marriage game itself, shifting the ideological basis of her treatment from issues revolving around marriage to larger ones that form the context of the "marriage question." She is moving closer to a skepticism about "what we wish for." After all, when Crawford is wooing Fanny—fruitlessly, we always know—it is her real love, Edmund, who is capable of hoping that Henry will persist. To be fair to him, it is Edmund's innocent blindness to the imperfections of both the Crawfords, as well as his merely brotherly concern for Fanny, that make his newly discovered love for her seem so odd. The match, long desired by Fanny but never occurring to any other character (except years before, when Fanny's adoption was being considered), including Edmund, is so strange that Austen's narrator points up its improbability: "I only intreat every body to believe that exactly at the time when it was quite natural that it should be so, and not a week earlier, Edmund did cease to care about Miss Crawford, and became as anxious to marry Fanny, as Fanny herself could desire" (429).

Austen's comic achievement in *Mansfield Park* is to create the illusion of a character ordering her destiny simply by foreseeing, hoping, deserving, and "desiring." Fanny sees more clearly than anyone else in the novel—often more clearly even than the reader, as in Fanny's objections to the domestic theatrical—and it does seem that at last she brings about the better world she has only dreamed of as an alternative to her sad experience. In this sense, *Mansfield Park* is Austen's most Jamesian novel, not just in its faith in the power of perception, since that belief is ubiquitous in the other novels, but in its identification of the process itself with its reward (although thinking of Fanny as an early Stether does seem farfetched). For example, Fanny's thoughts, especially later in the novel, often create the sense that she actually controls the entire household. At one point, Edmund "wondered that Fanny spoke so seldom" of Mary, little realizing that "it was this sister . . . who was now the chief bane of Fanny's comfort." The internal monologue continues: "If she could have believed Mary's future fate as unconnected with Mansfield, as she was determined the brother's should be, if she could have hoped her return thither, to be as distant as she was much inclined to think his, she would have been light of heart indeed." She then sadly contemplates how Edmund's objections to Mary's character, and hers to his situation, "seemed all done away," although "nobody could tell how." Still, Fanny sees, "independently of self"—that is, of her own love for Edmund—that there are "bad feelings still remaining" between Edmund and Mary. She then remembers how, at their last meeting, Mary displayed the same "mind led astray and bewildered" that, in Fanny's view, renders her unfit for Edmund: "She might love, but she did not deserve Edmund by any other sentiment" (a comment relevant to

Austen's innovation in *Persuasion,* in which Anne deserves Wentworth precisely because she does love him so much). If Edmund's influence on her were so scant "in this season of love . . . his worth would be finally wasted on her even in years of matrimony" (333–34). The rest of the novel seems to be the enactment of these insights, as if Fanny's clear sight, her objectively impotent "determination," and the reader's strong hopes must sooner or later be confirmed by external events. Fanny conspires with the reader to change her world. Although no one else in the novel sees her control—it is, after all, invisible—her perceptions have the power of vaticination.

Austen, of course, has prepared us for this strange pattern by showing Fanny's judgment confirmed at every step; for example, in the long moral comedy of the theatrical. Only Fanny fully understands how indecorous Sir Thomas would consider the whole affair. At that early stage of the novel, even the reader may be a bit at variance with her: what's so harmful about putting on *Lover's Vows?* Of course, Fanny is right to be uneasy about the position the play puts them all in, as she alone anticipates Sir Thomas's disapprobation. The novel, then, is a series of scenes that allow us gradually to identify with Fanny's moral perceptions, so that we may finally rejoice that all she wishes comes true. The wonderful illusion is that her desires are fulfilled because she has so clearly seen their rightness—and the wrongness of the alternatives. Even as everything is arranged so that Fanny is powerless, when all things come to her—not just in the conclusion, but as her vision is confirmed, time and time again—she begins to seem like the creator of her own happiness. If her self-willed fate has any "edge," if in its treatment Austen withholds full approbation, it is only in the repository of Fanny's love, Edmund. There is more than a little disdain in Austen's arranging for his coming to his senses, and Austen's narrator needs to "intreat" us to believe in an affection that only "became . . . anxious" because its earlier object disappeared. Of course, Austen is not the first or last novelist to find risible the vagaries of male infatuation.

If this, or something like this, is the special power of the novel, might we not explain some of its features that have puzzled critics? For example, to increase the emotional power of Fanny's success, would it not have been better to have her not only in an inferior position in the family but unappreciated, even mildly persecuted? Then too, since much of the pleasure of the novel's conclusion comes from our apprehension of the great change in her fortunes—again, seemingly because of her ability to enact her vision just by owning it—it would be nice if her powerlessness were frequently contrasted with the seeming power of the other members of the family, especially Sir Thomas. Since one of the most serious constraints on female fulfillment in this novel seems to be the will and blindness of males, the objective fantasy requires that Sir Thomas be a father who gives "advice of absolute power" (254). Good patriarch that he is, he tries to "recommend" Fanny "as a wife by shewing her persuadableness" (255), the way one might showcase the admirable tractability of a slave in Charleston or Kingston. Of course, despite all her docility, she is not persuadable. Her way of seeing things does the persuading. It is therefore all the more interesting, as part of the novel's unspoken subtext, that Sir Thomas, when he sails to Antigua, has on his hands, among other difficulties, a slave rebellion.[7]

On the one hand, there is *Emma,* a novel of character change that results in reward. On the other is *Mansfield Park,* with Austen's first static heroine, if not her last. Both novels, despite their being so different in form, reconfirm the connection between merit and happiness, although both do so with a sleight of hand that indicates Austen was having doubts about the "neatness" of novels like *Pride and Prejudice. Persuasion* calls into question the very comic conventions of representation while seeming, especially in its gratifying conclusion, to reaffirm them all. Once again, innovation brings into uneasy proximity the unreconcilable.

Anne Elliot and the Knowledge of Pain

In *Persuasion,* Anne's pain has a reality, if not a permanence, unlike that of any of the other women destined to be rewarded by Austen's comic art. It is too much to say that Anne's pain is indelible, since we are told, in that luscious moment of reavowal, that "they returned again into the past, more exquisitely happy, perhaps, in their re-union, than when it had been first projected" (240). No, Anne's pain is like a possession, and although she lays it aside when the novel is over, the reader cannot. Austen came finally to believe that employing misery as a plot device somehow belies its seriousness. All her heroines suffer. They may not "need" a man, but somehow their fate gets tied up with one. For reasons the reader always perceives as temporary, he is lost to her. Every Austen heroine is like Emma, "left to cheer her father with the spirits only of ruined happiness" (*Emma* 410; see Tave 1973:17).

In the action, these are temporary barriers to their playfully deferred fulfillment, serving to evoke only the mildest analogy of real excruciation for the reader. Somewhere along the line, however, they became real for Austen, and the formal beneficence of the comic action turned hollow. Virginia Woolf thought the reason entirely personal, and Woolf is a critic dangerous to ignore, especially when she is discussing a novelist whose efforts she likens to her own: "Her attitude to life is itself altered. She is seeing it, for the greater part of the book, through the eyes of a woman who, unhappy herself, has a special sympathy for the happiness and unhappiness of others." This new quality, for Woolf, "proves not merely the biographical fact that Jane Austen had loved, but the aesthetic fact that she was no longer afraid to say so" (147–48). The "unwritten" here is "loved and lost." Whether the reader is willing to accept Woolf's implication that Anne Elliot stands in for her creator's misery does not really matter. The "aesthetic fact" is that the pain of actual loss—the vanity of human wishes, "the way things can go awry or go nowhere at all" (Molan, 148)—is given a reality here that it possesses in no other Austen novel, indeed, in few novels, period. The novel's structure insists upon the continuing immediacy of bereavement, as if Austen had found some new meaning in the idea of "temporary." The very stasis of most of the book, the sense in which the reader experiences Anne's misery as if it were *not* temporary, is an innovation in the representation of human pain, as Anderson's reading of the novel so brilliantly discovers. Later authors found such suffering more appropriate to progressive tragic actions. Tess and Jude trace a slow path of decline to their fates. Here, a hundred years before Jake Barnes, unhappiness begins to look as if it might be endemic to the human state, a hint only partially taken back by the restoration of felicity. The ending does not erase memory, for the reader or for Anne.

For the first time, Austen takes her heroine's pain with full seriousness, as something closer in its irrevocability to tragic knowledge. While the novel issues "comically," of course, there is no possibility of ending on the same note she did in *Mansfield Park:* "Let other pens dwell on guilt and misery. I quit such odious subjects as soon as I can, impatient to restore everybody, not greatly in fault themselves, to tolerable comfort, and to have done with the rest" (420). Even in the very chapter in which Anne is delivered from her long prison, the reader is reminded of her bleak life and how easily circumstances might have conspired to condemn her, as they did Austen herself, to a life of eavesdropping on an unending succession of indiscretions uttered by an unending series of Mrs. Musgroves. As Nina Auerbach perceptively noted, the "blended tone of *Persuasion* brings us close to the elegiac lyrics of Jane Austen's contemporaries, Shelley and Keats" (128). Anne Elliot's wasted face and spirits are not just evidence of a temporary "mortification," an inevitable passage like Lizzy's to a better state, but also traces of the lost years. The reader knows—indeed, it is a kind of petty annoyance at times—that Anne and Wentworth will marry. Even in the ecstasy of the long-delayed embrace, the memory of the barren life Anne has *already* lived lingers for the reader as it does in no other Austen novel. Austen's next novel, had she survived to complete one, might not have been an exploration of unrelieved misery; but it would have been an even more drastic departure from the materials and techniques of comedy than even *Persuasion.* Sacks and Anderson were right to recognize the seeds of the lyric novel, as practiced by Woolf, germinating in *Persuasion.* So also are the seeds of what became another important form of the nineteenth-century novel, the "abated action," in which the terms of happiness are always problematic and the final state of the hero or heroine is itself ambiguous (P. E. Wilson). Austen might have turned, as Woolf suggested, to a larger drama, without the moral certainty projected by the earlier novels. The comic distance that permitted the triumphs of the earlier novels is no longer possible in *Persuasion,* which is precisely why Woolf—with the opposite problem, a fear of writing too personally, without sufficient distance— seemed so moved by Anne Elliot's story. Here is a secret sharer, another suffering woman drawing her likeness, trying to "discuss" what she finds so compelling without giving too much away.

The form of *Persuasion* is so unlike any of Austen's other novels that a special difficulty in describing it arises, especially in the work of those critics, like Walter Anderson, who are intimately conversant with the workings of her other plots. The temptation is to employ the terms of the comic action from the earlier works to describe *Persuasion*. While the model of the comic action seems to go far toward explaining the book, it does so at the cost of marginalizing or rendering extraneous or excrescent features that, viewed from the perspective of a different model, might count as the very things that make this novel uniquely new. The problem is compounded, I believe, when a novel is a departure from the generic principles that have informed the earlier works—as is almost always the case with innovations.

Anderson argues that one does not get far explaining *Persuasion* as a comic action, at least not as a coherent one. Lady Russell seems designed for a more important role than she plays, which accounts for the unexplained, almost casual, delay at the end of the novel in Anne's telling her about Mr. Elliot's true character. Mr. Elliot appears at first to be a comic barrier, a real alternative to Wentworth, but he is never given the chance to play that part. Mrs. Smith's revelations about Mr. Elliot, coming when they do, are wasted if Elliot is never really a romantic possibility. These elements, and others, may be dispensed with if the novel's real business is the fullest exploration of Anne's character. On the other hand, if the novel is a comic action, Lady Russell and Mr. Elliot are clearly underdeveloped. Too much, that is, is missing from *Persuasion* for us to react to it, much less interpret it satisfactorily, as a variant of the same kind of plot she previously perfected. On the other hand, the external events that impinge upon Anne's consciousness are too important for us to assume that Austen had anything but a positive intention in mind when she included them in the novel. Nor is it safe to conclude that Austen left the novel unfinished, since her revisions of the scene of reconciliation between Anne and Wentworth indicate an author who clearly recognized the formal demands of her structure.[8]

The most striking feature of *Persuasion*, one that has not been given close attention, is the degree to which the most important of all Austenean virtues, knowledge, is now the most difficult to obtain. Not self-knowledge: Anne is, quite obviously, in full possession of all three of Austen's triumvirate of supreme virtues, "self-knowledge, generosity, and humility" (*Mansfield Park,* 16); indeed, the striking disjunction between what she knows about herself and what she knows about anyone else may serve as a key to the novel's structure. Her lack of knowledge about Wentworth serves as a kind of delaying structure, rendered thematically functional as thoroughly in this novel as Lizzy's independence is in her story. At crucial moments Anne is blocked from even the simplest kinds of interpretations. Happy at her final happiness, some readers still wonder why it takes so long, why Anne does not sooner see what anyone else could, that Wentworth loves her still. Certainly the reason is not just that Anne's misery makes her gun-shy. In this novel, the very basis of knowledge is called into question just as the possibilities for exertion are canceled by past experience, not only in relation to Anne and Wentworth but as a specific thematic construct that affects the way "comic" elements function in this new kind of story.

I hasten to emphasize that I have no intention of suggesting that *Persuasion* is somehow "about" the "impossibility of knowing" or any of the other critical clichés so successful in dismissing morphological questions without explaining them. Probably every novel, play, and poem that raises the slightest interpretative question may be read as a metafiction, as being "about" itself or "about" the impossibility of being about anything. *Persuasion* is about Anne Elliot. The ideology of the book arises out of the way it is told and the values that are endorsed in the telling. They are "there," but only by implication. If Austen's innovation in *Persuasion* is the creation of literary consciousness, then it is not surprising that she would find her subject at least in part in Anne's perceptual difficulties. It is, one might venture, a short step from the "internality" of a Fanny Price to that of an Anne Elliot, although there is no touch of the whimsical in the inner view of Anne. In between, Emma's unreliability of judgment becomes another element in the equation that results in *Persuasion.* Even so, such a mechanical amalgamation should produce only another experiment in comic form, not a radical innovation. The truly new novelistic form arises when an author loses interest in what can be achieved with available resources. There is already evidence in the "surprise" ending of *Emma* and the playful ending of *Mansfield Park* that the probabilities of the comic action no longer compelled Austen as they once did. More basically, *Persuasion* issues from a sense of loss: for reasons buried in the mystery of her life, Jane Austen lost her faith in the beneficial effect of the exertions of even the most sensitive, intelligent women. This loss is signaled everywhere in the novel by a narrative structure that blocks even the simplest perceptions.

Anne is often unable to achieve certainty or even clarity of judgment, and not just about Wentworth; at other times, however, she is extraordinarily acute. In the wonderful scene in which Frederick comforts Mrs. Musgrove over the loss of the worthless Dicky, a scene Sacks takes as paradigmatic of the lyric power of this entire section of the novel (1976:S105–8), Anne's perceptions are faultless: "There was a momentary expression in Captain Wentworth's face . . . a certain glance of his bright eye, and curl of his handsome mouth, which convinced Anne, that instead of sharing in Mrs. Musgrove's kind wishes, as to her son, he had probably been at some pains to get rid of him; but it was too transient an indulgence of self-amusement to be detected by any who understood him less than herself" (67). Anne clearly learned in those brief weeks of bliss years ago to "read" Wentworth; indeed, it pains her now that she learned to read him so well then. If Austen is using such a static moment of self-revelation as a kind of comic reassurance—that is, by virtue of Anne's seeing the same noble qualities in Wentworth she once saw, the reader will be reassured that his love must revive—then why does she follow it with so many pages in which Anne seems unable to determine whether Frederick is in love with Louisa? First the reader learns, consonant with Anne's earlier precision of judgment, that "from memory and experience . . . Captain Wentworth was not in love with either" sister (82). Shortly, though, "Every thing now marked out Louisa for Captain Wentworth; nothing could be plainer" (90). One explanation may be that the novel's frequently shifting point of view is more "scenic," representing the cast of general opinion in its constant quest for "plain" truths, while the sentiments of the earlier paragraph are

Anne's. Yet why should a false scent be appropriate here? A couple of pages later, Admiral Croft expresses his conviction that Frederick "certainly means to have one or other of those two girls" (92), and, although he is usually reliable, here he may be an ironic commentator. Even after Louisa's injury, Anne believes that if Louisa should recover, "More than former happiness would be restored" (123). Anne does not seem to see, as the reader may, that Wentworth cannot possibly be in love with anyone but her. No convincing reason for the gap between her ability to read Wentworth in matters indifferent and her inability to perceive his affection for her—until much later—is ever presented. Only by implication can we explain Wentworth's opacity for Anne: she dares not speculate on his possible love for her because it would be too painful.

Anderson's explanation is that the confusion results because Austen consistently refuses to "distinguish between Anne's knowledge, which must be imperfect in order to sustain her pain, and what the reader knows and is made to feel." Yet, while each of Austen's heroines knows less than her readers, only Anne's ignorance is so complete, and so painful—in part because the promised fulfillment is not something to be discovered, as it is for Lizzy, but something lying wrecked in the past. Her problems with knowing what is going on extend into other areas and episodes and—more important for what finally emerges as Austen's overall intention— begin to involve the reader in confusion about everything *except* that Anne is intended for Wentworth. For example, what does Mr. Elliot look like? At the moment when Anne first encounters him, we learn only that he is "completely a gentleman in manner" (104). Soon after, a second meeting at the inn takes place and the reader learns that Elliot, "though not handsome, had an agreeable person" (105). This polite language means that his face is homely but his body is not malformed—nothing special, one notes, since from *Pride and Prejudice* "agreeable" has been reserved for the merely unobjectionable in looks and manners (Tave 1973:117–31). When Anne next sees him in Bath, Elliot is "quite as good-looking as he had appeared at Lyme, his countenance improved by speaking" (143). Has Austen forgotten Anne's perception of him as "not handsome"? Or is the distinction, part of Anne's subjectivity, between that negative state and "good-looking" too fine, at least for this reader?

Putting Anne's testimony aside, similar ambiguity is expressed through other characters. Amongst the "little crowd in the shop" in Bath, some unidentified speaker exclaims of Elliot, "What a very good-looking man!" (177). Earlier, Sir Walter expressed the "lament" that Elliot is "very much under-hung, a defect which time seems to have increased" (141). Now, Sir Walter's testimony is ordinarily to be despised, but in the case of male physiognomy he may perhaps be trusted: Elliot's jaw recedes! Here is a fine suitor for Anne Elliot and a rival for Wentworth, yet one Anne has found "good-looking." Does she see only what she wants to see when she is ever so briefly attracted to Elliot?

Even that attraction itself invites the reader's confusion, for where is Anne's heart? Sacks sees the comic action reestablishing its progressive nature immediately after Louisa's accident at Lyme Regis (1976:S105). The plot requires a contrast between Wentworth's truly amiable navy crowd and Anne's selfish relations to make her reunion with Wentworth all that much more desirable— if Anne's misery hasn't already made it so. Of course, Austen's method of constructing a comic action often entails the use of a romantic rival—therefore, Elliot. This does seem to be what is afoot because Anne, receiving Lady Russell's compliments on her improvement in looks since Lyme Regis, "had the amusement of connecting them with the silent admiration of her cousin, and of hoping that she was to be blessed with a second spring of youth and beauty" (124). What follows, however, of Anne's real attitude toward Eliot is enough to make the reader believe that Austen is either playing fast and loose or has lost her grip on the story. Within a chapter Anne is "not animated to an equal pitch" as her sister by the prospect of a reconciliation with Elliot, "but she felt that she would rather see Mr. Elliot again than not" (136). Within a few pages of this limp endorsement Anne is expressing reservations about his character. There must be "something more than immediately appeared, in Mr. Elliot's wishing, after an interval of so many years, to be well received by them" (140), since he has so little to gain. Taken with the testimony, on the next page, as to Mr. Elliot's weak chin, Elliot seems less and less a real alternative for Anne, especially given Wentworth's noble appearance. Again, Anne's perspicacity in judging character, here as fully engaged and accurate as Fanny Price's, may make us wonder where her capabilities begin and end.

At any rate, when Lady Russell ventures to suggest the connection, two chapters later, Anne's mind is made up: "Mr. Elliot is an exceedingly agreeable man"—once again, the Austenean red flag—"and in many respects I think highly of him . . . but we should not suit" (159). One could trace the pattern out until, for example, Anne reveals that no one could *ever* have won her from Wentworth (192), but it is already long clear: Elliot is not a threat, which leaves the "second spring of youth and beauty" passage hanging out on a limb.

Even so, it is a mistake to conclude that these are merely false echoes of Austen's older method of telling a story, that her attention is now so fixed on Anne's fluctuating consciousness and the new possibilities for narrative psychology it presents that she loses control of the rest of the story. In fact, it is much more reasonable to assume that these "inconsistencies" are themselves part of Austen's overall intention, that they are somehow expressive of her desire to tell a new kind of story.[9]

The Happiness of Misery, The Misery of Happiness

Austen separates her heroine, with the completest possible aesthetic and ideological effect, from the comic story that so concerns her. While doubtless there is a comic action, its possibilities are beyond Anne's perceptions for most of the novel. Even when Anne begins to see signs of Wentworth's returning love, Austen does not use those signs as she did in the previous novels. Of course, while none of Austen's heroines knows she is destined for happiness, Anne has less to do with the happy resolution of her fate than any of the others. There are no complications, and the resolution has little to do with any barriers, except the inability of the two lovers to speak, although it could be argued that this paralysis is hindrance enough and is certainly thematically consistent with Austen's overall intention. Indeed, at first glance it appears that the only "mistakes" in *Persuasion* are those moments at which Anne seems to be even on the verge of exerting herself in her own cause, traces of Austen's old way of telling a story.

The removal, or its promise, of something standing in the way of Anne's happiness is always followed, until the reunion scene, by Anne's continued suffering. For example, at the concert, Anne and Wentworth seem about to speak their minds for the first time since that long-ago parting. Wentworth, talking ostensibly about Benwick, says that a "man does not recover from such a devotion of the heart to such a woman!—He ought not—he does not." Anne now interprets correctly that his words and his uneasy manner in leaving his pregnant sentences unfinished "all declared that he had a heart returning to her at least." A little later, the resolution actually seems even closer, by virtue of Wentworth's reaction to seeing Anne and Elliot together. Anne concludes that Wentworth must be "jealous of her affection!" and for "a moment the gratification was exquisite." But how, she wonders, "in all the peculiar disadvantages of their respective situations, would he ever learn her real sentiments?" (183, 185, 190).

It is difficult at this point to explain precisely why Anne's difficulties seem somehow out of proportion to her situation. After all, it is possible to argue that this is still a comic novel and that the barriers, while different from those in the other novels, are still barriers. Even so, the precise comic difficulties Austen chooses are always indexes to her thought, and they are not less so now. All Anne needs is a moment alone with Wentworth, which should be easier for Austen to arrange than to postpone, and fully a fifth of the novel remains. Unlike *Pride and Prejudice,* in which Darcy's letter to Elizabeth removes most of the reasons for their estrangement somewhere near the middle of the novel, only to have new difficulties arise to keep them apart, Austen here has no new complications in mind. The next chapter, the long conversation with Mrs. Smith, is a smokescreen, in that Mr. Elliot has long been out of the running. In her final novel, Austen neatly reverses the relationship between her heroine and the comic action that promises her reward. Now the mechanics of the instability are muted, rendered ironic, while the "real" subject, Anne's unhappiness, continues to be highlighted. This explanation of the plot of *Persuasion* may strike some formalist critics as too "easy," too much a dismissal rather than a solution of the sticky problems often identified as resulting from Austen's attempts to write another comic action. The form of the novel, however, is itself Austen's own response to dissatisfaction with the implications of representing pain as a barrier to be overcome.

If, after the concert scene, Anne's ecstasy seems to subdue most of the former misery, for most of the story Anne is a tragic character in a minimalist comic action. Most of the reasons that keep Wentworth from Anne are hidden from her and from the reader, which is another indication of how the plot of the novel moves toward expressive form. Only at the end of the book is the reader allowed—at the same time Anne is—an understanding of why she has had to endure these additional months of excruciation. Wentworth's ambivalent attitude toward Anne, a result of his "angry pride" (242), and his conviction that he is committed to Louisa, especially after the accident, are explanations deferred until the conclusion, serving therefore as absent causes in Anne's drama of pain. His relief, after Louisa's surprise engagement, at now being at liberty to "exert" himself, to put himself "in the way of happiness," and his "agony" at the "eligibilities and proprieties" of her match with Elliot, his mistaking her relaxed manner with him for "the ease which [her] engagement to another man would give" (243–45), are all elements, much like what one finds in *Pride and Prejudice*, of a traditional comic action. The only difference is that, as barriers, they are either all chimeras, like Anne's involvement with Elliot, or already inert by the time they are revealed, like Wentworth's obligation to Louisa. If Fanny's happiness issues from the power of her imagination, Anne's is always available. Austen's refusal to abandon Anne's misery, her commitment to the immediacy of bereavement, results in a predicament: how to "get out" of the "comic" novel that (inevitably) decenters that pain. It is the continuing *aporia* of the novel.

This separation of the circumstances of Anne's reunion with Wentworth from her own apprehension results in a kind of double vision for readers. There is no reason to doubt that Anne and Wentworth will eventually come back together, but at the same time there is no reason for the reunion not to occur on the next page, no reason for one or the other lover not, even with a bare word, to "exert." During much of the novel, then, the reader is as "deep in the happiness of such misery, or the misery of such happiness," as Anne is. The happy conclusion of the novel evokes emotions in the reader very different from those normally associated with a comic action. Our encounter with Anne's deep misery has been more than just watching; it is more like experiencing, so when Austen finally, reluctantly it almost seems, stops deferring Anne's restitution of happiness, there is a tremendous rush of relief. This effect is as much a part of the ideological innovation of the novel as it is the result of a new formal arrangement.

Critics who have seen the reader's encounter with Anne's consciousness as somehow at odds with the "comic" paraphernalia have missed the crucial connection. The comic action is in the novel to comment ironically on the impossibility of Anne's perceiving that she is a part of it. In simpler terms, the novel portrays a heroine whose fate is sealed in misery finally reaching a happiness which there is no necessity she ever attain but from which she is never impossibly divided. Austen strips the comic action of much of its freight of causality. Even so, the novel is a more radical departure from Austen's earlier works than these attempts at description imply. Anne Elliot has little to do with the happy reversal of her fate. Her heartbreak so determines the way she deals with the world that she cannot bring herself to act on the possibility that Wentworth still loves her until it is all but confirmed. All of the actual barriers (internal and external) to fulfillment have nothing to do with Anne: she is still frozen in her situation by the loss of Frederick.

Persuasion has, then, one story—Anne's. It is the story of a woman whose pain of separation has defined her life for more than seven years—one-sixth of Austen's own life, as it turned out, but no mean span for anyone. Its dominant feeling and tone are expressed by this much-quoted passage: "Anne, at seven and twenty, thought very differently from what she had been made to think at nineteen.—She did not blame Lady Russell, she did not blame herself for being guided by her; but she felt that were any young person, in similar circumstances, to apply to her for counsel, they would never receive any of such certain immediate wretchedness, such uncertain future good" (29). To be a wretch is not only to be miserable, it is also to be despised, and Anne is both. Before Wentworth, she endures the loss of a darling mother and the contempt of her father and sister. Since Wentworth, she is doubly cursed. The happy ending of her story by no means cancels those years. What the reader is allowed to see—what composes the material action of the story—is Anne's suffering, even as she is on the threshold of its termination.

It may well be that the comic elements of the story, including the welcome ending, are not fully subordinated to the presentation of Anne's state of mind. It does not seem to me crucial whether they are lingering vestiges from the earlier actions or conceived separately for this novel. Wherever they come from, and however much they continue to elicit comic expectations somewhat at odds with the lyric plot, they serve to comment on the ideological constrictions of comedy, including *Persuasion*. There are, in fact, two sets of comic expectations. One set involves Wentworth and is hidden from Anne and the reader until Frederick reveals at the end how committed he has been to Louisa, how easy it might have been for him to have slipped away from Anne a second, even more hateful, time. The other is a set of ambiguous signs—Mr. Elliot the most important, but Mrs. Smith too—that serve only to suggest how powerless Anne is to affect her own fate. That Mr. Elliot, weak-chinned varlet that he is, comes close to attracting Anne Elliot—some readers see him as a real possibility, others dismiss him, with both sets reacting to ambiguous textual evidence—suggests the precariousness of the most powerful of loves. That he never "really" has a chance with Anne and that she can still "just acknowledge within herself such a possibility of having been induced to marry him" (211) is frightening. After so many years of seeing happiness as a matter of personal responsibility and perception, Austen now sees it as more a matter of luck. In this final novel she is closer than ever before to Charlotte's Way. In 1817, might she have emended Charlotte's assertion to read "Happiness in life is entirely a matter of chance"?

Nowhere do we see Austen's innovative intention in her final novel more clearly than in her attempt to bring the conclusion of

Persuasion, the actual coming together of the lovers, more into alignment with her own conception of the novel's formal demands.[10] Here Austen's attempt to create an ironic, self-reflexive action is inscribed in revision.

In the original version, Admiral Croft pulls Anne in from the street so that a reluctant Wentworth can ask her about the rumors of her impending marriage to Elliot, the ostensible reason being Croft's willingness to give up Kellynch if Anne and Mr. Elliot wish to reside there after their wedding. She firmly denies the rumor and, suddenly, "all suspense and indecision were over. They were reunited" (258). Then follows his explanation of what I have suggested is the hidden comic action—all those things that have delayed him. This ending provides a perfectly satisfactory sense of closure to the novel in that it has the suddenness of a reconciliation long delayed by silence. In another regard it is completely at odds with the fact that Anne always has available to her the option of speaking to Wentworth and is unable to do so. Wentworth's question also refers to an external barrier that is never really a barrier, Mr. Elliot, so that the inquiry is impertinent, especially now.

What is needed is a reunion that comes about with similar speed but much more indirection. To be thematically consistent with the object of representation, Anne's suffering, the conclusion must emphasize the continuing strength of that pain and indicate, ironically if possible, that despite Wentworth's original misery of rejection, over the years he has not suffered as Anne has, that indeed, no one could have suffered so deeply and so silently. So Austen invents the brilliant scene of Harville and Anne contending over who, the woman or the man, suffers and continues to love longest "when existence or when hope is gone" (235). Wentworth overhears them talking, writes his letter, and together they share their renewed love in a stroll to Camden Place. This ending has the virtue of indirection that mirrors the entire history of their estrangement. Nothing is ever clear and straightforward, from Anne's motives for giving him up to his own feelings, years later, upon returning to the neighborhood. All but the earliest of Anne's pain results from a pitiful misunderstanding that could have been straightened out years ago. In addition, the dialogue between Anne and Harville has another virtue lacking in the original ending, in that it makes two points: Anne's suffering extends right to this very moment (which is why she argues so forcefully about woman's portion of pain), and it is not something she ever could do anything about. In a paragraph that echoes most of the concerns that have arisen during the novel, Anne says, "Yes. We certainly do not forget you, so soon as you forget us. It is, perhaps, our fate rather than our merit. We cannot help ourselves. We live at home, quiet, confined, and our feelings prey upon us. You are forced on exertion. You have always a profession, pursuits, business of some sort or other, to take you back into the world immediately, and continual occupation and change soon weaken impressions" (232). Anne's fate—it is her merit, her curse, and her redemption as well—is not to forget her love. As in Virginia Woolf's *The Waves*, it is the tree she could not pass. Her loss comes close to ruining her health; it preys upon her. Her exertion has been devoted to mediating the marital squabbles and disciplining the children of others. She has been condemned not to change but instead to endure the unweakened misery of her estrangement from Wentworth.

The revised ending reemphasizes all of these things, and something more. It suggests, in the depth of its feeling and in its tangential reference, an author who saw herself in Anne and who in Anne's final happiness commemorated the ruins of her own life. "All the privilege," Anne tells Harville, with Wentworth in hearing, "I claim for my own sex (it is not a very enviable one, you need not covet it) is that of loving longest, when existence or when hope is gone" (235). Anne is, of course, arguing generally here; the reference to "existence" being "gone" is inert in reference to her own situation and does not apply to Benwick, too light a presence to be more than the proximate cause of these discussions. The lover whose existence ended was, perhaps, the "youngish, intelligent, charming, and handsome" clergyman "greatly attracted to Jane" in Devonshire in the summer of 1801; the young man who, "on the verge of proposing marriage when the holiday came to an end," went away and had the ill grace to die (Halperin, 132). Jane Austen was twenty-five. Anne Elliot's romantic life begins again, with a letter, at about the same time in her life that Austen's died forever, for want of a letter.

Persuasion is the most ideologically paradoxical of Austen's novels. On the one hand, it is not even about love, but rather love's fragility. From the moment Anne gently sighs to herself, "a few months more, and *he* perhaps, may be walking here," there is little reason—nothing, indeed, that is not illustrative of how easily love may miss its object—for her happiness to be deferred. That is how it seems, at least, with the real comic action hidden from our eyes and the illusory one falling apart right before us. Given how little seems to divide Anne and Wentworth—a tissue of fear and misapprehension that could have been lifted by a little talk, even by the right sort of gesture or facial expression—the length of time it takes them to reconcile suggests how easy it is for the most powerful of feelings, the most devoted of attachments, to whimper away into ruin. All it takes is pique, a sudden departure with a word unsaid, and lives are crippled. It is this almost tragic understanding of the world's ability to arrange for the lover to be in the wrong place, to overhear the wrong word or not hear the right one, that informs the novel. Anne's near decade of sharp bereavement may have lost its sting. She will be, finally, happy. For the reader, however, her unhappiness is not erased from history just because Wentworth finally enfolds Anne in his healing love.

On the other hand, the book is perhaps Austen's most romantic. Despite its skepticism about our ability to know anything that will help us secure happiness, and its unsettling belief in the reality of pain, it takes love as seriously as any of the other books. Wentworth's return to Anne's arms is a "revolution" (237), all the sweeter because it came so close to not happening. It is perhaps fitting that the proud Wentworth, who very nearly throws love away, finally sees how important and how precarious his rewinning of Anne has been. He has the last speech in the novel: "'I have been used to the gratification of believing myself to earn every blessing that I enjoyed. I have valued myself on honourable toils and just rewards. Like other great men under reverses,' he added with a smile, 'I must endeavour to subdue my mind to my fortune. I must learn to brook being happier than I deserve.'"

4

Eliot, the Reader,
and Parable

Innovations take place in an "extended" situation involving previous work, present composition, publication, and (implied or expected) reception. While they may originate in private concerns, they immediately generate unexpected influences. For example, they modify the taste of their readers and then serve as an impetus to further innovation. New forms foster the attitude that authors, painters, and composers *should* innovate. This was so even in the eighteenth century, when neoclassical decorum and the burden of the ancients weighed so heavily on the present that Pope thought of invention as linguistic "dressing" of oft-told truths. Even so, almost every neoclassical poet, from Dryden to Gray and Cowper, sought ways to meld the purely personal with a kind of poetry expected to be essentially impersonal. It is, therefore, poetry with its "didacticism" often "closely associated with the representation of inward experience," lending it a "powerfully lyric cast" (Feingold, vii). These poets tried to wedge their lives—decorously, of course—into structures whose standards discouraged such private commentary. The roundabout path Pope takes in the "Epistle to Miss Blount" to convey what appears to be a commonplace is puzzling at first. In Pope's hands, however, the decorum of the epistle makes room for the gentle message that Pope will be at loose ends until Miss Blount returns to town. Forms yields to personal urgency (see Rader 1976; Feingold).

The dialectical relationship between the effects of innovative forms on readers and whatever the innovative author chooses to do in subsequent works is too complex and too haphazard to serve as a reliable basis for a theory. Each case is different. Even so, one might conjecture that the more strenuous the readers' reaction, the greater the stimulus for an authorial response, although no "simple causality" would be involved. Some authors seem impervious to public reaction, while others, like Hemingway, are painfully thin-skinned. The site of innovation will always vary on many axes, including the degree to which an author respects or disdains the capacities of his or her readership. Hemingway's attitude was hardly avuncular in the 1930s, while Eliot's was almost always benevolently auntilary, to appropriate Amanda Cross's long-needed neologism. In this chapter I examine the interaction of a shift in George Eliot's perception of her readership with a change in her own beliefs about their needs, which resulted in an attempt to design a more effective novelistic structure. *Daniel Deronda* does not, as is sometimes argued, traverse in turns the boundaries of romance and the novel. Instead, Eliot designs a structure that takes on the public task of instruction always implicit in her earlier fiction. She tries, once again, to enact the moral goals for fiction that antedate even the rise of the novel and which, as Janice Carlisle put it, "by the 1870s, must have seemed both still inescapable and almost impossible to live up to."[1]

This chapter and the next show two antithetical sides of the moral dialectic of innovation. Eliot comes out on the opposite end of the process from Hemingway, whose adventure with his readership resulted in the 1930s in the accusatory, adversarial operation of satire.

As George Eliot neared the end of her career as a novelist, the bounds of serious fiction had been so expanded by Dickens, Thackeray, and herself that a shift occurred. Social mimesis, with which an entire fictional society may be established and made to obey the moral laws of its creator, had brought the action to the boundaries of coherence. As Henry James put it, novels like *Middlemarch* set "a limit . . . to the development of the old-fashioned English novel. Its diffuseness . . . makes it too copious a dose of pure fiction" (Miller, 154).

Although it is not merely a matter of space, the very size of the Victorian novel is the single most apt metaphor of its intention. Austen's plots all represent the travails of an individual trying to make her way through a maze of choice involving self, family, and society to arrive at some sort of personal happiness. Eliot's realism, on the other hand, begins with the idea of a better society. She could not achieve her goal with anything less than a plot that takes in a large range of socially relevant possibilities for right and wrong choice. The amalgamation of story and moral with which the novel had been cursed, or blessed, since Defoe's *Roxana*, now presented the Victorian reader with a profound problem of interpretation. The materials Austen tried to subordinate to the fate of a pair of lovers, Eliot opened up to a much larger cast of central characters, requiring many more shades and degrees of requisite approbation and blame, all of which constitute the complex "message" of the novel's smooth surface of experience. How is one to judge the lives of so many important characters, how come to the "right" conclusion about this unwieldy world? Having discovered in *Romola* that the more complex the relationship between story and ideology, the more readers were left behind, what now? Put complexity aside to compose more "simple" novels like *Silas Marner*? Eliot, of course, was incapable of offering her reader simplified realism, as the imponderables of Silas's story indicate. The very match of realistic story telling—which is better the more it renders the experience rather than just telling about it—and moral intention becomes problematic, at least from the standpoint of a reader (still) in need of moral instruction. Of course, in the 1870s, with Walter Pater's star barely above the horizon, no novelist of stature had yet tried to apply in narrative Blake's warning that to generalize is to be an idiot.

Eliot certainly was not that novelist. She had to find or invent a narrative form that would enable her to emphasize the ideological content of her massive mimesis. One almost inevitable pitfall of such an intention is mixing incompatible ideological intentions in the same novel. As I try to show, Eliot usually had the clearest idea of the moral structure of each novel before she began. Then too, since she was committed to representing mixed characters, neither villains nor saints, she usually needed only to observe the kind of consistency that would lead to convincing characters. The configuration of their fates, and particularly *how* they come about, make her overall moral point. Through *Middlemarch*, Eliot was almost always successful in combining mixed character with moral purpose, although the result is no obvious homogeneity from novel to novel. All of her novels, including *Daniel Deronda*, may be present as potentialities in *Scenes of Clerical Life*, but it is also possible to see each as an innovation—the old persistent paradox of the sui generis nature of each example of a genre. The separate newness of Eliot's last novel—its urgency—resides in the fact that Eliot changed her mind about what Daniel meant to her as she was writing the novel. The result is a complexly innovative intention that she never quite worked out.

Like Austen, George Eliot is not often seen as an innovator of narrative forms, even though from the beginning of her career her very method of writing fiction was itself new, in fact almost a reversal of the "normal" pattern in realistic fiction. Nevertheless, a strong case can be made for her career being unwrinkled by obvious attempts to "start over." Despite the heavy freight of moral commitment and the willingness of each of her narrators to engage in overt commentary, she developed the potentialities of psychological realism in her repeated attempts to dramatize relationships of necessity—the interplay of events and character. Even as late as *Middlemarch* she still believed in the general, albeit slow, betterment of the human lot, the way in which many manage to make the world at least a little more livable. Indeed, *Middlemarch*, still perfectly in the realist mode, serves as a kind of nineteenth-century handbook for amiable feeling about oneself in the midst of consequential error. Who would think that such good could come out of marrying a Casaubon? Eliot did not end her career with *Middlemarch*, however. She wrote one final novel, *Daniel Deronda*, which has puzzled critics since its appearance in 1876.

First, the novel seems to fall into two parts, in a much sharper and more noncoalescing manner than any of her previous fiction. It begins with a plunge into the middle of the action, as if Eliot wants to show her heroine at the height of her career before going back to see how she will get there—an unusual procedure for Eliot. The first scene, after some preliminary cautionary teasing about the "make-believe" nature of "beginnings," seems to suggest inevitable romance between a young gambler, Gwendolen Harleth, and Daniel, through whose eyes we see her. Gwendolen loses her money and must pawn her necklace. Deronda takes the opportunity to redeem the necklace, and the reader sees what will probably be their relationship: no matter the vicissitudes of Gwendolen's fortunes, Deronda will save her in the end. He will be her more perfect Ladislaw. Deronda, however, pursues his own separate fate and never becomes more than a kind of sympathetic adviser to Gwendolen. Like the characters of a later writer, also committed to showing her readers how to be better, Gwendolen and Daniel "rise," but they do not "converge." The narrator's preliminary suspicion about the illusionary nature of "beginnings" is finally confirmed: whatever else it leads to, the opening scene in the casino is not the start of a picture-book romance. From his youth enamored with finding his origins and a purpose, Daniel finally discovers he is a Jew, marries a Jewish woman, and at the end of the novel is poised to go in search of a Jewish homeland—promising Gwendolen he will write. She is left still wondering what she should do with her life, having discovered only her own emptiness and the glimmer of a realization—the "seed" of the final book's title—that her male-dominated society, with its genteel and facile corruption, has destroyed her life.

This lack of convergence of the two main characters, or of even resolution for Gwendolen, bothered early readers, and it continues to do so. F. R. Leavis went so far as to wish the Deronda part excised from the novel, although he later repented a bit, and many critics since Leavis have felt compelled to echo his strictures, as when H. M. Daleski called the Gwendolen part "among the best things George Eliot ever did" and the Daniel part "among the worst" (27). All of the novel's elements, character, plot, technique, and theme seem radically bifurcated. Mary Ellen Doyle spoke for many critics when she said that no "one statement of what-it's-about will define its subject" (Doyle, 160). While some critics manage to view the novel as unified, they have to employ explanatory hypotheses so flexible or so general as to be relatively unhelpful in explaining the novel's details. Finally, as one might expect, readers may be found who experience no difficulty with seeing *Daniel Deronda* as just as unified as Eliot's previous novels, like the anonymous reviewer in 1876 who praised the "powerful construction" of the novel's "plot" (Carroll 1959:369).

In addition to the lack of convergence there is a second problem, partly a matter of subject, partly a matter of treatment. Although Gwendolen's story achieves a startling psychological intensity—and even, according to many critics, tragic sublimity—Deronda's story is relatively uncomplicated, and his character, despite his successful search for his identity, remains largely static. Gwendolen's "spoiled" nature, her blindness to humanity both specific and general, leads to her disastrous marriage, while Deronda seems to be a paragon: handsome, intelligent, sensitive to the needs and feelings of others. What flaws he does have, noted by some recent critics like Carlisle, may be easily ignored by most readers. Like Sir Charles Grandison, Deronda strikes some as a bore, although Daniel certainly is more interesting than Richardson's paragon. Moreover, although Gwendolen reveals herself to the reader from the brilliant opening, in multiplicitous act and thought, Eliot often fails to dramatize Deronda. Although readers today may be as inclined as their Victorian counterparts to excuse a bit of summary story telling, Deronda's flatness is all the more disturbing precisely because Gwendolen is so successfully drawn; the rich texture of her story contrasts sharply with the inertness of the paragon's fait accompli. One hopes, even suspects, that the contrast is carefully engineered, but to what end?[2]

Even though Eliot and other authors of her time were blessed with critics sensitive to the range of formal possibilities in the novel, and with space aplenty to speculate about her aims, only two of her contemporaries, Henry James and David Kaufmann, really appreciated what she was trying to do. To their insights I shall turn later. In our time, a number of general critical assumptions about Eliot and her novel influence the direction of specific readings. One is that *Daniel Deronda* is basically just a variant *Middlemarch*, a view first encouraged by George Saintsbury's comment, in 1876, that "Gwendolen is at heart a counterfoil of Dorothea, animated by an undisciplined egotism instead of an undisciplined altruism, and by the fanaticism of enjoyment instead of the fanaticism of sympathy" (Carroll 1971:372). Second, although critics have been assiduous in exploring the ideas Eliot employed, only Leon Gottfried is sufficiently interested in formal innovation in fiction to suggest that Eliot's last novel is a radical formal departure. Gottfried sees *Deronda* as a combination, in the Deronda and Gwendolen parts, of romance and novel. The problem is that in Northrop Frye, Gottfried's source, the concept of romance has little to do with novelistic function or structure. I can see how Eliot might have wanted to "develop in the novel an art form fully answerable to all the demands of mythic expression and fully equal to poetry" (Gottfried, 165). At the same time, recognizing that the Deronda part of the story is somehow more "mythic" does not take us very far toward understanding *why*, given her steadfast ethical intentions, Eliot wanted such a different structure after the success of *Middlemarch*. Finally, dividing the book into novel and romance, even if the terms were more than just "empty carriers," only names what all along has been perceived as divided. Eliot believed she was writing a unified novel. Some remaining questions then are what she intended, why *Deronda* is the result, and what goes right or, possibly, wrong in the book. Those questions are not approachable without some attempt at understanding the nature of Eliot's achievement through *Middlemarch*.

Eliot and Moral Panorama

From *Scenes of Clerical Life* (1858), written when the author was in her late thirties, to *Middlemarch* (1872), her masterpiece of panoramic social portraiture, Eliot's novels take as their subjects the effects of the actions of a large number of characters on each other and on society's prospects for moral betterment. It is true that each of the *Scenes* is named for a single character, as are *Adam Bede, Silas Marner, Romola,* and *Felix Holt*. It is possible to argue, however, that Eliot wrote only one novel, *The Mill on the Floss,* with the aim of subordinating all elements to the representation of a single character's fate. Even *Silas Marner* divides our attention between Silas and Godfrey Cass. To the extent that her novels are unified, it is the unity of equivalent parts working to the same end, and not, as in Fielding or Austen, a hierarchal relationship of subordination. This is not to say that her novels aim at only a kind of coordinate unity, or, much less, are inevitably disjunctive, although with George Eliot assertions of unity are always easier than explanations of how such diverse materials might actually become *one*.

Unlike Austen, Eliot first arrived at a coherent moral purpose that provided a rationale for every scene. Long after she gave her novel of fifteenth-century Florence, *Romola*, to the world, she still remembered why she had included the odd irrelevancy of the frenzied monkey and its antics: "The whole piquancy of the scene in question was intended to lie in the antithesis between the puerility which stood for wit and humour in the old Republic, and the majesty of its front in graver matters" (Haight, *Letters*, 5:174). Her ready memory of what she had in mind for that single scene reinforces what Eliot's friend Lewes understood—that she always knew exactly what she was trying to do in her novels, always had a working principle of unity.

Eliot's fictional form is an idea-charged realism, a thematically dense medium that nevertheless uses ideas without letting them displace the concrete story. Indeed, so concerned was she about the realism of her novels that she laboriously worked out their historical and situational problems of plausibility. She often expended so much labor on representing the backgrounds of her characters' actions that her powers of invention—what shall the people of the book *do?*—failed her. From burrowing through mountains of historical material about Italy in order to construct the Florentine society of *Romola*, she got "into a state of so much wretchedness in attempting to concentrate my thoughts on the construction of my story that I became desperate and suddenly burst my bonds, saying, I will not think of writing" (*Letters*, 350). Part of her difficulty arose because she was committed to a narrative "pattern" she invented herself, not one "ready made" like comedy or tragedy. She employed tragic sequences (Maggie, Hetty, Gwendolen) and happy endings (Dinah, Dorothea, Daniel), but her novels as wholes, as prolonged experiences—the side of them she was most concerned about—do not usually take care to satisfy conventional generic expectations, which at any rate began to disintegrate after Austen, Scott, and then Dickens. Eliot wished to represent the true state of sublunary happiness and misery in all its gradations. For this reason, many readers feel that her novels provide an experience equivalent to reading about real people. While it may seem liberating for an author not to have to worry about generic constraints, the task is maddeningly difficult, as Eliot's miserable anxiety—shared with Woolf and many another writer—in completing each of her novels indicates. It was not just her paralyzing "diffidence," as Lewes so often called it, that hindered her. Her diffidence was the result of the difficulty of dreaming up imagined lives for variegated characters while carefully keeping in view the overall ideology of the realistic stream. Despite the autobiographical elements in her fiction she was not a Virginia Woolf, elegantly disguising confession under fiction. Constructing fictional reality on Eliot's principle may seem like poor Hetty in her wanderings, sensing a possible destination, but with no map or knowledge of the way.

Eliot, of course, had much more to guide her than did Hetty. First, the societies (Florentine, English, or Zionist-in-exile) constructed on her pages carry with them carefully designed limits on human development, and therefore on the theoretically possible fates for each of her characters. It is curious that someone who wrote as many letters as Eliot did engaged so rarely in aesthetic discussion, "shop talk." Even so, she left us a passage, frequently quoted but seldom analyzed, that is a precise description of her own process of creation: "The psychological causes which prompted me to give such details of Florentine life and history as I have given, are precisely the same as those which determined me in giving the details of English village life in 'Silas Marner,' or the 'Dodson' life, out of which were developed the destinies of poor Tom and Maggie" (*Letters*, 4:97). While it is possible to make a case that "psychological causes" is ambiguous, I do not believe this is a formula for social mimesis, at least not if Eliot's description of her practice is accurate. The societies represented are responses to, equivalents of, her own internal states—"successive mental phases," as she elsewhere put it. These a priori attitudes toward her materials generate each novel. Put in slightly different terms, each of Eliot's novels reveals an attempt to represent the consequences of morally complex acts and attitudes; but the design of the signifying plot, in its origin, is traceable not to fidelity to existing institutions, or to a desire to achieve realism for its own sake, but to her own vision of a better world. It is moral realism. The events in her books obey laws of ideational as well as verisimilar probability. In that ideological intention is something like a ruling hypothesis, a philosophical reference point for the construction of the fictional society. From that construct spring characters, scenes, and the entire causal structure of social action. Gordon Haight has suggested, in regard to *Romola,* that "from her immersion in all these primary materials George Eliot hoped that a story would somehow emerge" (350). This is just how she worked, except that her "immersion" was the second, not the first, stage of the artistic process. Her moral conception predated the painstaking, sometimes antiquarian research; from that welter of facts and impressions came the represented society; only after it was embodied in a fictional arena, a context, did she go on to "construction," to peopling the fictional society. Eliot constructed her novels as many people do their moral lives, by making the facts fit a prior conception of their significance. More important for *Deronda,* her process of creation—idea, represented society, and material action—actually seems more to resemble certain neoclassical notions of fabulation than it does realistic story telling. It is not surprising that Eliot and Lewes loved to read Samuel Johnson. What is surprising is that, given her wholehearted approval of the moral nature of story telling, she remained so thoroughly and so long committed to the indirections of realism.

Lewes, George Eliot's best critic and the only person to whom she confided her full artistic intentions, understood the necessary relation of her stories to their represented societies. When Blackwood, her publisher, complained about "Janet's Repentance" that it contains "characters who do not seem likely to assist materially in the movement of the Story," Lewes replied that the "descriptions of character are not so alien to the drama as they possibly appear" and that their function would "become clear as the story proceeds" (*Letters,* 2:344, 353). Blackwood's objections, soon stilled as he was better schooled to his new author's ways, show that he expected the plots of novels to exhibit a kind of unity not possible in Eliot's new plan. Indeed, the genesis of plot in Eliot's works—to the extent that any certainty about such a slippery question might be available—differs from that of most other realists. For example, when James came to invent Isabel Archer, the "germ" of the idea was "altogether in the sense of a single character . . . an engaging young woman, to which all the usual elements of a 'subject,' certainly of a setting, were to be super-added" (Miller, 70). Eliot's procedure is almost the opposite. She thought from large to small. First come her own conceptions of a better world; then the fictional society where she shows small additions to the general good by individuals and the competing tendencies toward ill that might be just as instructive; and then, only then, the specific characters whose lives enact the struggle to be good. Having begun what would become *Middlemarch*, Eliot realized that she had assembled the proper cast of characters and concerns to "frame" the separate story about Miss Brooke's efforts to be good.[3] It is only in the context of other efforts to live well, such as Fred's and Lydgate's, that Dorothea's yearnings to reach beyond the "nibblings and judgements of a discursive mouse," the lot of most of Eliot's thinking women, not only make full sense but have their emotive power. Never in the business of providing "pleasing pictures," Eliot resembled in this regard, she thought, "the most powerful of living novelists," Thackeray (Haight, 236). Dorothea's efforts to find a way to "do"—"what ought she to do?" (*Middlemarch*, 27)—are usefully seen from Eliot's own lively sympathy with the imperfect successes of the human comedy.

Given Eliot's earnest acceptance of fiction's responsibility to improve the world, it is a little surprising that her beginning with the moral underpinning of her stories did not result in more overtly didactic narrative structures. She declared to Blackwood that she "always exercised a severe watch against anything that could be called preaching." She envisioned a morally efficacious totality in fiction: "Unless my readers are more moved towards the ends I seek by my works as wholes than by an assemblage of extracts, my writings are a mistake. . . . and if I have ever allowed myself in dissertation or in dialogue [anything] which is not part of the *structure* of my books, I have there sinned against my own laws." In this same letter she denies that her books are "properly separable into 'direct' and 'indirect' teaching," which is one reason she was always so uneasy about Alexander Main's extracts from her writing—they might "encourage such a view" (*Letters*, 5:458–59).

Even with their genesis firmly in ideological concerns, then, it is still not surprising that Eliot's novels before *Deronda* do not yield readily to analysis as examples of what David Richter has called "fables," that variety of didactic structure the eighteenth century knew as "apologues," fictions whose highly stylized elements of character and action are rigidly subordinated to ideological propositions, as they are in *Rasselas* and *Candide*. Nor do they resemble such experiments in ideological fiction (before and after Eliot) as *Frankenstein* or *1984*, in which the reader understands that the elements of the fiction, realistic as they might be, are just as surely at the service of a message as they are in earlier, more obvious parables (Richter 1974). Eliot was committed to representing the process of betterment, what it *feels* like "on the page" as well as the moral propositions that might be extracted, which means that while the novelistic society she designed was craftily formed to point a moral, she never sacrificed the complexity of individual lives like those of Bulstrode, Casaubon, and Lydgate for the sake of the "argument."

All of Eliot's novels are experiments in representing morally determined character. Discussions of her fiction often concentrate quite properly on its realism as an element of its moral force. She found, for example, that she could represent consciousness in such a way that the moral implications she wanted to convey are a part of the experience itself, not superadded. Hetty, in the marvelous chapter 15 of *Adam Bede*, is a real advance in the portrayal of unusual states of mind. The meditative point of view, concentrating on her impressions and thoughts, unironic, uncondescending in the face of this monstrous vanity, creates a chilling portrait. In this work Eliot, as she so often does, offers a disturbing portrait and then challenges the reader to bring the malefactor into the circle of his or her compassion. The fact that one purpose of the chapter is a comparison of two feminine natures—one amoral and only barely capable of salvation, the other the angelic Dinah's—does not overpower the mimetic effectiveness of Hetty as a reluctant object of the reader's pity. Mimesis, in the sense of a possible reality, in Eliot's hands becomes inseparable from belief.

It seems obvious that such a method of representing so as to encourage a gradually bettering world, which her characters pay for in the coin of suffering and in which her readers are tested at every turn, requires the largest possible canvas. Like Lewes, Blackwood soon came to understand that judgment about matters like coherence must be withheld where Eliot was concerned until the reader might survey every floor of her spacious edifice. To read George Eliot requires leisure and patience. The first was provided by the method of publishing in successive volumes, which Lewes and Eliot hit upon as financially advantageous but which also perfectly suited the formal and ideological ends of her fiction. It is characteristic that Eliot's intention to induce readers to ponder her characters' fates rather than rushing to anticipate them helped decide even the method of publication.

Yet even these modest aims are often frustrated by the impatient dynamics of reading. That readers, even with time to digest each volume of the novel, still insisted upon leaping to judgment is indicated by Eliot's exasperation at attempts to predict the endings of her stories. Alexander Main made the acquaintance of Eliot and Lewes when he proposed assembling the best quotations from the novels into a "wit and wisdom" volume. Eliot, who was acutely aware that her house of fiction was not best shown brick by brick, lectured Main on his tendency to rush ahead in his imagination to possible endings: "Try to keep from forecast of Dorothea's lot, and that sort of construction beforehand which makes everything that actually happens a disappointment." One might think such an activity innocent enough, and certainly Eliot's imaginative largess would cheerfully grant such freedom to the reader. On the contrary, she seems to have been seriously annoyed when Main's comments indicated that he was ignoring her advice: "I never felt so inclined to scold you [for] . . . constructing the future of the story. . . . Nothing mars the receptivity more than eager construction" (*Letters*, 5:261, 324). Although one can fully appreciate Eliot's desire that her readers receive the full impact of her fiction, this is an odd view of the reading process, especially considering how she published her novels after giving up magazine serialization. Bringing out a multivolume novel, sending forth an installment every month or two, seems almost to ensure that readers will leap to predict the futures of characters in whose fates they invest so much time and care. Why does "eager construction" lead to "disappointment"? Don't readers always eagerly look forward, especially in the midst of traditional novelistic structures that seem to require anticipatory knowledge for their plots to be understood? Of course, Eliot had in mind here *Middlemarch*, so it is likely that she was thinking of the reader's attempt to guess the ultimate fates of Dorothea and Lydgate. However, since she planned to unite Dorothea with Ladislaw and continue Lydgate's domestic unhappiness so that the thematic point about professional endeavor persisting in spite of marital misfortune might be enforced, how could the Mr. Mains of the reading world lose out? One is tempted to conclude that it is *how* her characters arrive at their fates that carries Eliot's thematic message as much as the ultimate fates themselves—which are left largely unnarrated anyway. By rejoicing at Dorothea's happy future, might the impatient reader lose sight of the moral implications of her present pain, or rush heedless through the succession of small changes that leads to her marriage to Will and constitutes, for Eliot, the subtle "lesson"?

As her career progressed, Eliot more and more rebelled against the generic constraints that tend to make happy endings "inevitable" and that, at the same time, furnish the conventions innovative form may undermine. When confronted with a problem of narrative probability, for example, she was careful to temper extremes of expectation, beating the Mr. Mains of the world to the punch. In this regard she reversed the practice of many novelists who published in installments by refusing to end each episode with a mystery and a clue. Eliot was instead carefully anticlimactic. In chapter 4 of *Middlemarch*, for example, when Dorothea agrees to marry Casaubon, much of what we learn about the match—that he is twenty-seven years her senior; that she acquiesces with no real emotion, admiring and honoring but clearly not loving him; that she wants a husband above her "in judgment and in all knowledge" (40)—makes fully, ominously apparent in advance the marital disaster she is contracting, even if the reader didn't already know from the wasteland of Casaubon's letter of proposal, a serio-pompous version of what Austen's Mr. Collins orated to Lizzy Bennet. The reader's task is not to anticipate the unsatisfactory state of Dorothea's marriage; Eliot anticipates it herself. Many women, after all, make just such bad marriages; but here, unlike Austen's use of Charlotte Lucas, the *fact* of the mistake is not the focal point. The reader's task, carefully designed, is to attend to *how*—that is the morally operative word—something might be salvaged, not in the future but right here with Casaubon sitting next to her. There is no suspense about the outcome of the marriage because our knowledge that it is a horrible mistake is necessary if we are to pay attention to what is really important to Eliot: how an idealistic woman will act when she discovers, quickly, as it turns out, that she has married a desiccated pedant. In the moral terms of the novel, and in contrast to James's intentions in *The Portrait of a Lady*, our attention should be not on Dorothea's fate but on the "gradual action of ordinary causes," specifically, how some good may come out of events much like the ones James uses to certify Isabel's austerely majestic fall from innocence. Typical of Eliot's human comedy, the situation seems to contain both pitiful and ludicrous elements. Casaubon is a comic masterpiece, a mincing, scholarly amateur—most scholars still were amateurs even in the 1820s, but Eliot establishes the "type" for all time—the unwriting author. Being married to him is, however, no joke.

Yet the strongest indication of Eliot's desire to short-circuit the generic expectations of earlier fiction, how even in *Middlemarch* she was moving toward the anticlimax and stasis of exemplum, is how she handles the question of Casaubon's health. Eliot could have built up a great deal of suspense about it. If she had, the reader's attention would have been directed at Dorothea's fate, at whether she would end happily or find a way cheerfully to suffer her martyrdom, a lifetime married to her dismal husband. Instead Eliot gives us two clear indications as to how long Dorothea will have to put up with Casaubon. Mr. Brooke mentions that "his health is not over-strong," and later we learn, in one of those leaps forward Eliot uses to redirect our attention back to the moral present, that "Dorothea remembered . . . to the last" her first real quarrel with her husband (40, 204). Foreknowledge that Casaubon will die allows the reader to concentrate on Dorothea's responses to her new misery. Freed from anxiety about her ultimate fate—although the reader does not know what it will be, Casaubon's prospective removal allows a hopeful attitude, which was the inadvertent cause of Mr. Main's prospective reading—the reader is supposed to watch Eliot's real drama, the moral dilemma of a bright woman forced to realize that she has made a horrible and irrevocable mistake and must now make the best of the bargain.[4]

In other words, Eliot shifts the probabilities of the realistic novel subtly toward the parable, relinquishing the luxury of suspense. If Eliot's handling of probability in this case serves to deflect normal anxiety about a character's future into concern about her present conduct, it also has another effect. Eliot forestalls possible resentment of Casaubon for ruining Dorothea's life, leaving the reader free to concentrate on something far more important, the poor man's humanity. Eliot felt more than a little affinity with this failed scholar, "in whose life" she "lived with much sympathy," and she seemed disappointed at how harshly readers reacted to him.[5]

This imaginative sympathy with characters many readers dislike is a key to Eliot's fictional methods, as well as to her hopes for her readers. Never content simply to inscribe reality, she involved the reader in a process of understanding, a heuristic dynamic that demands as much as it gives. Readers tend, just by virtue of thorough knowledge, to excuse conduct they might readily condemn from a greater distance. When Eliot's readers showed by their comments that their own moral imaginations were commodious enough for her purposes, she was almost spiritually moved, her fiction serving for her as a kind of religion: "What one's soul thirsts for is the word which is the refle[ction] of one's own aim and delight in writing—the word which shows that what one meant has been perfectly seized, that the emotion which stirred one in writing is repeated in the mind of the reader" (*Letters,* 5:374). In Crocean terms, to which Eliot's comments bear resemblance, her intuition is embodied in an objective structure which then allows the reader to reduplicate her generative intuition. Eliot meant for her readers to sympathize with Casaubon, and the fact that many readers despised him must have indicated to her that something fundamental went wrong with her formal intuition in *Middlemarch.* One possibility is that the very expectations she tried to prevent by providing foreknowledge led to the predictive reading she wanted to prevent. Her next novel, *Daniel Deronda*, demonstrates that if beginnings are only delusions, anticipating satisfactory conclusions is an even more treacherous venture.

Flight from Realism

In 1873, with *Middlemarch* behind her, Eliot's thinking frequently revealed an anxiety about the recalcitrance of her readers, their refusal to activate their sympathetic imaginations, their insistence upon reading for the plot. Given the sales and translations of her novels, by 1873, even with her famous diffidence, it would be hard for her not to have perceived that her fiction had a powerful potential for benign influence. However many novels she might be vouchsafed to write in the remainder of her days—and her health was not good—each would be a kind of moral duty from which it is death to hide. Her "universal and private" religion—it is not too strong a word—involved an active concern for the "just and loving deed of every day" by which one's "heart" is carried "strongly to every other part of the world which in its need of love and justice is just in the same predicament." The little acts by which a person improves, "the daily conquest of our private demons," constitute "the most difficult heroism," not the "slaying of world-notorious demons" (*Letters*, 6:112, 126). Yet just those subtle acts were the most difficult to get her readers to address, in her novels and in themselves. Perhaps she wanted more than readers of any age could give. If she could by her magic make readers feel that Casaubon is not just a literary function, not just a barrier to Dorothea's later fulfillment, but instead a suffering man doing his mediocre best, then she and her readers might with their bare imaginations do something to thaw the frozen sensibilities that made possible the Franco-Prussian War and the brutality between British soldiers and Zulu warriors. Everywhere she looked she saw intelligent people refusing to extend their humanity, and her reaction was dismay. She disliked Pater's *Renaissance* because it seemed to encourage just those tendencies toward selfishness that she saw at the heart of the worldsickness. Pater's critical principles encourage a false view of life, sundering philosophy and the moral imagination from the artistic process, making art irrelevant to the secular sacredness of bettering the world (*Letters*, 5:455). When she wrote to Harriet Beecher Stowe that what the world needs is a "more perfect" religion, one springing from "a more deeply-awing sense of responsibility to man" and from a "sympathy with . . . the difficulty of the human lot," her sense of urgency arose from seeing both "abroad and . . . at home . . . how slowly the centuries work toward the moral good of men" (*Letters*, 5:31).

The personal genesis of *Daniel Deronda*, I suggest, is a sense of the inherent liabilities, the indirection, of realistic fiction. In her hands it had become too multiplicitous a genre, too demanding. She now needed to find or invent a new, more powerful fictional vehicle, one whose efforts at moral rejuvenation would be, if not less complex, then more forceful. Almost by definition, a mode of realistic fiction that attempts "to show the gradual action of ordinary causes rather than exceptional" is in danger of trying the patience of reader and author (*Letters*, 5:168). The better it is as fiction, the worse it is as morality. More disturbing, readers made a habit of refusing to enter into the humanity of so many of her "mixed" characters, from Hetty to Tito to Casaubon, that Eliot's faith in her readers, or her own fictive practices, was finally shaken. It is not that George Eliot changed her mind. That shift occurred only after she began to write *Deronda*. She had her "little store," her "two or three beliefs which are the outcome" of her "character and experience." Then too, she feared "harping on these too long, and taking up other strains which are not at all our beliefs, but mere borrowing and echo" (*Letters*, 5:212). Actually, with her coherence of moral vision, she was not in much danger. She saw everything with the same eyes. When she witnessed the gambling at Homburg, the real-life scene so often pointed to as the genesis of the brilliant opening of *Daniel Deronda*, she saw the gamblers failing as some of her readers do—in the exercise of their moral imaginations. The gaming tables were "the most abject presentation of mortals grasping after something called a good that can be seen on the face of this little earth," the players' "dull faces bending round the gaming tables," and the "saddest thing to be witnessed"— "Byron's grand niece . . . completely in the grasp of this mean,

money-raking demon." For Eliot, the casino was the perfect metaphor of the inhumanity that led to war in Europe and Africa, and
watching Byron's niece made Eliot "cry to see her young fresh face
among the hags and brutally stupid men around her" (*Letters*, 5:312,
314). From this horrific vision of a lost woman came Eliot's intention of writing a work whose moral intention would not escape her
readers whether they liked her new story or not. It became, in the
end, crucial that the "young fresh face" she saw at the tables was a
niece and not a nephew. That connection between insensibility,
gambling, and misery provided the catalyst of Eliot's moral vision:
a kind of misfortune finally defined as preeminently feminine.

Realism and Parable

Henry James was the first to note the formal consequences implied
by Eliot's moral intentions: for Eliot, the novel "was not primarily
a picture of life, capable of deriving a high value from its form, but
a moralised fable, the last word of a philosophy endeavouring to
teach by example" (Miller, 94). While the split between form and
moral intention is not one everyone would accept today, even in
regard to James's own novels, it is clear that he recognized something important about Eliot's fiction. As wholes, their parts are
explainable only by reference to Eliot's ideological design. Even so,
most of her novels do not owe their formal configurations to the
tradition of parable; they are not later versions of *Rasselas*. Tito, in
Romola, exists as a character so that Romola may have her confrontation with the deepest duplicity. Eliot's intention seems to
require that the reader resist tying Tito up in a neat package and
dismissing him, at least not until his life and fate have been
experienced whole.

Eliot did finally turn to the parable, in the Deronda substructure, but the result is a novel even more complicated than *Romola*
or *Middlemarch*. Having assumed all along that readers can relate
the multiple parts of her realism to each other and come out at the
end with a changed view of the world, she now assumes that they
will see what she is doing when, basing her new kind of fiction on
the firmest psychological principles, she juxtaposes only two sto-

ries. One, Gwendolen's, is a carefully plotted tragic action, with the heroine's fate turning on both character and circumstances. The other, involving Deronda, is a static exemplum of a fortunate life, with the ordinary probabilities of realistic fiction turned upside down. While Gwendolen's descent into the abyss obeys fictional laws so strict they seem almost Pavlovian, Deronda's entire life reads like an exercise in knowing before the fact. No one would accept such a portrait as novelistic art by itself; but when all the elements of the exemplum are made to serve as rhetoric for the tragic story, then, as a substructure, it becomes a powerful lesson. Not least, the novel as a whole is an undeniably effective vehicle for moral instruction. With the Deronda section fully subordinated to the main action, the novel satisfies Johnson's prescription for morally efficacious fiction:

> In narratives, where historical veracity has no place, I cannot discover why there should not be exhibited the most perfect idea of virtue; of virtue not angelical, nor above probability, for what we cannot credit we shall never imitate, but the highest and purest that humanity can reach, which, exercised in such trials as the various revolutions of things shall bring upon it, may, by conquering some calamities, and enduring others, teach us what we may hope, and what we can perform. (*Rambler*, no. 4)

While Diedre David's contention that the novel "falls apart" needs to be tested—there is much evidence that she is right—it seems accurate to say that Eliot's general intention in the Deronda section is for it to serve as "a moral alternative to its representations," in both story lines, "of a corrupt upper-class society" (David, 135). The blatancy of the parable corrects the indirections of realism. The Deronda part is necessary for the full comprehension of Gwendolen's story, serving in its lucid directness as the positive analogue Eliot never before offered so fully or so starkly. The values that make the Deronda story recognizable as an exemplum, as an alternative to the mess Gwendolen makes of her life, or has made for her, are to remain at the end of the story as the bedrock of a new social morality of purpose and benignant exertion.

David Kaufmann, who wrote an entire book in 1877 attempting to "appreciate" *Daniel Deronda*, argued that the lines of subordination run in the other direction, from Daniel's story "down" to Gwendolen's. Her selfishness serves as a negative contrast to his "love and resignation. . . . And although unselfishness may sometimes succeed in bettering and ennobling selfishness, the two are not the less contradictories, which can never be entirely reconciled." Kaufmann concluded that the "meditative reader will guess for himself how deep a lesson, from a moral and national point of view, is inculcated by the circumstance that Gwendolen and Deronda are not finally made one" (60–61). While Eliot seemed specifically to be endorsing this reading when she wrote to Kaufmann of the "sympathetic discernment" manifested by his "clear perception of the relation between the presentation of the Jewish element and those of English Social life" (*Letters*, 6:379), all the evidence points in the other direction. As Kaufmann himself noted, although "from boyhood beyond the reach of care, [Deronda] early accustoms himself to take an interest in others, and to help and aid them as occasion offers." His only failing is that he has never had occasion or opportunity to "bestow his own confidence upon another" (61–62). Only in this last trait is Deronda a clear product of his past, like every other major character Eliot ever drew. His perfections spring, it seems, from his nature, not from his experience. The reader sees little of the process by which his character is formed, except in regard to his attitudes toward the man he erroneously suspects is really his father, Sir Hugo. Deronda springs almost fully developed from a kind of experiential vacuum. To understand Lydgate, for example, one must see him in Paris, following his false romantic ideal and losing his illusions. Deronda is not conceived in the same way. His hidden origins only confirm him in the tendencies of his character, much as what the travelers see in *Rasselas* confirms their suspicions about human happiness and misery. Deronda is a function whose reason for being, given all we know about Eliot's ordinary novelistic methods, must be as an aid to achieve something else. The criticism of the novel, from the beginning, confirms this view; it was not his Jewishness that turned Leavis against him, but rather his obviousness as an ideal.

That Eliot's intention does not remain unmixed is clear, although plenty of readers take Deronda seriously as a paragon. The question of well-being, of making one's life, which in Eliot's view is always a cooperative endeavor between men and women, takes on in this novel a specifically gendered cast. The Deronda substructure, capable of signifying as an ideal of masculine virtue and exertion, comes to mean something else, too: the vastly easier task of making his way in the world that is the fortunate lot of the British male in easy circumstances, a type George Eliot knew by heart in the late 1860s and early 1870s. By the time Eliot came to "cast" the opening of her novel—to show us Gwendolen through the eyes of Deronda and the other males in the casino—the metaphor of life's gamble, always interpreted with specific reference to Gwendolen and the marriage game, had expanded to take in Deronda and the whole of society. The exhortation to provide whatever small doses of good one may do along the way—the thematic burden of the plot of *Middlemarch*—is replaced by a much more austere view of life as designed for the fortunate and, as it seems usually to work out, the male, with female exceptions in *Deronda* only pointing up the rare abilities and good fortune necessary for a woman to thrive (and even then insisting that they must pay a price the Derondas of the world do not). The straightforward exemplary plot, whose character gives his name to the whole novel because he is its initial ethical center, acquires a heavy dose of irony. The Deronda plot ends up having two not entirely compatible functions. On the one hand, he serves as a positive alternative to the sterility of Gwendolen's life, in his active identification with and sympathy for the Jews. As she wrote the book, however, Eliot discovered that her hidden text questions the basis of male perfection. Her fictive society has no room for male paragons and women at the same time, for the terms of male success are predicated on female distress. The original male-female split, designed to generalize the ethical issues, now serves instead to point difference. What began as complementary stories become warring antinomies, the woman in bondage and the man at liberty.

A few critics, such as Elizabeth A. Daniels, have seen that Eliot changed her mind about women. Daniels perceptively noted a "pervasive feeling of ambiguity and futility about women's efforts, together with an accompanying sense of powerlessness and psychological distress" constituting "a new and changed note" (29). How that new note may relate to the Deronda section, however, how it may even generate the new structure and cause changes in Eliot's attitudes toward her subject in the very act of writing, are questions largely unexplored. The novel attempts to signify "in between" its story lines.[6] For this reason its structure is very difficult to specify. Eliot is one of the first novelists, along with Dickens, to attempt to tie dependent and coessential stories together. In the history of the many forms of the novel, this kind of amalgamation is perhaps the hardest to pin down, as the criticism of not only *Deronda* but also a later novel involving a multilineal plot, William Faulkner's *Light in August,* shows. It seems clear that the meaning of Faulkner's novel depends on the reader's apprehension of the relationship among the Lena/Joe/Hightower/Byron lines of the plot. What, for instance, do Lena's "getting around," Byron's stolid dedication, and Hightower's gesture of brotherhood have to do with Joe's tragic destiny? It will not suffice simply to argue that Faulkner is portraying a society in all its diversity. As with innovation, the relationship of multiple plots—or story lines that become one plot—cannot be effectively approached by applying general "laws" to unique examples.

Deconstructive criticism of *Deronda,* for example, has been prevented from even hypothesizing an explanation of the novel's formal features because of an explicit "faith" in the inevitability of narrative treacherousness. Instead of looking for the "doubleness" unique to Eliot, what specific circumstances might have induced her to split her novel, Cynthia Chase, for example, starts with some presumed duality inherent in story telling—or language—and then finds it exemplified in a novel. When it comes to innovation, however, such "laws" prove only that they work because they carefully choose what not to take seriously, like the idea of "the author," or of probability. Fixing on the omissions of novelistic texts, they succeed only by virtue of their own exclusions. Frequently, as in Chase's reading of *Deronda,* the new and exciting (at least in 1978) deconstructive procedures only mask much more "traditional" critical operations, if not assumptions. Chase's dismantling of the novel's basis of probability depends on a crucial "impossibility." Deronda could not have failed to discover that he is Jewish, unless during all the years of his growing up "he never looked down," a witty observation Chase borrowed unexamined from Stephen Marcus, who himself didn't examine it very thoroughly (Chase, 226, n. 13). It never seems to occur to Chase that there might be reasons, supported by the text she wishes to undermine, for Daniel never having been circumcised.[7] It should be granted, however, that Chase—perhaps deconstruction itself—can dispense with almost any specific argument about any text, since she is interested in universal properties that may always be discovered, as it were, by definition. My complaints about evidence would be deemed paltry, but my uneasiness here is owing to my view of innovation as an act always unique to time and place and often a tentative ideological exploration. While urgent innovations may, of course, be deconstructed like any other act or product—more easily, perhaps, since they so often leave obvious traces of their author's mixed purposes—I do not think that one understands them any better as innovations by applying to them, even with care and precision, universalist procedures, even ones designed, like deconstruction, to frustrate efforts to "totalize." Eliot's experiments with plot almost seem, in their singular complexity, to deconstruct the critical theories that would deconstruct them.

If *Deronda* were another *Middlemarch*, the two plot lines would have independent meanings, but at the same time Gwendolen's and Daniel's stories would qualify each other in more or less stable ways, as do Dorothea's and Lydgate's. For example, even though both characters marry less than happily, marriage opens up new possibilities for exertion and service. There is no reason Eliot could not have achieved such a subtle synthesis in *Deronda*, unless she was committed to a radically different plan. While the magnitude of the Deronda part, given its function as exemplum, is a problem, there is no inherent necessity for the Deronda plot to be overdetermined. Yet it is. The static parable of a paragon becomes so complex as positive analogue, in itself and in its interpenetration with the tragic action, that its hermeneutic function is overwhelmed, buried under specification. Even so, the basic structure of the novel remains. The best indication is that, while Deronda never becomes a hollow man, his advice near the end of the novel to Gwendolen to take her sorrow as a "preparation" for life, to find her "duties in what comes" to her and "not in what we imagine might have been," has the empty sound of platitude, uttered by lips never salted by tears of remorse. Whether Eliot wants her reader to see through this advice, or whether her earnestness has betrayed her, Gwendolen would be perfectly right to reply: "Easy for you to say."

The Novelistic Society

The full significance of Eliot's last novel resides in two incommensurable intentions: in the way the Deronda section enables the reader to interpret Gwendolen's realistic tragic story, to generalize it beyond its concerns; and in the way her story renders ironic the parable of the "Good Man" and problematic any "assistance" such a man can offer a woman in such a society. Even so, the parallels between the two characters are carefully established to demonstrate that their differential, gendered fates result from the same social situations. Gwendolen and Deronda are from the same "place," both partially orphaned and both looking for some mission in life. It is easy to forget, given Daniel's discovery of his Jewish parentage and the even earlier interest in Jewish thought and culture sparked by Mirah and Ezra, that the novel's title character derives fully as much from English society as does Gwendolen. If he escapes, therefore, it signifies as much as Gwendolen's remaining trapped. Eliot's primary task is to establish the preconditions in the society for Gwendolen's character and fate, and then to show the same conditions leaving Deronda almost untouched, his undeniable virtues free to make their rounds. The reader's admiration for him is then qualified by the ease with which his life falls into place, and the irony generated shifts the significance of the Gwendolen story from the personal to the social.

Eliot establishes the inhumanity of this society, particularly its antipathy to women, in many ways. One indication of Eliot's shift in formal method, the closer "match" between character and overt ideology, is Captain Gaskin, Gwendolen's uncle. Even the characters that populate Gwendolen's realistic action, while imbued with complex humanity, are more or less obvious "functions." Gaskin, who "took orders and a diphthong but shortly before his engagement" to Mrs. Davilow's sister (26), represents all those well-meaning fathers whose view of the world makes for widespread unhappiness. Sir Hugo is another, as Eliot reveals that even the most amiable of fathers may be a misogynist. Gascoigne unites in one breast the manly virtues of soldier and priest, two professions that serve as red flags in Eliot's novels. Gascoigne's faith is "such as became a man who looked at a national religion by daylight, and saw it in its relations to other things," principally in a light "likely to be useful to the father of six sons and two daughters" (26). To his niece, who appreciated his "fine person," any "failings that were imputed to him all leaned toward the side of success" (25). His views of the duties of womanhood, however, are as pernicious as his influence on poor Rex's happiness. Even so, Eliot's gentle, forgiving narrator refuses to condemn Gascoigne, and only two women in the entire novel, Miss Arrowpoint and Deronda's mother, understand the destructiveness of such misguided male prerogative.

Gascoigne's wife certainly does not. She has "decided" opinions, but only as a result of "imitation and obedience." Gascoigne's timid daughter, Anna, must endure her father's obvious pride in his niece while hearing that her own "growing days are certainly over" (27). And while Gascoigne is right that Gwendolen is the one who will "grow," he is incapable of foreseeing what horrors will accompany the process and how he is, in part, their cause. When his son falls in love with Gwendolen—a love that in another society might be harmless, and even in this one would be far better than what Gwendolen falls into—he does everything he can to discourage it as a social mésalliance.

Even his words of domestic counsel drip contempt for women, as when he advises Gwendolen to "make a little sacrifice for a good style of house . . . [e]specially where there is only a lady at the head" (28). Like most men who secretly disdain women, Gascoigne refuses to take even their pain seriously. The reader may know that some demonic selfishness inhabits Gwendolen's soul, that her "fits of spiritual dread" (57) betoken an emptiness—that she was actually capable of strangling a canary in her unguided, willful childhood. To Gascoigne, "young witch" that Gwendolen is, still "there is no harm" in her. All she needs is to be "well married"; not, of course, "to a poor man, but one who can give her a fitting position" (69, 71). Gascoigne's avuncular solution to a "troublesome" young niece becomes Gwendolen's "last great gambling loss" (411), her marriage to Grandcourt. As a pillar of society and upholder of the establishment, Gascoigne erects an elaborate politico-moral justification for Gwendolen's alliance. "This match with Grandcourt presented itself to him as a sort of public affair; perhaps there were ways in which it might even strengthen the Establishment. . . . aristocratic heirship resembled regal heirship in expecting its possessor from the ordinary standard of moral judgments. . . . There was every reason to believe that a woman of well-regulated mind would be happy with Grandcourt" (124–25). Like Austen's misguided, self-trapped Charlotte Lucas, who believes marriage to be the "only honourable provision for well-educated young women of small fortune," Gascoigne finds it "the only true and satisfactory sphere of a woman." He is not completely cynical—he wants his niece to discover in that state "a new fountain of duty and affection"—but the order of the moral imperatives reflects his priorities. The prospect of "parks, carriages, a title" leads Gascoigne to conclude that such "considerations are something higher than romance" (127). He is "not disposed to repeat . . . gossip" about Grandcourt, even if he had heard any. He refuses to look into Grandcourt's character—if he did he would hear about Mrs. Glasher—even though it is the customary thing to do, and even though it is his responsibility to his fatherless niece to do so. "He held it futile, even if it had been becoming, to show any curiosity as to the past of a young man whose birth, wealth, and consequent leisure made many habits venial which under other circumstances would have been inexcusable" (80–81). Worship of money and status leads to a spurious male decorum based on a cynical moral relativity. In Gascoigne, it is a complex, social failure of simple humanity.

Taken out of the context of Gascoigne's overall representation, my version of him turns him into a monster. It is Eliot's considerable accomplishment that, in the flow of the novel, he and his advice seem only decidedly worldly. That, of course, is the deadly point: the more attractive men like Gascoigne are, the more harm they do. Even to his creator Gascoigne is not to be scorned: it "would be a little hard to blame the Rector of Pennicote that in the course of looking at things from every point of view, he looked at Gwendolen as a girl likely to make a brilliant marriage. Why should he be expected to differ from his contemporaries in this matter, and wish his niece a worse end of her charming maidenhood than they would approve as the best possible?" The "why should he" implies its own answer, which is at the moral heart of the novel, but in everything he and many of his male "contemporaries" do for "their women," their "feelings on the subject [are] entirely good-natured" (31). Some critics, like F. R. Leavis, miss the point and fall headlong into Eliot's bland trap. For Leavis, Gascoigne is "a fine figure of a man and an admirable person" whose advice to Gwendolen involves a "snobbery that isn't merely ignoble" (Leavis, xx). It is, Eliot's narrator reminds us a few pages after Gascoigne's advice to Gwendolen, only "perspective" that allows us to tolerate "horrors": "What hymning of cancerous vices may we not languish over as sublimest art in the safe remoteness of a strange language and artificial phrase! Yet we keep a repugnance to rheumatism and other painful effects when presented in our personal experience" (140). It is only Gascoigne's distance from his niece's plight, his inability to enter into her pains or even to recognize her faults, together with his professionally useful bonhomie—to which Leavis so sympathetically responds—that allows him to compose such a "hymn" to this carcinomatous marriage. Deronda is a better man than Gascoigne, but the latter's "safe remoteness" is an advance warning to the reader that Deronda's goodness needs a carefully arranged perspective to be "safely" viewed.

Since this is a large and complex novel, designed to represent the consequences of institutional as well as individual uncaring in many different corners of the characters' lives, it would be possible to go on for many pages showing how Eliot builds (largely in the first book, "The Spoiled Child") her represented society into a machine for female destruction. Clearly, however, Eliot's main "target" is a socially determinant maleness specifically British, a point one must understand to see why Eliot creates the Jewish substructure and why Deronda's fate lies abroad. It is English patriarchal society that is the great offender, the reader is often reminded, as, for example, in Sir Hugo's three daughters. They are a "melancholy alternative" whose birth "involves no mystery," unlike Deronda's, who can't inherit from Sir Hugo (159). Fixated on property and power, most of Deronda's adopted countrymen are cynical or dull. Examples of male vivacity, enthusiasm, and inspiration, such as Herr Klesmer, come from other countries or, if they are English, are dilettantes like Hans. The "prevailing expression" of the "English," the narrator informs us after Klesmer enters the archery field, "is not that of a lively, impassioned race. . . . The strong point of the English gentleman pure is the easy style . . . he objects to marked ins and outs in his costume, and he also objects to looking inspired" (92). Any opinion exerted must be at a "small expense of vital energy" (141). This is a purposeless race, and Eliot comes as close as she ever does to presenting it without compassion, "gentleman pure" verging on the rhetoric of disdain. Even dear Hans defuses Deronda's objections to Mirah's being painted as Berenice by exclaiming that his "pictures are likely to remain as private as the utmost hypersensitiveness could desire" (429)—no purpose, no moral consequence.

Deronda as Success Story

Deronda, it seems, is the happy alternative to this general malaise. His very virtues, however, more and more tend to highlight Gwendolen's misfortunes and deepen the reader's apprehension of the problematic nature of male virtue and opportunity. Handsome, intelligent, generously supported by Sir Hugo, whose affection for him testifies to Deronda's basic goodness; displaying "far-reaching sensibilities" (579) and a knack for judging character, so much is admirable in Daniel.[8] Even early in the novel, however, the narrator's attitude toward him is not exactly unqualified approval. For example, when he returns to London from his travels on the Continent, he begins to read law in part to "fence off idleness," which only serves to "deepen the roots of indecision" about his future. His problem is "common in the young men of our day." He must decide "whether it were worth while to take part in the battle of the world." This is not a decision faced by everyone, and here Eliot's first ironic undercutting of Deronda takes place: such leisurely looking around is part of the preparation only of those "young men in whom the unproductive labour of questioning is sustained by three or five percent on capital which somebody else has battled for" (169). This passage occurs soon after we have seen the new limitations on Gwendolen's hopes—constraints that will force her to marry Grandcourt—and it therefore takes on the force of an implicit indictment, as does, retrospectively, his redemption of Gwendolen's necklace. It begins to seem a gratuitous and facile act, and her anger and humiliation at his easy presumption are not at all the reaction of a human "demon" or "witch" but rather that of a proud woman wanting to be beholden to no one.

Daniel has been called both prig and messiah (*Letters*, 6:337; Carpenter, 131–53). Both of his names may signify: "Daniel" in its associations with Protestant apocalyptic history (Carpenter), and "Deronda" in other ways. The consonantal echoes of the names of Grandcourt and Deronda evoke an ominous alliance, but with an important sonic difference. The *g, c,* and *t* of Grandcourt's name suggest his obduracy, while the mellifluous combination of the other consonants in Deronda expresses something more difficult to pinpoint. Eliot may be implying that Deronda is a product of forces not so different from those which produced Grandcourt, but that his humanity allows him to make the best of his chances for doing good, as one whose name means "rounded" should. Of course, such a difference is in a sense everything to Eliot. There may, however, be two sets of contrasts at work in the plot: one, between male and female freedom—with both Mallinger and Daniel contrasting with Gwendolen—and the other, more usual in Eliot, between freedom and what may be done with it. In this complex parable the two almost constitute separate systems. Although Eliot seeks, like most Victorian novelists, allusive suggestiveness with her character's name, she may not be quite certain what to allude to. If one follows out the Continental associations of *de-ronda,* one must conclude that Eliot presents her hero as a near-perfect man. However, *de-* in English often cancels what it prefixes, or at least diminishes it. In one system of ideological "probability," involving the presentation of an unattractive English society, Deronda's foreign origin is fully functional. In the other, more specifically male-targeted series of associations, Deronda could have been born on the moon and the thesis would still hold that men are freer than women. The specific meaning of Daniel, "God is my judge," may also be read as vindication or condemnation of the hero.

The possible musical associations with Deronda are if anything even more problematic. As early as 1859, Eliot testified that she "owed . . . many thoughts and inspirations of feeling" to music (*Letters,* 3:71). Is it possible that she had a musical metaphor in mind, to the rondo, when she named her hero? She certainly knew the form, which by Mozart's time was standardized as the appropriate celebratory or whimsical closure to concertos and sonatas, for in the winter of 1866 she and Frederick Lehmann "played together every piano and violin sonata of Mozart and Beethoven" (*Letters,* 8:385). It does seem unlikely, I admit, that Eliot would derive a negative analogy from anything as sublimely beautiful as the last movement of Beethoven's Eighth Piano Sonata. The form, however, has two features that might be relevant to Deronda. While there is plenty of room in the rondo (especially in a larger work like Beethoven's later violin concerto), it is still a repetitive form. Second, in between the three presentations of the main theme, one or more "irrelevant" themes may be introduced. The form is, then, a singular mixture of rigid adaptability. It is ready for anything, no matter how unexpected the couplet material might be and how unconnected to the musical context of its general structure. Deronda's life, viewed from this perspective, seems rounded and regular, but with much that does not seem to "fit," especially when his story is compared, as it must be, with Gwendolen's. The problem is, as Eliot taught her readers from the beginning of her career, in her fiction nothing is irrelevant.

If these speculations leave my reader cold, the novel's interpretative history from the beginning indicates that some sort of doubleness in the way Deronda is portrayed disrupts readers' ready acceptance of his more obvious virtues. The most fundamental difference between Deronda and Gwendolen is that Deronda at every step of his career is free to choose his way, and she is not. Perhaps his fate is as determined as Gwendolen's, but it never seems so. Even his birth, of which there are "mysterious tokens," turns out not to be the kind of puzzle the reader is originally led to suspect. The young Daniel turns from reading his history to ask his Scots tutor why the "popes and cardinals always had so many nephews." He finds out, of course, that their "own children were called nephews," which raises in his mind the suspicion that what he is called is not what he really is. The reader, of course, suspects right along with Daniel—there is no distance, no situational irony here—that he is Sir Hugo's son. Here we have a very different novel from the one Eliot ended up writing, although there are indications, like her excessive concern about the law of inheritances as she was writing, that perhaps she had in mind Deronda's turning out to be a Mallinger (*Letters,* 6:100). It does not really matter, however, since this false trail fits in very nicely with the novel Eliot did write. Deronda's origins do not signify, except insofar as his mother turns out to be an image, twenty years later, of Gwendolen's fate. Deronda's Jewishness, as many have sensed, has very little to do with his fate, although one need not therefore conclude that Eliot herself was indifferent to the fate of Judaism. It may indeed be argued Eliot took it very seriously, in that Deronda's Judaism is precisely what makes him equivalent to Gwendolen: his religion leads to his social exclusion, just as her gender puts her out of reach of most careers. Parallels, however, are not the same as equivalences. In this case, the significant difference is that although both are excluded, Deronda is free to pursue his fate and Gwendolen is free to be miserable. Even within the comparison, crucial to the success of the parable, Eliot knows precisely what to subordinate to what. She took Judaism very seriously, but in this book its function in the plot is as a powerful and convenient "alternative" to English society. It issues from a "deep *impersonal* historic interest" (*Letters,* 6:317, my emphasis), although after she finished the book, Eliot saw that she had in addition been able to "widen the English vision" toward Jews (*Letters,* 6:304).

To take Eliot's concern for Jews as crucial to the *structure* of the book is like suggesting that Swift wrote the Fourth Voyage in order to say something vitally important about horses, or that, were Austen alive today, she would be drawn to a career as a marriage counselor. Put another way, in terms of the necessities of the novel's ideology, Eliot can do without Deronda's Jewish heritage, can do without Mirah and Ezra. Any opportunity distinctly not British, any future separating Deronda from the corruption of British male society and involving him in a community of caring and purpose, will serve. Eliot was fortunate to find an ideological and historical structure, in Judaism, that intrigued her. Even so, whether as

Englishman or Jew, Deronda's fate will inscribe male success, since the repeating theme of his "rondo" is the freedom to choose his fate.

Even the use of probability in his story reinforces the certain and self-fulfilling nature of Deronda's fortune, as if somehow he is not subject to the same environmental laws that constrain Gwendolen. Deronda's story exhibits only an illusion of progression, carefully built up through the novel. As a boy of thirteen, he has his first intimation that his "uncle" might not be an uncle at all. Daniel, however, is patient, as it is not hard to be for a young man nourished by a kind and intelligent if somewhat whimsical "uncle" on one of the finest estates in England. While Eliot is careful to motivate his reticence and pain about his origins—his mistaken belief that he is Sir Hugo's illegitimate son—it still strikes some readers as odd that he waits almost ten years to find out what they are. Along the way he grows into a fine manhood and wishes for a purpose, and it comes to him unbidden. He discovers he is a Jew when that discovery is the only thing that stands between him and his quest, not to mention his bride. As Chase notes, causality is turned upside down. Eliot's narrator tells us, "That young energy and spirit of adventure which have helped to create the world-wide legends of youthful heroes going to seek the hidden tokens of their birth and its inheritance of tasks, gave him a certain quivering interest in the bare possibility that he was entering on a like track" (479). Yet Deronda's "tokens" must hardly be hidden, since two people recognize him as a Jew before he even knows he is one. Even though Eliot became more and more interested in the history of the Jews, Deronda's origins end up not mattering except in the specific activity he chooses to round out his life. In addition, the terms of his discovery of his origins speak much more to Deronda's qualifications as a paragon, and to his status as privileged male, than to the Judaism his mother repudiates.

Whether Eliot ever came to see that she had fractured her portrait of male superiority is impossible to say. She seems to have intended Deronda to have a more dynamic being than he ends up with, for the reader learns that in Gwendolen's "ideal consecration" of Daniel "some education was being prepared for Deronda" (401). Janice Carlisle suggests that Deronda is "the last in the long line of increasingly secular clerics who epitomize the aims of George Eliot's fiction." She sees him, however, as ineffectual, except in his relation to Mirah, who "is less in need of moral guidance than almost any other character in the novel." With his mother and Gwendolen, he fails: "Deronda's mother dismisses as nonsense his claims that his imagination allows him to participate in her suffering," and "his efforts to help Gwendolen are no more conclusively satisfying" (Carlisle, 217). Even his relationship with Mirah has its disturbing side. Indeed, the entire scene in which Deronda objects to Hans's historical painting seems designed to suggest that Deronda and Mirah are not ideally matched. Hans paints Mirah as the notorious Berenice and Deronda as her brother Agrippa, with whom, according to Suetonius, she had an incestuous relationship. It is bad enough that Deronda, having saved this waif's life, ought to treat her as a cherished sister instead of looking to wed her. Worse, however, are the terms of his objection to Hans's painting. Hans should desist because this "frail" world traveler "should be kept as carefully as a bit of Venetian glass" (430). Now, Grandcourt and Deronda could not be more unlike; one is a monster and one is a model of affectionate disinterest. In one regard, however, a crucial one, they are uncomfortably alike: their attitudes toward "their women." Isn't Eliot, as she nears the end of this novel, bent on portraying the impossibility of any man in this society achieving self-knowledge sufficient to avoid a demeaning overprotectiveness? This seems to be one of Deronda's main purposes throughout the novel; he serves as a kind of illustrative "foil." In every situation in which he is aligned or contrasted with someone else, his situation opens up the impenetrable for inspection. It is Grandcourt, for example, who is the novel's overt representative of male dominance, and he dies, although not exactly at Gwendolen's hands. As a male paragon and the strongest contrast to Grandcourt, isn't Deronda still subject to the same gendered distinctions that have called for his presence in the first place? If he is, then Grandcourt's fate is not a repudiation of male dominance but the hint of something perhaps less dramatic and sudden, but just as unpleasant, awaiting Deronda.

The contradictions in Deronda's character never align, never fall into a pattern that allows us to see what he *is*. Deronda is not a coherent character, unlike earlier creations such as Adam, Felix, and Dorothea. On the one hand, he is a standard of conduct and right thinking, a positive alternative for the unfortunate Gwendolen and the erring reader. Nevertheless, his very pupose contains within it the potentiality to create a parallel and variant Deronda in the reader's mind—and perhaps in Eliot's as well—a Deronda whose virtues and happy fate are somehow rendered irrelevant next to Gwendolen's wasteful trek. To call one or the other the "real" or the "intended" Deronda seems irrelevant. Both are there, giving the novel its peculiarly rich, complex confusion. It is doubtful if Eliot ever settled the matter in her own mind. Deronda is, for example, masterfully in control of his own feelings, as little given to impulse as Grandcourt. True to this trait, the narrator argues that to "say that Deronda was romantic would be to misrepresent him" (189). Many pages later, however, the narrator concedes that "if you like, he was romantic" (479).

"And Gwendolen? . . . The Slavery of Being a Girl"

Pure and clean things may rot no matter what is done to prevent it, but they rot faster in a noxious environment. The environment Eliot designs for Gwendolen has all the earmarks of benevolence but ends up impoverishing her emotionally and intellectually. While giving Deronda to the reader as almost a kind of narrative "fact," Eliot establishes Gwendolen's nature with care. The selfish, willful young woman at the gaming tables, peered at by the surrounding males as if she were horseflesh, has grown up without the "tender kinship," the "blessed persistence in which affection can take root" (18). Before moving with her mother and four half-sisters to Offendene she had been "roving from one foreign watering-place or Parisian apartment to another . . . meeting new people under conditions which made her appear of little importance." Her "two years at a showy school, where on all occasions of display she had been put foremost, had only deepened her sense that so exceptional a person as herself could hardly remain in ordinary circumstances or in a social position less than advantageous." She has "no notion" of her grandparents and is only dimly aware that "her father's family was so high as to take no notice of her mamma" (19). Knowledge of her father was shut away after the twelve-year-old Gwendolen had the indelicacy to ask her mother why she had remarried.

Gwendolen's "improper" question is the same one about origins that Deronda is always too reticent to ask Sir Hugo. But Deronda, it turns out, doesn't need to ask, since everything is finally provided for him, and this is one key to the opposite set of probabilities under which each character labors. Gwendolen's deep egotism, which makes her want to know even at twelve why her mother has divided her affection by marrying again, is a defensive reaction to an upbringing that has left her just another girl amidst "hired furniture," with only enough education—"her knowledge being such as with no sort of standing-room or length of lever could have been expected to move the world"—to reinforce her own good opinion of herself without giving her the intellectual resources necessary to make her way under reduced circumstances. At twenty, there is "more show of fire and will in her than ever," but she has learned self-control and "calculation." Her intention is to do what is "pleasant to herself in a striking manner; or rather, whatever she could do as to strike others with admiration and get in that reflected way a more ardent sense of living" (34). Instead, she will be the one struck.

The source of Gwendolen's egotism is not solely her society, although her family pampers her like a "princess in exile" (34) because she is a valuable economic resource for them all. Her duty is to bridle her spirits long enough to secure a superior marriage. It is not at all clear, the narrator asserts, "whether even without her potent charm and peculiar filial position Gwendolen might not still have played the queen in exile." Nor is it only a matter of being born a woman, the only "resemblance" among egoists being "a strong determination to have what was pleasant, with a total fearlessness in making themselves disagreeable or dangerous when they did not get it." Gwendolen is, after all, an example of an "inborn energy of egoistic desire" (36). Eliot constructs her character not to suggest that it originates in the misogynist practices of society but rather to show what happens to the specifically female egoist when she finds herself in a society in which most of the resources for the gratification of ambition are in the hands of males. The force to make her way isn't available to Gwendolen, whose arsenal includes only "her beauty, a certain unusualness about her, a decision of will which made itself felt in her graceful movements and clear unhesitating tones." Gwen is useful to companions on a "rainy day when . . . the use of things in general was not apparent to them," for then her charm seems a "sudden, sufficient reason for keeping up the forms of life." She fits in, that is, as the tiniest of cogs in the gigantic machine of English, leisurely gentilesse forged on the backs of colonial and domestic workers. Or, to employ Eliot's pointed imagery, Gwendolen comes in handy "when everybody else" is "flaccid" (35).

Marriage is the most striking example of how the British male-in-power keeps on keeping on, and nothing is more pitiful in her story than Gwendolen's belief that she can control a man like Grandcourt. Gwendolen's ignorance and massive, misguided self-confidence lead her to many false notions, but one that is not false is her desire to avoid marriage, even with Rex. Without the "independent life," the only preventative for a tendency toward "living too exclusively in the affections," the leisured wife is stuck in "helplessness" when those "affections are disappointed" (*Letters*, 5:107)—and Gwendolen has no such independent life. When Eliot presents Gwendolen with the "choice" of a husband, she stacks the cards so adroitly against her heroine that the best Gwendolen can hope for is that "the less" Grandcourt has "of particular tastes or desires, the more freedom" she is "likely to have in following hers" (122). Only much later, after seeing the "passionate affliction" Gwendolen endures and examples of the only two ways to avoid such a heartbreaking marriage, other than not marrying at all—the Alcharisi's and Miss Arrowpoint's—can the reader understand the unavoidability of the snare. Given her character and history by the end of the novel, she can never escape and "may well be emotionally and intellectually, if not morally, crippled for life" (Daniels, 31).

The trap is sprung, then, not because Gwendolen is a woman whose particular kind of upbringing has unsuited her for happiness in this society, while Deronda, as a man with his own very different character and background, fits in. For he doesn't "fit" either, and his happiness must be sought elsewhere. The differentiation, and the social basis of the novel, lie in the way English, and more broadly, European, society systematically steamrolls those not strong enough or ruthless enough to get their way. The sharply ironic differentiation of the two stories, however, cuts through that ideology of gender, for Gwendolen cannot escape, while Deronda's liberation seems like a lark, even contrasted, in "his" story, with Mirah and Daniel's mother, who are victims too. Mirah, who knows the world and has learned to let its destructive forces help keep her afloat, still arrives at the desperation of suicide, only to be saved by—a man. The Alcharisi remains true to her art only at the cost of any sort of happiness, arriving at her end bitter but unrepentant. None of the women in the novel really provides an "alternative."

So pervasive is the social trap Eliot sets for Gwendolen that no escape is possible. In the careful parallels and contrasts between Gwendolen's and Daniel's characters and circumstances, the way they look at times to be made for each other and at others to be forever estranged, are Eliot's fullest social meanings. In *Middlemarch*, the general standards for male excellence are proposed in Ladislaw, and Dorothea appropriately finds love as well as her long-looked-for opportunities for expression. Since Eliot's endings always point us in the direction of the novel's larger meanings, it should perhaps have surprised more readers that she does not unite Gwendolen and Deronda. Gwendolen's solitary misery at the end of the novel is, however, fully expressive of the novel's entire system of action. Eliot's handling of marriage as a kind of fulfillment is much more subtle and complex in this novel than in her earlier fiction. It is almost as if she somehow ceased to believe in its possibilities for feminine happiness in her society unless a set of almost impossible conditions were met. This is not to say that she did not portray successful marriages or that somehow she had despaired of men and women ever learning to live happily together. She knew only too well how fulfilling marriage can be, especially when a couple contrives to ignore society's unreasonable expectations. It is the terms of marriage in this society—the one Eliot devised, at least—that make it anathema to women, unless it is a marriage of perfect sensibilities, "determination," and luck, like

Miss Arrowpoint's. Their match is close to being a paradigm of Eliot's own marriage of affinities.

The Klesmer/Catherine Arrowpoint episode in the novel is one of Eliot's most Fieldingesque in structure and tone, which is a clue to its function as an exemplum of alternative conduct and, even more, as another example of how Gwendolen's story is surrounded by "qualifications" to its meaning and emotional power. As in Fielding, the characters play their parts and then largely disappear. Then too, Eliot's narrator engages in the kind of irony she usually denies herself elsewhere, and that humor keys the reader to the "unmixed" state of this prospective marriage, its promise of stable happiness. The contrast, on the basis of choice, to Gwendolen's horrid, forced choice of Grandcourt is striking. For these lovers make their fate where they do not find it. When Catherine goes to her rich father and belletristic mother, the narrator turns to the reductio hypothetical language that introduces so many absurd situations in *Joseph Andrews* and *Tom Jones:* "Imagine Jean Jacques, after his essay on the corrupting influence of the arts, waking up among children of nature who had no idea of grilling the raw bone they offered him for breakfast . . . or Saint Just, after fervidly denouncing all recognition of pre-eminence, receiving a vote of thanks for the unbroken mediocrity of his speech." One can almost hear Fielding's treatment of Parson Trulliber. Catherine's mother, that is, like so many a failed priest in Fielding, is faced with a challenge to her principles, and like them she fails the test of humanity. The resistance she and her husband put up to the marriage, the weak arguments, comic versions of good Mr. Gascoigne's serious ones in favor of Gwendolen's marriage to Grandcourt, culminate in Klesmer's dismissal from the house and Mr. Arrowpoint's comic lamentation—Catherine is an only child—"It's all very fine . . . but what the deuce are we to do with the property?" (227–31).

Klesmer and Catherine carry all before them because they marry for love *and* art. As musicians—Klesmer is, of course, an avant-garde composer—they plan a life of high, sweet professional cooperation, much like Lewes's and Eliot's. In addition to being suited to each other, however, they are principled, tenacious, and care nothing about losing the fortune her parents hold over her head as, it turns out, an empty threat. Catherine and Klesmer, that is, get their way because they disregard everything that induces Gwendolen to marry Grandcourt. Even so, it is impossible for the reader to take this episode only as a coyly inserted instruction packet on assembling a marriage. For, like Deronda, these two are lucky in their assertions. Eliot is not saying to young English women: Learn music, then go out and find yourself a vivacious, talented German or Italian, for there resides your only attractive alternative to the bare-pated, empty-headed Englishman—any more than with Deronda she is counseling her reader to be born handsome, sensitive, and rich. Nor can she be implying that all women need to get by in the world is talent, although she certainly believed women needed something more than domestic affections for a full life. Whether Eliot realized it or not, the Klesmer/Catherine substructure really teaches that, in addition to possessing an independent spirit and talent, one needs to be at the right place at the right time. Then too, although it is hard to imagine Gwendolen doing as Catherine does, it helps to have a fortune to give up in the first place. Marrying Rex, for example, will not extricate her family from its financial woes.

Interactive Stories

It should now be clear that Gwendolen's story, as fully coherent as Isabel Archer's, remains the core of the novel, the basic situation of pain the Deronda plot is to help clarify and render as tragic action and "point" to the parable's general significance. His character, and the entire secondary action, become problematic as Eliot's intentions shift under the pressure of her attraction to Deronda and his possibilities for exemplifying an "alternative" to Gwendolen. Deronda has not one function but two, contradictory and incompatible. As positive standard, his very virtues, while never disappearing, finally become bitterly ironic counterpoint to the story of a woman drowning as surely as her husband will. The reader's attitudes toward Gwendolen, then, are shaped less by conventionally subordinated substructures than by the seemingly independent Deronda story. It is his happy fortune, in particular his finding purpose and affection apart from Gwendolen, that provides the rhetorical force to "convert" her story from stark, individual, idiosyncratic mimesis into even bleaker social commentary, tying the two distinct stories together and giving them their working power. Eliot intends, that is, to create a more effective social plot than she had in *Middlemarch*. The mechanism of conversion I speak of is David Hume's discovery, and it is the principle that lies behind the many successful attempts, from Dickens to Faulkner, to unite seemingly unconnected stories into a single plot, not by mere thematic allusion but by a relationship of necessity based on the deepest of psychological structures. Students of tragedy will remember Hume's elegant little essay "Of Tragedy," although it may be less well known than "Of the Standard of Taste," with which it was published in *Four Dissertations* in 1757. In this essay Hume attempts to explain the age-old "unaccountable pleasure" of tragedy, how such emotions as "sorrow, terror, anxiety, and other passions, which are in themselves disagreeable and uneasy; the more they are excited, the more the spectator is pleased" (185). Hume argues that the unpleasant subjects of tragedy are "converted into pleasure" by the "delightful movements" of representation: "The impulse or vehemence, arising from sorrow, compassion, indignation, receives a new direction from the sentiments of beauty" and the force of "imitation" which "is always of itself agreeable" (Hume, 191–92).

It is important to the art of tragedy, Hume insists, that the subordinate set of impulses, those involving pleasurable story telling, become predominant. If they do not, all the forces of eloquence and imitation have the opposite effect. For example, "though novelty of itself be agreeable, it fortifies the painful, as well as agreeable passions" (Hume, 193). *Deronda* might very well have been a novel in which the Deronda story served, along with the other means of telling the story, to convert Gwendolen's tragic action into fully pleasurable art, in which her fate was more sublime than bitter. Yet this is just what does not happen. Deronda's massive story only serves to revivify and reinforce the most galling aspects of her fate, leaving the reader at the end with a deep sense of waste not usually associated with tragic art. Put another way, whatever the difficulties readers may have with the conclusion of

The Mill on the Floss, all of the novel's means are employed to convert Maggie's pitiable virtue "into a noble courageous despair" appropriate to a tragic action, while all of the resources of Eliot's last novel contribute to the strongest sense that Gwendolen has simply been ground into the dirt while Daniel marches off to reestablish Zion. The central paradox of the novel's form is that what is originally intended as a substructure takes on the magnitude of an independent exemplum that then, by virtue of its interaction with the main action, converts that action into Eliot's most powerful representation of female oppression.

5

Innovation as Pugilism
Hemingway and the Reader
after *A Farewell to Arms*

The image of Hemingway as a cool, self-conscious craftsman needs some revision, especially in regard to his writing in the 1930s. "Hemingway," we learn from Robert N. Wilson, "was an exceedingly self-conscious writer who knew precisely what he was doing. One might say that, among his peers, Fitzgerald, Faulkner, and Wolfe, were often possessed by their material; but Hemingway possessed his" (51). While there can be little quarrel with this view of the early Hemingway, it is not accurate for Hemingway in the decade between *A Farewell to Arms* and *For Whom the Bell Tolls*. Literary history, striving to make sense of an entire career, plasters smoothly over the rough surface of difficult innovation. That invaluable fiction "the author" is only probable, like its twin "the reader," in the plural. Something happened to the "earlier" Hemingway to undermine his relationship with his reader. Perhaps it is more accurate to say that he was forced to deconstruct his own fiction of a trusting, competent reader and invent another. His activities throughout the 1930s are symptoms of a writer badly in need of an exorcism.

After his initial critical success, Hemingway spent most of the 1930s attempting to rediscover the art that permitted his earlier triumphs. This site of innovation differs markedly from the others I have treated, especially in that Hemingway did not become disenchanted with his own earlier formal innovations for aesthetic or ideological reasons. Instead, he abandoned his favored methods of composition to appease and then to attack readers and critics who, in their numbers and temperaments, formed an audience markedly different from George Eliot's. Unlike Eliot, Hemingway's attempts to define and accommodate his readership did not result in a more "readerly" fiction. On the contrary, from his persistent annoyance at critics who demanded that his art represent the social realities of the 1930s came an intention to "punish" those who did not appreciate the "cosmic" basis of his stories. At the same time, he retained his desire to continue to write so as to please those who knew and approved of his art. The rhetorical situation, if I describe it accurately, was virtually untenable for him and resulted in schizophrenic fictional structures that defy critical comprehension.

This "phase" of his career ended in 1937 with *To Have and Have Not*. From *A Farewell to Arms* until then, Hemingway produced a number of works that seem to divide their readership into the worthies and the fools, fiction that continues to appeal to the initiate while wreaking revenge on his (its) enemies. While this impulse seems to be what Frank Kermode posits as the beating heart of all narrative, it particularly defines Hemingway's work in the 1930s. Hemingway provides us, then, with a striking example of an author of realistic fiction who turned to Frye's bitterest alternative, the mythos of winter—satire. From this unstable mixture of artistic integrity and satiric rage came a number of new forms that demonstrate their uneasy genesis by their incoherence. While the most ambitious of his attempts to come to terms with his newly defined readership is *To Have and Have Not,* traces of compositional anxiety surface as early as *Death in the Afternoon* and are present in many of the short stories. The decade from *A Farewell to Arms* to *For Whom the Bell Tolls* represents, then, a continuing readjustment to the changing perceptions of his readership, a succession of response, new effort, and new disillusionment. Compared with the writers I have already discussed, Hemingway in the 1930s often innovated out of a sense of outrage and rebellion.

Hemingway's achievement in the 1920s, in two novels and a number of fine stories, established his reputation for the rest of his life. Having learned an ideology of universal tragedy somewhere between Oak Park and Paris, and having achieved two brilliant and very different structures for imparting fictional life to that ideology, he was prevented from extending and refining those discoveries. Instead, after two brilliant tragic actions that captured the imagination of thousands of readers, he followed his success with a book that is the equivalent of the self-portrait of a man sitting with a sick bull—one of the photos Hemingway rejected for *Death in the Afternoon.* Then, and worse, he wrote a book whose climax is hunting the unglamorous eland, the African equivalent of the moose. The explanation of Hemingway's strange transmutation is contained in the social situation in which he found himself in the early 1930s and in the critical response to those early successful fictions.

Many of Hemingway's early critics, even those disposed to be hospitable to the author, suggested that something absolutely necessary to serious art is missing in Hemingway's works. The charge arose in 1932 in regard to *Death in the Afternoon* when Malcolm Cowley complained that "Hemingway is a master at not drawing implications. . . . To do so would force him to think about the present and the future, and he has fallen into the habit of writing with his eyes turned backwards" (Meyers, 168–69). Cowley denied Hemingway both universal and specific meaning. Jake and Frederick, he thought, are caught in idiosyncratic situations devoid of general significance; and, in persisting in writing about Caporetto and Paris, Seney, Michigan, and, worse still, Africa, Hemingway's fiction is socially mute. The first objection was anticipated and countered by critics like T. S. Matthews, who argued in 1929 that "there has always been . . . in the implications of Hemingway's prose, and in the characters themselves, a kind of symbolic content that gives the least of his stories a wider range than it seems to cover" (Meyers, 122). Wyndham Lewis, who took up the second charge, found it difficult "to imagine a writer whose mind is more entirely closed to politics than is Hemingway's" (Baker 1972:203). Among these various charges and defenses one may chart the rhetorical terrain, or battleground, on which Hemingway's writing in the 1930s occurred, on which his hopes for success arose and his rhetorical strategies evolved. His earliest successes divided his readership into those who believed in the significance of his fiction and those who argued that it had none.

As is usually the case in examples of drastic critical divergence, there is some truth in both views of Hemingway's early work. Early on he discovered a method of telling a story that did not depend upon commentary, on the kind of overt fictional rhetoric George Eliot and Hardy used so often, and which, since James and especially Ford, was discredited as destructive of the fictional illusion. Hemingway's methods were not, however, a mere accommodation to aesthetic taste, but particularly suited to the kind of story he wished to tell. In the beginning, with short stories like "Big Two-Hearted River," and even with *The Sun Also Rises,* Hemingway's achievement was the result of a complete trust in his reader. He had no fear in 1925 that his austere anatomies of shattered personalities like Jake's and Nick's would be too difficult for his readers by virtue of the indispensible freight of meaning small details must carry. This confidence extended to his subject matter. He was not trying to "depict" life, much less to "criticize it." He wanted "to get the feeling of the actual life across . . . to actually make it live," as he wrote to his father in 1925 (*Selected Letters,* 153). Even as late as *A Farewell to Arms* he was leaning on the reader, as a rereading of the first chapter of the novel will demonstrate.

It is important to emphasize, especially given the later criticism that his subjects were merely visceral, that he knew exactly what he was doing. Even so, to reduce a story like "Big Two-Hearted River" to sensation is absurd, as most critics and readers have always known. He was not writing for *Outdoor Life* when he took Nick into the Upper Peninsula of Michigan, dropped him off in the burnt-out town of Seney, and sent him in search of brook trout. I do not know if Matthews was right to call Hemingway's fiction "symbolic." Hemingway expected his reader to appreciate the title—which he borrowed from a river fifty miles to the northeast of Seney—the incinerated town, the blackened grasshoppers, Nick's uneasiness when he speaks aloud to himself in the empty forest, the various "needs" left behind, the postponing of difficulties like fishing the swamp, as indications that, at the very least, Nick is a man who has suffered some kind of severe shock that has left him unfit for anything but solitude. Any response that fails to generalize the action in some way is inadequate, and not just different. Even so, Hemingway's method is a realism so strict that at times it borders on the behaviorist. He really believed in the uniqueness and at the same time the complete integrity of characters and "moments," if only the right details could be found. "I've written a number of stories about the Michigan country—" he told his father in that same letter, "the country is always true—what happens in the stories is fiction."

The achievement of his ends has little to do with literal truth, of course, and everything to do with internal, artistic probability, the function of a narrative element and not its origin. When the two are confused, it is really between things that only look the same. The novel, for example, is not necessarily equivalent to fiction; nor is it a single form. Hemingway wrote—all the authors I am studying, except Defoe, habitually wrote—actions, complex and progressive structures based on a probable sequence of events. Even when the representation appears to be "spatial," to proceed without the step-by-step decline of traditional tragic patterns, as it does in *The Sun Also Rises* and in many of the stories, all of the reasons for the destruction of happiness still have to be revealed somewhere along the line, and *Sun* is therefore as pervasively a "causal" structure as *Pride and Prejudice.* The material of the action may originate anywhere; what matters is how it is transformed into probable fiction. The confusion of material action with novelistic plot is so pervasive that it has assumed the status of truism: "Of course," stated Bernard Oldsey, "the more realistic a novel is (like Joyce's), the more it tends to be autobiographical (or biographical); the less realistic (like Wells'), the less it tends to be so" (Oldsey, 37). Hemingway's artistic "psychology" is much more complicated than this. In 1934 he wrote Fitzgerald about *Tender Is the Night,* which he "liked" and "didn't like." His objection was that, having started beautifully with Nicole and Dick, who are based on Sara and Gerald Murphy, Fitzgerald then "started fooling with them, making them come from things they didn't come from, changing them into other people." It is fine to "take real people and write about them," but you should not "give them other parents than they have (they are made by their parents and what happens to them) you cannot make them do anything they would not do." Hemingway made it clear that he was talking about novelistic probability, and in a way George Eliot would be perfectly comfortable with. If an author chooses to write about real people, "liberties" must not be taken with their "pasts and futures." Otherwise one ends up with "damned marvelously faked case histories" and not novels (*Selected Letters*, 407).

Hemingway always appreciated how something may be "true" in more than one way, if all his critics do not. Often his characters had real people behind them, but they and the "country" and what happened became fiction and therefore more compelling by virtue of his choices as an artist, his ability to make probable that which is only latent. Even in Hemingway's most coherent fictions, like *For Whom the Bell Tolls,* if the distinction between subject and creative intention is not observed, it is easy to see Hemingway as writing about "himself." Robert Jordan, for example, remembers the circumstances of his father's suicide. It is too tempting, perhaps, to assume that Hemingway's father is behind the portrait. Hemingway, however, wrote a fiction in which his main character needs a compelling personal reason to be indifferent to his own fate, a reason to bestow his life as if it were a casual gift. Where Hemingway got the particular suicide he used for Jordan's father is aesthetically irrelevant, as one may see by speculating about what the fictional suicide would mean if perchance it were our *only* clue to Dr. Hemingway's fate.

Hemingway had a strong faith in his ability to describe "country" so that the sight of it and what it means, for the sake of the aesthetic structure, would come across. If he lived it and understood the precise steps that generated the emotion in him, he could re-create the steps for a reader. This much is commonplace, but it is not usually recognized how closely Hemingway's relationship with his readers in this early fiction describes the successful Crocean paradigm already mentioned, with an authorial intuition given objective form in an aesthetic structure, which then serves to provoke in the reader the same intuition. This faith in the reader is not a common modernist practice, but then not every belief and technique associated with modernism affects writers of different generations and nationalities simultaneously. For example, like other writers, Hemingway had his own brand of ironic nihilism, the thematic equivalent of shadowboxing with the Grim Reaper. At the same time, he habitually resorted to an "old-fashioned" fictional pattern, tragedy, even in many of his short stories, in which only a "slice" of the tragic pattern, or its consequences, is usually represented. In another seeming contradiction, while everything else may have gone to hell, art still represented for Hemingway his own clean and well-lighted place. Like T. S. Eliot, he used the order of form to enact the fragmentation of modern civilization, which he and most everybody else outside comfortable Oak Park knew was never the same since that day near the Somme.

One nice paradox involving the practice of tragic fabulation in the first decades of the twentieth century is that modernist narrative tragedy, with its frequent ideological commitment to the impossibility of transcendence, depends for its powerful effects on the author's implicit faith in meaning. Hemingway's tragic art relies on a readership that shares certain beliefs and knowledge—including knowledge of horrors. It also depends on habits of reading, many of them learned from close reading of modern poetry like Cummings's and Eliot's, as Hemingway said he did. He was fully aware of the "rhetoricommercial" complexity of his age: "The classic example of a really fine book that could not sell," he wrote Horace Liveright in 1925, "was E. E. Cumming's [sic] Enormous Room. But Cumming's book was written in a style that no one who had not read a good deal of 'modern' writing could read. That was hard luck for selling purposes." The canny way around this problem was to write about things that "anybody with a high-school education" could understand, but in such a way that it "will be praised by highbrows" (Selected Letters, 155). More than anything else Hemingway wanted for his art, this goal indicates the extent of his initial faith in his reader.

This "solution" to the now-discernible problem of a fragmented reading public seems sensible. The success of his early work indicates that his trust in his readers was not delusory. Even so, it was never as simple as dividing readers into two groups based on the height of their brows, and Hemingway's success in actually "molding" with his fiction a kind of existential common ground eroded later on. While Hemingway's honeymoon with his readers was brief, early in his career he knew with the firmness of the religious belief he somehow missed that he must not overwrite. His marvelous fishing story concludes, in one version Hemingway tried out, with a long "coda." It is mostly "interior monologue by Nick Adams, full of reflections about his old friends in Michigan and his new ones in Europe," but it also contains thoughts on Joyce and the craft of the writer (Baker 1969:131). As he much later told George Plimpton, the "most essential gift for a good writer is a built-in . . . shit detector" (Bloom, 1985:136). From the beginning, he turned the detector on his own work. He wrote to Robert McAlmon in 1924: "I have decided that all that mental conversation in the long fishing story is the shit and have cut it all out. The last nine pages. . . . I got a hell of a shock when I realized how bad it was and that shocked me back to the river again and I've finished it off the way it ought to have been all along. Just the straight fishing" (*Selected Letters,* 133). Not only does the coda make explicit Nick's sojourn in Europe, it also calls attention to the writer's craft, an amateurish thing to do in a seamless story like "Big Two-Hearted River" and something he knew to avoid in fiction, even if he didn't always do it. This is not to say that the young Hemingway would not talk about his art—that refusal belonged to an older author, spooked by wound-hunting critics like Philip Young—or that he was critically naïve. Indeed, when he wanted to be, and despite the scatological vocabulary, he was a better critic than many of his critics, especially when he was engaged in that kind of nuts-and-bolts "how-to" talk almost invariably more interesting to the novelist or poet than to the academic critic. Early in his career, however, he knew that inclusion of such chat marred the seamlessness of his fiction, and he was not interested, as many postmodernist writers are, in reflexivity, the fiction about making fiction. Even so, he gave up a great deal in cutting that coda, leaving intact only Nick's reference to the "need to write." The problem is that silence about his craft, while good artistic sense, cost him a great deal, especially after critics started telling him what he really *ought* to be doing. By 1929, for example, he was already joking about "correcting" his detractors: "I saw in the World that some citizen was *lecturing* on Farewell to Arms. God it would be fine to walk in and ask a few questions and then say, 'Shit, Sir I do believe you are mistaken!'" (*Selected Letters*, 311). He was fascinated by how most things are done, not least by his first love, writing. Of course, he knew that such artistic discussion is for very few, mostly writers, and he wanted his fiction to be "readerly" art, as one might say today. What he noted of Joyce one suspects he wanted equally to apply to himself and to his "ideal reader": "The better the writers the less they will speak about what they have written themselves. Joyce was a very great writer and he would only explain what he was doing to jerks. Other writers that he respected were supposed to be able to know what he was doing by reading it" (Plimpton, 126). It is significant, even in this late interview with Plimpton, that it is only "jerks"—not just ordinary readers—who need explaining to.

Hemingway's hope all along was not that by using things he had actually experienced he would somehow give his reader a kind of translation of that experience, a verbal equivalent. That is good journalism. He wanted the third and fourth dimensions, "not a representation," a word he used in a much stricter sense than is usual for an author. For him, representation was a lesser skill, a presenting again. While there may be many reasons for writing "that no one knows," he saw his task clearly: from everything he did and knew and some things he didn't, to "make something through . . . invention that is not a representation but a whole new thing truer than anything true and alive." This is one of those things, like "quality" in Robert Pirsig's *Zen and the Art of Motorcycle Maintenance,* that is impossible to define and yet always apparent when present, a kind of superior "life" in writing. The life comes from the art, "you make it alive, and if you make it well enough, you give it immortality" (Bloom, 1985:136). Since death was for Hemingway the central, certain reality, nothing was more important to him than conferring universality, and therefore permanence, on his work. His early faith in his reader to conspire in the creation of that universality was the basis of whatever success he had.

His first novel employs a tonally complex first person that permits unobtrusive ethical complication. Experimenting with the kind of contextual rhetoric he meant his coda to "Big Two-Hearted River" to supply, and having rejected it as too distracting from the unitary effect he habitually sought in his own writing and in things like the *corrida de toros*, he discovers that a surer way to "place" his tragedy is to have the characters do it themselves. The first two novels are told by their protagonists so that Hemingway may convey an entire world of tragic implications without committing himself to any sort of overt authorial "stance." The problem is related to what eighteenth-century authors faced when burdened with the need to express the purely personal in poetry: how to do it with decorum. A fiction ideologically based, as it were, on the necessity for dignity in the face of the void cannot very well risk erasing itself by undignified authorial intrusions, a lesson Hemingway knew, forgot, then relearned. Many of the reviews of Hemingway's first two novels confirm that he achieves this special kind of decorum by virtue of his refusal to speak for, or even through, his characters—although, as in all fiction, the choice of what and what not to have a character say is itself full of meaning. Like T. S. Eliot, he conveys his tragic view of life without the awkwardness that accompanies so many literary expressions of personal doom.

The first two novels therefore establish their extraordinary authority as much from the way their protagonists speak as from what they say. As ideological structures representative of the high modernism, they are innovations, but "serene" ones. What he discovers are two very different ways to present a tragic action, with a covert but pervasive causal substratum. While there seems to be more thought in *Sun* than in *Farewell*, that is in part because the books have a purposeful intertextual relationship. Hemingway clearly depends in the second novel on most of his readers remembering what they were "taught" in the first one.

A great deal of the immense authority Hemingway's fiction still seems to project derives from his protagonists' misery issuing as naturally and inevitably from experience as agony from a wound. There is no extended analysis of the mysterious ways of the universe, much less of society. His critics in the 1930s found his silence on the sources of unhappiness evidence of the author's stupidity or callousness, but this was doubly an error. Hemingway knew exactly why, apart from the casual, proximate reasons such as cholera and bullets, humans are miserable—they have to die. And he reveals this causality to the reader everywhere without ever "telling" about it. Jake inherits the world Frederic first falls afoul of in the retreat from Caporetto, but neither has any choice in the matter. Unlike the Hardy of *Tess,* who sometimes seems unsure whether the tragedy might have been avoided by adopting a different sociology, or theology, Hemingway is certain that life is a tragedy. So, while Hemingway's first two novels abound in "thought," most of it is used for the exercise in difference on which his fiction is based: proper and less proper, dignified and less dignified, ways of responding to an ideological given, requiring only the barest of exposition, the emptiness of the universe. Ideologically, Hemingway's novels are therefore impeccable modernist documents. That unity of modern thought, which is probably a chimera anyway, often falls apart when critics face Hemingway.

His favorite metaphor for fate is, of course, war. Its appalling impersonality, its verbal and situational perversions of the old verities like duty and honor and heroism, are perfect equivalents for a cosmos that treats its inhabitants the same way Twain's visitor does ants, with the toe of his boot. In Hemingway's first novel, the war is a distant but always present influence, for structural as much as ideological reasons. In *Farewell,* it revisits the idyllic, almost comic Switzerland in the guise of biological necessity: "Now Catherine would die. That was what you did. You died. You did not know what it was about. You never had time to learn. They threw you in and told you the rules and the first time they caught you off base they killed you. . . . Stay around and they would kill you" (327). If this was not, as philosophy, to the taste of many critics in the 1930s, it certainly was to many readers in the 1920s. I leave it to the historical demographers to determine who was reading Hemingway in 1929, although I shall later make a stab at who was reading him in 1936. It is a good bet, however, that most of his readers, not necessarily including his mother, agreed with him not only that World War One was the ugliest of environmental pranks but also that it made jokes of many of the old beliefs and ways of transmitting them, like authorial commentary. The identification of "author" and "authority" may be spurious etymology, but even so, readers may have tended to stop listening carefully to anyone offering guidance after General Haig sent sixty thousand men to march unquestioningly to evisceration. The "agreement" between author and reader Hemingway depended on, to the extent that it really existed, therefore marks an exception to the times, an old paradox I'll not pursue here but which had consequences for at least the public Hemingway. Writing for "nonbelievers," he convinced them to accept his view of the world, at least temporarily.

The authority of the fiction, then, the willingness of his readers to accept Hemingway's as somehow a "correct" version of the world, was aided by the dignity of Hemingway's sufferers and the prescience the fiction projects. It is silent about matters like economics and politics—although more is implied than some of Hemingway's critics thought. The rhetorical stance, an effective one if the reader will abide it, is closer to Conrad than to Hardy in its enactment of but refusal to explain the mystery of human misery, although, curiously, it is closer to Hardy in viewing tragedy as almost an inevitable part of life. Much of Hemingway's public authority, established in a strikingly brief period of time, came to him precisely because he stood behind tragic novels that refuse to see tragedy as a social aberration. The power of the stories, for a reader like Allen Tate, lies in their "careful rejection of 'ideas,'" and Tate was admirably percipient to compare Hemingway with Defoe, another author whose power in his early fiction came from his refusal to "say anything" in his own person (Meyers, 70). *The Sun Also Rises* and *A Farewell to Arms* are thematically mute about any such matters as why we are damned, although they are full of "advice" about what we might do about it. There is nothing particularly naïve about Hemingway's view, at least not in the sense that if he had just looked at life more closely, he would have seen things the way the Marxists do and set about the political reformation of the world. I shall have to return to this question later. For now, it should be pointed out that whatever Hemingway and his critics believed about the universe—and it is clear that Hemingway's beliefs became a political question soon after *Farewell*—tragic causality in the novels is for the author and his "successful" readers as much aesthetic and rhetorical as it is ideological. His artistic faith was with the representation of pain, early and late in his career, and he saw that he could create a great deal of dignified pathos, the "feeling" of the misery, by showing undeserved suffering in ways never attempted before. Once grasping how completely expressive of his beliefs and how perfectly suited to his aesthetic aims his first two novels are, it is difficult to see how he might have avoided the "disaster" of his confrontation with politicized readers in the 1930s. Had he continued to write novels like *Sun* and *Farewell,* critics would have competed to see how far he could be pushed into the margins of fictional discourse.

Hemingway's rhetorical situation, then, after *A Farewell to Arms,* became increasingly complicated. First of all, his view of life, like Eliot's, was deeply conservative, in the sense that both believed in the universality of experience, apart from the local modifications of time and place. Hemingway's intention, whatever his effect, was not to catch a particular historical moment in *Sun.* His use of Gertrude Stein's "You are all a lost generation" is therefore ironic in one way not always appreciated. The "you . . . all" was simply the universal, second-person plural for him, not, as it seems to have been for Stein, a reference to one group of Paris expatriates. The implications of this ideology could be missed in Hemingway's first novel but not in his second, in which, because of the different demands of the tragic sequence, he must represent a specific, proximate cause for Catherine's death, the biological "trap" that kills her and lies waiting for everyone else. Now the tragedy is not conveniently hidden in the past, where it may exert its mysterious influence on the simplest act. It is in front of the reader's eyes, something that Frederic ought to know but does not. What destroys Catherine and Frederic? Childbirth. Narrow hips. Hemingway now has to commit himself to a specific example of what he conveniently disguised under "life" in the earlier novel.

To put it another way: the ideology of Hemingway's first two novels—and, it turns out, their newfound liability in the 1930s—is equivalent to his ascription of human misery to causes incapable of social solution. It is not that he is unaware of social causation, or forgets to include it. In *Sun* and *Farewell* he studiously avoids anything like "social tragedy" because it would reduce the significance of suffering to the much smaller arenas of class conflict and economic exploitation. Part of his famous quarrel with Fitzgerald came from Hemingway's insistence that, in writing about the rich,

Fitzgerald was squandering his talent. It is clear, in one way at least, that Hemingway was right, in terms of fictional conception if not execution. When Daisy weeps over Gatsby's beautiful shirts, or sits with Tom at the kitchen table, munching cold fried chicken and quaffing ale as a suitable repast after reckless homicide, it is hard not to conclude that Gatsby, if not Fitzgerald, has badly mistaken the American dream.

The success of Hemingway's first two novels depends much more on readers sharing Hemingway's assumptions about the omnipresence of suffering than it does even on traditional novelistic emotions like empathy. The reader need not, for the sake of the experience, think particularly highly of Hemingway's characters—admire them, for example—as he or she must do in some other kinds of tragic action. Hemingway needs pathos, but not too much of it. The ending of *Farewell* is exemplary in this regard, with the tremendous resonance of the rain falling, again, as it always must on human happiness. There is none of the highly particularized concern, much less bitterness, one associates with the end of one of Hardy's tragic actions. This is the tragedy of the inevitably ordinary, the death of love. Somehow the reader must accept this overarching necessity, either from prior experience or as a kind of temporary narrative given, to be adopted for the nonce of the story. Since the bleakness of the view, even tempered with Hemingway's stoic humor, was fairly potent in 1926, and again in 1929, as it is for some readers today, there were probably many who did not see it his way and whose pleasure at having the story confirm the sad truth was denied.

Thus the seeds of the divided audience Hemingway wrote for and against in the 1930s were planted early—by his own beliefs, generously supplemented, of course, by a drastic change in the concerns of his readership. Here, and not in any perverse desire to alienate critics, was the beginning of Hemingway's long struggle to write for those who, seeing, understand, and his equally strong frustration with those who, seeing, refuse to extend to him the generosity of their acquiescence. The same situation drove Hardy from the field. Hemingway raged and then shifted the way he wrote, away from the confidence in his reader that permitted his first successes and toward a kind of style that is "readerly" only if you are the right kind of reader. "You could if you wanted be proud of me sometimes," he wrote his father in 1927, "—not for what I do . . . but for my work. My work is much more important to me than anything in the world except the happiness of three people and you cannot know how it makes me feel for Mother to be ashamed of what I know as sure as you know there is a God in heaven is *not to be ashamed of*" (*Selected Letters*, 259). Hemingway's bright, scrubbed place was his substitute for God. Perhaps for the first time he was faced with the fact that his parents were shut off from his view of the world by the very beliefs that sustained them, running up against the convictions his fiction could not do without. Their faith in Providence must have made their son's work seem as if it had tumbled down from some strange, ghastly planet. Splitting the world into highbrows and lowbrows, even finding a way to please both, won't solve the problem if both groups are not reunited, even temporarily, by the pressure of authorial rhetoric and belief.

Death in the Afternoon

Where was Hemingway to go after these two very different tragic novels? If tragedy is a matter of simple biology, what more is left to portray after one has shown one "hero" trapped inside the consequences of what the next hero-victim will move inexorably toward discovering? One may tell the story, perhaps, only twice, especially if one believes that the novel is "an awfully artificial and worked out form" (*Selected Letters*, 156). Hemingway wrote to Max Perkins in 1932, "I am certain of doing better work than I have ever done." At the same time, he said impatiently, the "one thing I will not do is repeat myself on anything so the new ones [i.e., the latest stories] are rarely as popular—people always want a story like the last one" (*Selected Letters*, 377).

Hemingway was not, of course, the first author to displease his readers by doing something new. Hardy's work polarized readers along similar lines. Hemingway aroused such strong feelings, starting with *Death in the Afternoon*, that it is clear that the climate of reception changed drastically between 1919 and 1932, as indeed how could it fail to? Much of what he wrote subsequently—although some of the stories are exceptions—until *For Whom the Bell Tolls* was received with one or another kind of "refusal," either to accept that what Hemingway was doing might be a valid next step in his career or, more vehemently, to grant worth to the entire enterprise, going back to the beginning. One interpretation of this shift in Hemingway's career is John Raeburn's, in his fine book on Hemingway's reputation. Raeburn argues that in *Death* Hemingway gave the world "a portrait of the author as he wished to appear." He knew the chances he took in doing so, but his "desire for heroic celebrity overrode his misgivings" (Raeburn, 38, 44). It is difficult to argue with this view, except to point out that as usual with Hemingway it is not by a long stretch the whole story. For example, it does not take into consideration the fact that Hemingway was bursting with ideas about life and art that he had not yet expressed in his fiction, given its inherent demands for authorial reticence; or that he wanted, as much as Faulkner or Fitzgerald, to be remembered as an innovator in fictional form, like Conrad, whose fiction he venerated. Hemingway does his share of posturing in *Death,* but what of his serious ideas about art? They bear directly on his attempt to write, later on, an innovative antisocial novel.

He long kept *Death in the Afternoon* on a back burner, and he was bitter when critics sneered at it. After all, the *corrida* and his writing are two expressions of the same view of the world: imitations, with emotion and wholeness, of the tragedy of life. His serious intention here is to inform his readers about a new "art form" and reveal in it the same universal "truth" to which he always aspired in his fiction. Whatever one might think of Hemingway as a thinker, in *Death* his comparative method is sophisticated, similar in method and assumption to Hume's discussion of tragedy I mentioned in the previous chapter. Hemingway locates the causes of aesthetic response in common mental "structures." One properly reacts to the bullfight, as to a novel or a symphony, not as a series of discrete elements but rather as a whole. So, in discussing the grotesque goring of the horses that for some spectators seems gratuitous, Hemingway says:

> I believe that the tragedy of the bullfight is so well ordered and
> so strongly disciplined by ritual that a person feeling the whole

tragedy cannot separate the minor comic-tragedy of the horse so as to feel it emotionally. If they sense the meaning and end of the whole . . . the business of the horses is nothing more than an incident. If they get no feeling of the whole tragedy naturally they will react emotionally to the most picturesque incident. (8–9)

In discussing the attitude of the enlightened spectator—the "*aficionado*"—it is clear that Hemingway is thinking also of how best to read, to be an "afictionado": "The aficionado . . . may be said . . . to be one who has this sense of the tragedy and ritual of the fight so that the minor aspects are not important except as they relate to the whole. Either you have this or you have not, just as, without implying any comparison, you have or have not an ear for music" (9). He goes on then to make what seems a bizarre analogy. One without an ear for music might very well, at a concert, fix his or her attention on "the movements of a player of the double bass." Those motions may be "grotesque" and the "sounds produced . . . by themselves, meaningless." The response of such a listener, having fixed on the double bassist, is to be concerned about the "wages and living conditions" of the musicians! In watching bullfights and listening to symphonies—as well as in reading literary tragedies—there are aesthetically appropriate and inappropriate responses.[1]

Hemingway works out in this book a literary aesthetic based on many of the same assumptions about human nature contained in his fiction. In his novels, characters either know the terrible truth about life—know it "whole"—and use the *nada*, paradoxically, to bestow the purposiveness of denial on their lives, or they do not know and spend their time moaning and flopping about. The "logic" of the bullfight is the same logic that informs the lives of his tragic characters. If one takes a part of the whole—like excessive drinking or use of unpleasant language—and puts it under a microscope, the unity of the whole disappears, and with it the reader's ability to understand how the part fits.

With the increasing fragmentation—or his impression of it, which had the same effect—of his own reading public, Hemingway sought to make sense of his art the only way he knew how: by relating it to the largest and most serious questions of human existence. Discovering that some readers, like some spectators of the bullfight, failed to appreciate the whole, he tried to account for the failure. That is not the totality of his task in *Death in the Afternoon,* for, as in his fiction, the subject inherently interested him, in part because he felt its wholeness. If it is ironic that one of the prophets of modern despair saw the world in this holistic manner, it is nevertheless as true for Hemingway as for the skeptic Hume. As Hemingway's "narrator" informs the "Old Lady" who serves as his interlocutor, sometimes a bull abandons his accustomed polygamy to abide with a single cow. At this point the cow may be removed from the herd, and if the bull does not go back to his unfaithful ways, he is sent to the ring. It is a seriocomic account, but the Old Lady misses the humor, finding it "a sad story." The narrator replies: "Madame, all stories, if continued far enough, end in death. . . . There is no lonelier man in death, except the suicide, than that man who has lived many years with a good wife and then outlived her. If two people love each other there can be no happy end to it" (122). The bullfight, for Hemingway, contains all of life, but the parts of any complex art become grotesqueries when viewed in isolation.

Hemingway's interlocutor, his ideal afic(t)ionado, shows that she does not understand either what Hemingway means by "love" or what all this has "to do with the bulls" (122). While she says she is an aficionado of the corrida, she is blind to the significance of its parts and, predictably, to the tragic totality of life. This figure arises often in Hemingway: Cohn, the younger waiter in "A Clean Well-Lighted Place," Gino the "patriot" in *Farewell.* Here the deficient onlooker is a rhetorical invention. The Old Lady, significantly, is alert and, superficially at least, a good reader. She has seen bullfights and her attention "does not flag" (179). Yet there are things she does not understand, in the bullfight and in the "stories" Hemingway's narrator tells her. Hemingway's playful "character," designed to help him deal with questions about the reception of the bullfight, therefore also represents his reading public. With all the best intentions, she is neither a skillful aficionado nor the adept reader Hemingway wrote for. Is Hemingway implying that he needs only to "school" his readers, as he is doing here, for them to perform their task of reading his fiction properly? Or is he conceding that his fictional enterprise is misguided, that readers skillful enough, initiated enough, to profit from his implicatory method and share his view of life are not to be found? If it is the latter, what will he do when he turns to fiction, with that "deficient" reader in mind?

Most of the "theory" in *Death* is only implied. Even so, it is the "clearest statement yet heard of Mr. Hemingway's point of view," as Robert Coates put it, only in the next paragraph to lament that the book is "morbid in its endless preoccupation of fatality" (Meyers, 162). Reactions of critics like Coates—his "morbid" is as irrelevant as the Old Lady's "sad story"—should not have surprised Hemingway too much, since his fiction, with its reticence, runs a built-in risk of being misunderstood. Only Max Eastman really took up Hemingway's aesthetic argument and directly countered it: the bullfight is not an art, and suggesting it is amounts to "sentimental poppycock" (Meyers, 173). The attempt to argue from art to life and back again, without passing through the departments of sociology and political science, were not easy in 1932, when seeing life whole, in universal terms, unless they were Marxist ones, was "naïve." Unlike Camus, who tried to elucidate the philosophical basis of his art in the 1940s, Hemingway's "explanation" ends in no implied program for dealing with immediate political questions. When the philosophical generality of his fiction began to be deconstructed as the author's avoidance of difficult social problems, Hemingway's quarrel with his readers became inevitable. His "solution" lay in narrative's readiness for duplicity.

The Reader in the Short Stories

In 1933, the same year he composed the story that became the first part of *To Have and Have Not*, the oft-quoted Hemingway of the "readerly" fiction wrote, "I am trying, always, to convey to the reader a full and complete feeling of the thing I am dealing with; to make the person reading feel it has happened to them. . . . Because it is very hard to do I must sometimes fail. But I might fail with one reader and succeed with another" (*Selected Letters*, 380–81). In the terms worked out in the bullfight book, he always tried to convey the totality of represented experience, even if some readers proved incapable of feeling it. Whether he succeeded or failed, most of his fiction attempts to live up to this ideal.

Even so, there were extraordinary pressures on his work. The effect of such continuous scrutiny, especially on a man of such strong aesthetic convictions, was a defensive stance toward his reader. At the same time, a realization of just how many readers his implicatory method might be wasted on led him to write more than once in ways that indicate he no longer trusted them. I hasten to add that Hemingway never tried, as far as I can tell, to put anything over on a discerning reader. Even so, his exasperation at being misunderstood, at being accused of social irrelevancy, and at having his personal character attacked in a manner that reduced his fiction to mere "macho" posturing, contributed to an already strong tendency to be more conscious of the effect of his fiction on the stubborn or the impercipient, two different classes of reader in his mind, and deserving of separate treatment. For one thing, the almost ritualistic authorial silence his early fiction required set him a difficult, frustrating task. What is so often praised in early criticism of his short stories—their bare, mute impersonality—is not the specific strength associated with the earlier novel, even in the hands of Conrad. It is this liability that some critics, then and now, have in mind when they suggest that Hemingway's talents were ill-suited for the novel. This is confusing ends with means, since, while it is not merely a historical accident that the novel engages in social commentary, James had already shown in his later fiction that a represented society need not be foregrounded in long fiction—might be left in Woolett, so to speak—and Joyce's *Portrait* and Ford's *The Good Soldier* confirm the fact.[2] Even so, sustaining evocative impersonality demands much greater effort in three hundred pages than in twenty and entails a tremendous sacrifice of expressive freedom. It is not so much a question of what may or may not be done in the novel: genre is relatively obsequious. If Hemingway had not held such strong beliefs about the proper way to write fiction, he would not have felt so much pressure both to explain and to defend his ideas in nonfiction, nor would he have experienced the creative anxiety he did in writing for his readers in the 1930s.

That anxiety is nowhere more evident, until *To Have and Have*

Not, than in a story usually pointed to as one of his high achieve-ments, "The Short Happy Life of Francis Macomber." Seldom in Hemingway is a site of invention so cluttered with so many extra-literary influences. Here surfaces perhaps the clearest fictional equivalent of Hemingway's attitude toward his readership in the mid-1930s, an attitude compounded of the old respect, an uneasi-ness about how much inferential capacity he can require, and a new note, a strident contempt. The latter is manifested, as it would be in the novel to come, which he was already working on, by an identification of some of the traits of his characters with what he most hates—which is not new, of course. What is new is a further identification of characters with types of readers. Hemingway's realistic fiction came to take on some of the aspects of satire—in the strict sense of a genre that has specific "targets." Never before had he written to heap scorn for its own sake, if not on the people themselves, at least on what they stood for. This is another way of saying that he almost always managed to give his biographical materials fictional rather than biographical significance. Carlos Baker perceptively notes that "as Hemingway's scorn rises, the satirical steam-pressure rises with it and the result is often close to caricature" (Baker 1972:191). In "Macomber" and in part of *To Have and Have Not,* the fiction chooses its targets from the pool of readers, separating the worthies from those deserving contempt.

The potential for converting fictional subjects into targets is always present, and Hemingway from the beginning used his art as a punitive tool—a view perhaps uncomfortable to those who think of satire as somehow artistically impure. Hemingway's own words, if his brother Leicester is trustworthy, indicate a blurring in his mind between literary and historical people.

> Never hesitate to call a spade a dirty unprintable shovel. And regarding unsympathetic characters, blast the unprintables with everything you have and let them dare to sue. Nothing is worth a damn but the truth as you know it, feel it, and create it in fiction. Nobody ever sued me in England over *The Sun Also Rises.* Yet the characters in it had very real origins. Some went around pleasuring themselves literarily for some time. So slip it to them, every one. If a writer cannot do with words what a cartoonist does with lines, he

should write political speeches where the premium is on volume without insight. (L. Hemingway, 275)

Although the Swiftian hatred of the world is here, one should not assume that Hemingway sacrifices art when, in "Macomber," he fashions a word picture designed to discredit a whole group of readers, damned in advance by the fact that they subscribed to *Cosmopolitan*. Hemingway admired exceedingly the artistic genius of effective "spittle-painting." A. E. Hotchner remembers standing one day in the Prado with Hemingway, who put "particular emphasis on Goya's huge portrait of the royal family of Charles IV." It is indeed an imposing work, with its fourteen figures stretched in various poses over a canvas measuring nine by eleven feet. Wyndham Lewis calls it a "masterpiece of effrontery"—it would be a wonderful illustration for the frontispiece of a lampoon—with the "pursy benevolent stupidity of the King; the tight-lipped shrewish malevolence of the Queen . . . the nullity of the rest of the family" (Lewis, 135). Hemingway gazed in awe at Goya's "masterpiece of loathing. . . . Look how he has painted his spittle into every face. Can you imagine that he had such genius that he could fulfill this commission and please the King, who, because of his fatuousness, could not see how Goya had stamped him for all the world to see" (Hotchner, 187).

What is it about the very ordinary Francis Macomber that suggests that his story is not another example, like "The Killers," of "pure fiction," but rather the character assassination Hemingway so admired in Goya? Put another way, what in the story cannot be explained by reference to Hemingway's practices as a realistic storyteller? As R. S. Crane long ago pointed out, in an essay too often ignored, there are obvious "lapses" from Hemingway's usual compositional methods. He resorts "too much to inferior and makeshift devices for keeping the reader aware of what is going on," including the flashback, "flat narrative statements" (e.g., "his wife said contemptuously, but her contempt was not secure. She was very afraid of something," and others I shall examine in a moment), and the "shift to the lion's perceptions." For Crane, these are all "crudities," failures of the implicatory subtlety Hemingway employs in stories like "The Killers," in which the author does not feel the need to explain why Andreson looks at the wall. Crane also objects to the story's hackneyed cuckold-turned-hero plot, but what bothers him most are Hemingway's violations of his normal grace and economy of representation. Crane concludes with an explanation that has never been properly appreciated and certainly never refuted: "I can explain these lapses only by supposing that, having begun to write like himself in the opening section, Hemingway then suddenly became aware of the limited intelligence, in matters of art, of his prospective readers in the *Cosmopolitan* magazine!" For Crane, that is, writing in the late 1940s, much closer in time to Hemingway's reading public of 1936, its probable effect as a rhetorical task on the author cannot be ignored (1967:326).

Indeed, this story contains some of Hemingway's most awkward and intrusive narrative "guiding," after the brilliant, understated opening. He begins to write "down": "The fear was still there like a cold slimy hollow in all the emptiness where once his confidence had been and it made him feel sick. It was still there with him now"; "He could not know that Wilson was furious because he had not noticed the state he was in earlier and sent him back to his wife"; and, perhaps the worst in all of Hemingway, "He expected the feeling he had about the lion to come back but it did not. For the first time in his life he really felt wholly without fear. Instead of fear he had a feeling of definite elation" (1936:129, 136, 148). This is a Hemingway who seems to have forgotten what gave stories like "Big Two-Hearted River" their magic. One will search the rest of Hemingway's oeuvre in vain for a phrase as awkward as "really felt wholly" or one as dead as "definite elation."

The question, which may as well be brought out immediately, is whether these and other problems with the story are best seen as evidence of artistic failure, compromise for the benefit of an inept implied reader (as Crane suggests), or something else: a deliberate attempt to damn the "flabby" reader by giving him or her a blatantly overwritten story, like so many others featured prominently in *Cosmopolitan*. That is, knowing the story is destined for the magazine, Hemingway "redesigns" it for its readership in such a way that acquiescence in the story's overt strategy becomes self-damning evidence of the reader's incompetence.[3] The question that immediately arises is whether this isn't a needlessly complicated explanation for something better viewed as an artistic lapse. The vexed interpretative history of the story, however, is one clue to its duplicity, indicating that Hemingway may have written with two very distinct kinds of readers in mind—the benefactors and the victims, one might say—although competing interpretations certainly do not automatically signal a divided intention. It does seem, at least since the 1950s, that critics are reading, and not just interpreting, at least two different stories. For example, for all of Crane's perspicacity in sorting out technical matters, he seems not at all disturbed by the central and enduring crux of the story, one that has been "explained" by almost every competing critical framework devised: "Mrs. Macomber, in the car, had shot at the buffalo with the 6.5 Mannlicher as it seemed about to gore Macomber" (1936:153). This statement has caused more consternation and critical "revision" than any other in Hemingway, simply because it seems to cancel everything the story has taught us about Margot Macomber's hatred of her husband and her clear self-interest in seeing him either gored or, perhaps to make sure of things, headshot. There is, additionally, no possible justification for ambiguity at this point in the story; as Robert B. Holland succinctly put it, "Who was there to deceive? No one was watching her shoot" (Holland, 139–40)—no one, that is, except the reader. The entire system of probable action—Macomber's initial degradation in fleeing the lion, the further humiliation Margot inflicts on him, the stages of his gradual discovery of courage, endangering Margot's hold over him—seems to point toward her interest in his death but, at the same time, is called into question by the narrator's unequivocal "shot at the buffalo."

Some revisionist interpreters are so disturbed by the inconsistency that in effect they turn the story inside out. Margot is really the one who deserves our sympathies at the end. Despite her earlier nastiness, repeatedly compounded, even to the point of sleeping with the white hunter and taunting her husband with the fact, she now "wanted to save" Macomber and, as the first revisionist, Warren Beck, put it, "might well have felt he had never been as worthy of her whole effort as he was now" (Beck, 36). The narrator's statement will not go away, and Mark Spilka's ingenious solution, that Hemingway's language is simply unable to convey the complexity of Margot's mixed feelings at the moment, does not account for why Hemingway, so unwontedly generous with his descriptions of internal states in the rest of the story, cannot arrange for one more to enlighten the reader at this crucial point (Spilka, 250, 253).

In the traditional interpretation of the story, such disturbingly untidy details may be ignored in favor of the strong overall plot— the disturbing chiasmus in which deconstructionists do delight. As Crane specifies it, the principle of unity revolves around a simple change of "moral character" from cowardice to a "brief moment" of "achievement." Humiliated in the field by the lion and in camp by his wife, Macomber turns courageous during the buffalo hunt and stands fast, ending his cowardice and, Wilson, the white hunter, thinks, "probably . . . cuckoldry too" (1936:150). Crane gives us three reasons why we must believe that Margot means to kill her husband. First, if we were not certain of her intentions, our final emotion would not be centered on what the story is all about, Macomber's triumph. Second, any mystery about Margot renders "retrospectively ambiguous" all the signs of her antipathy revealed earlier. Finally, doubt would be cast on Wilson's reliability, and what, Crane asks, then becomes of our "confidence in him as a trustworthy chorus which has been built up through the story?" He concludes that "in spite of the narrator's statement . . . I think we can no less easily rule out the possibility of accident" (1967:315–16).

The problem with all this, as the revisionists are quick to point out, is that Hemingway ordinarily did not leave such loose ends lying around. Robert Holland put it admirably: "It was Hemingway's virtue to report with exactitude what he saw, to render the thing as it was in all possible clarity. This is not to say that ironies and paradoxes and ambiguities and all sorts of shadowy implications do not exist in the fictional world Hemingway created, and in the real world upon which he based his creations. It is merely to say that the ironies and paradoxes and ambiguities reside in these worlds and not in Hemingway's reporting" (Holland, 138).

All this revisionist activity, from Warren Beck forward, has resulted in the creation of a completely different story from the one Crane and other later interpreters read. There seems to be no way to "refute" such an interpretation, since it is self-contained in its assumptions and "explains" just as much as other readings. It seems improbable that Hemingway would write a story that condemns his favorite sport and asks for sympathy for someone like Margot, but this is just because I *read* the story in such a way as to render that interpretation improbable. Every work of literature may be revised or "unwritten." Browning's Duke becomes the sympathetic, pitiable hero of the poem, a wronged husband, if the reader will just accept the hypothesis that the last duchess was a conniving adulteress. While it is possible to see such readings as arising from a healthy recognition that "impatience for singleness of soul is deadly" and an aim "to suspend rather than resolve" opposing interpretations, it is also possible to see them as resulting from a "will to bafflement" (Christensen, 443, 440).

While I do not have the space here to go into all the details of the revisionist reading, it may be noted that accepting "shot at the buffalo" as a statement of fact leads the revisers to do just what Crane said it would: to ignore or make retrospectively ambiguous everything earlier revealed. The story becomes a more "humane" document—even, incredibly, an antihunting tract—and certainly an exculpation of Margot, as in the work of one of the most recent of the revisers, Kenneth Lynn, who joins the others in blithe indifference to both the probabilities of the story and to Hemingway the man and artist (Lynn, 431–36). Realigning the story with "shot at the buffalo" costs too much for this reader to pay.

The critical attempt to remake the story, to change it into Margot Macomber's vindication, implies that Hemingway at the very least succeeded in duping one whole set of readers, whether by intention or inadvertence. Anyone who buys into the revisionist interpretation is forced, for example, to take as aesthetically purposeful a great deal of just the kind of overt, guiding rhetoric Hemingway usually scorned. It would be one thing if Hemingway just did not have confidence in the *Cosmopolitan* reader, as indicated by the narrator's comment that Margot spoke "contemptuously, but her contempt was not secure" (1936:151). Something much trickier seems to be going on at the end of the story, something so positively misleading as to suggest that Hemingway does indeed intend to deceive any reader who is not paying full attention. Margot's contempt is directed at her husband's new courage.

She says, "You've gotten awfully brave, awfully suddenly," and then we learn that she "was very afraid of something." All this fits snugly into the standard interpretation, since she must fear his surge of manhood if she is plausibly to murder him. Her next speech is, "Isn't it sort of late," spoken "bitterly." Of course; having led a shallow, spiteful life, now she is about to lose the only thing that made it worthwhile, a whining husband to ridicule and betray. What immediately follows, therefore, is an incomprehensible appeal for sympathy: "Because she had done the best she could for many years back and the way they were together now was no one person's fault" (1936:151). This is a patently false signal, one Hemingway ordinarily is incapable of sending. Nor is it finally conceivable, especially given his frustration with those who cannot understand what he is doing, or, worse, seem intentionally to misread, that he would allow himself to "write down" to the *Cosmopolitan* readership—not, at least, without exacting revenge for having to do so.

Even if one did not know that Hemingway wrote the story with *Cosmopolitan* in mind, there are plenty of clues in the story itself—as Crane has pointed out—to Hemingway's consciousness of his readership. Practiced readers of the magazine, for example, expect authors to use the flashback as a reliable device of disclosure, often providing information about the heroine's past love life. They expect such glimpses to be brief and direct, since they replace rather than aid the imagination, confirming the reader's apprehension of the situation. How is the technique used in "Macomber"? Francis is first seen after he has run from the lion, when his cowardice is the central fact of his character. Yet, in Crane's view, when the reader understands precisely what Macomber faced, it is hard to feel that his behavior has been so very cowardly after all. Instead of a contemptible poltroon, Macomber becomes a victim of circumstances. The story's rendering invites a disjunction between earlier and later estimations of Macomber, one that cannot possibly help Hemingway if he really is doing what the traditional interpretation says he is. See, the flashback seems to be saying, it really isn't as bad as Wilson thinks for Macomber to bolt like a rabbit. The repeated roars of the lion, the deadliness of the situation once the lion is wounded, emphasized by the "very grave" looks of the gunbearers, the "pitiful"—not frightened—expression on Macomber's face as he tells Wilson he'd just as soon skip the whole thing, the suddenness of his flight—"The next thing he knew he was running"—all serve to induce most readers to pity rather than condemn Macomber. For the *Cosmopolitan* reader, the flashback is a lavish invitation to release Macomber from the unreasonable bonds of a "code" that now seems unnecessarily harsh. If a number of practiced critics go ahead and do just that, how must the "naïve" *Cosmo* reader have reacted? It is misreading as Hemingway's revenge.

For such a misreading, the story's subversive substructure—its ambiguous signals that allow for systematic "error"—invites exculpation, even pity, for Margot too. Her nastiness, which the reader sees before witnessing its cause, is easily forgotten in the flashback, in which she acts in a way that allows an inattentive reader to sympathize with her. She reassures Macomber, who is already scared witless, that he will kill the lion "marvelously . . . I know you will. I'm awfully anxious to see it" (1936:131). In the traditional interpretation, these words must be scornful. After the lion fiasco, when Margot robs her husband of the last sliver of his self-respect, there is little room to excuse her, especially since the flashback weakens the reader's tendency to condemn his coward-ice. Even so, the entire progression of the story's duplicitous plot, after the flashback, is in the direction of inducing a misguided pity for Margot, permitting the naïve reader to identify with her— fulfilling the strong generic expectations that the story's appear-ance in *Cosmopolitan* guarantees—and opening up possibilities for excusing her conduct.

Macomber is precisely the sort of man Hemingway despised, or pitied, which may have been the same to Hemingway. He is also an antitype of the man who usually adorns the pages of *Cosmopolitan* romantic stories, like those by Ursula Parrot and Agnes Sligh Turnbull in the same September 1936 issue in which Hemingway's story appeared. The two paragraphs recounting the Macombers' past life are perfectly in the *Cosmo* manner in their flat matter-of-factness, and they are scathing enough to anyone familiar with the Hemingway "code." For a reader on the outside, one who herself perhaps "would not leave" her husband because he has "too much money," the narrator's invitations to sympathize with Margot must be tempting. It is Macomber's failings that are emphasized, after all, "sex in books, many books, too many books," his "great tolerance which seemed the nicest thing about him if it were not the most sinister" (139–40), a curious statement until one realizes that it is aimed at the wealthy *Cosmo* reader who resents the passivity of the "typical" wealthy American husband, a type Hemingway thought he knew perfectly well. After all, the woman on whom Margot is modeled, Jane Mason, had just such a "tolerant" husband. Hemingway, who apparently had an affair with Jane, said that he "invented" Margot "from the worst bitch I knew (then)" (Baker 1969:284).

It is in Margot's sleeping with Wilson—who is, pointedly, not American—that Hemingway invites his female reader to project and fantasize, bringing together the "worst bitch" with all those other "bitches" who will read the story. The knowing reader, male or female, will incorporate Margot's casual adultery and most of the other details into the code reading. Another kind of reader, a member of Margot's class, or even an aspirant to "the international, fast, sporting set, where the women did not feel they were getting their money's worth unless they had shared the cot with the white hunter" (1936:144), will condemn Margot only at the risk of condemning herself, and may even take a certain amount of vicarious pleasure in Margot's successful exploitation of a "tolerance" so "sinister." Hemingway's intention with this episode is especially clear, in terms of sexual satire. While many other things in the story relate to his experiences hunting in Africa with Philip Percival, who sits for the portrait of Wilson, the white hunter's sleeping with Margot is not (Baker 1969:284).

Hemingway, then, goes out of his way to make Margot a bitch, in conformity with his opinion of Jane Mason, and then includes details in the story that permit the attack to be sidestepped. For example, when Macomber has finally gained his courage, one might expect the most unambiguous evidence of Margot's sense of the new threat to her dominance. What Hemingway does is quite the opposite. The very last weighted comment by the narrator, powerful for the *Cosmo* reader in its finality, is a sentimental extenuation, worth quoting again: "she had done the best she could for many years back and the way they were together now was no one person's fault." She does not reenter the story as a presence of any sort until she fires the bullet that hits "her husband about two inches up and a little to one side of the base of his skull" (1936:153). The rhetoric of extenuation opens the door for one kind of reader to see this as a lamentable accident.

Why Hemingway's narrator says "shot at the buffalo" should now be clear. Macomber, modeled on a "nice jerk" Hemingway knew, is to be slain by his wife, modeled on Jane Mason. Hotchner reports that Hemingway talked about the prototype of Margot, "a woman whose sole virtue was an overeagerness to get laid" (164). The antipathy accompanying Hemingway's later memory of her origins as a character, however, is totally at odds with the way he softens her characterization as the story concludes, just as much at odds as the conflicting "versions" of Jane/Margot are within the story itself. It is as if she exists, independently, for different readers, in several dimensions. Based on a real person, like Cohn and Brett, she is therefore an example of Hemingway's fondness for calling a "spade a dirty unprintable shovel" (L. Hemingway, 275). Like Cohn and Brett she also has an independent fictional existence, a narrative "function" in a subsuming plot. As a satiric representative, she is the kind of American woman Hemingway despised— greedy, domineering, and emotionally dishonest—at least in the code reading! It is a horrid type and may have had more reality in Hemingway's imagination than in fact. His treatment of her in the story indicates that he is issuing a blanket invitation to at least one kind of reader, identified in Hemingway's mind with Jane/Margot, to engage in self-damning identification. Hemingway devoted much of his artistic life to discovering ways to induce readers to infer the "clear" truth about the world. In this story, however, he writes so as to ridicule the kind of reader he mirrors in his characters, turning away from "straight action" to covert satire. He aims his competing, ambiguous set of signs at those Mark in his Gospel calls "outside": "so that they may indeed see but not perceive, and may indeed hear but not understand" (4:11–12). As Frank Kermode has pointed out, in reference to Mark's words, this kind of "formula of exclusion" is a certain invitation to narrative obscurity (1979, chap. 2) Like the perplexing passage in Mark, Hemingway's story is mostly beyond his critics. For in trying to design a new kind of story that might compliment the inferential skills of readers he respects and bewilder those he does not, he fragments his story to the point that a single interpretation of it, one that assumes a unitary reader response, is impossible.

This, of course, is the most disturbing part of this entire scene of innovation: the legacy of confusion. "Macomber" was one of Hemingway's favorite stories, which is not at all surprising given its duplicitous but brilliant strategy.[4] Even so, it is a story that issued from frustration and anger and carries with it, like *To Have and Have Not*, the need to be understood as an intensely personal, time-bound document.

To Have and Have Not

Hemingway's third novel has its genesis in a return to the barest of tragic stories, the tale of Harry Morgan in the short story "One Trip Across" that Hemingway wrote in 1933 and published in *Cosmopolitan*—one of the greatest mismatchings of story to readership in history. His intention, once the story grew into a novel, seems to have been to represent a tragic decline in the barest possible descriptive terms, as if, at about the same time he was writing "Macomber," he decided to give no quarter to the reader in this story. He used every narrative technique and device at his disposal to render this simple tragic story so that it would not only be understandable to what he saw as a diminished reader but would also be a novelistic tour de force, an experiment in point of view like *The Sound and the Fury*—no mean task. Hemingway was acutely attuned to possibilities for innovation. The year before, he wrote to Bill Lengel that he had invented "a new form for a story," the tripartite "Homage to Switzerland." He clearly hoped from the multiple views to achieve his usual high goal: "Anybody will have been [in Switzerland] when they read the Homage" (*Selected Letters*, 367). Hemingway's ambitious task in the novel, however, goes largely unrecognized, as Baker points out: "Few of Hemingway's critics, either in 1937 or since, seemed able to appreciate the difficulty of the technical experiments in *To Have and Have Not* or the skill with which some of them were overcome" (Baker 1972:216). Baker's is easily the best account of Hemingway's experiment in the novel. What also remains largely overlooked is how very unsuited to his habitual outlook the entire enterprise of writing a novel of social commentary is. His beliefs effectively "ironize" the social basis of the entire story. Like "Macomber," *To Have and Have Not* is just as much a product of rhetorical accommodation as many of the other works of the 1930s. It too posits a divided readership and was written for one kind of reader and against another.

At some point, for example, Hemingway decided that Harry's story would not stand alone and thus accompanied the central action with seemingly unrelated scenes. Examples of bad marriages, bad sex, bad authors, and bad government—these "digressions," as they were once called—generalize the meaning of the main action as well as elevating Harry's stature by contrast, an important task in a modern narrative tragedy. When the novel finally appeared, the few critics who liked it seemed to discern a new awareness of the burdens of class; here was Hemingway's first attempt to write a novel with a social ideology. What Hemingway really gave his readers, fully in the rancorous spirit of "Macomber," is his most antisocial novel, for the Morgan story actually refutes the possibilities for collective action. The rhetorical commentary of *To Have and Have Not* does not open up the Harry Morgan story to social significance. It closes it in a cloud of vituperation masquerading as social commentary.

Again, however, Hemingway had an overt intention, a serious desire to generalize the particularity of his bare-bones action, to "place" the story of his proletarian antihero in an America that causes Harry's demise. The problem is that it calls for precisely those talents Hemingway least possessed. Whenever, in the 1930s, he seemed to heed the urging of his critics to be more "relevant," it resulted in his mistaking what I call satire for social commentary. Criticized for remaining silent about the American scene, he wrote a story that "shows up" Jane Mason and anyone who sympathizes with her fictional portrayal for the "rich bitches" they are. Hemingway would not have composed "Macomber" as he did unless he thought the subscription list of *Cosmopolitan* was replete with other Jane Masons, and it was a magazine he knew much better in 1936 than he did when it first published "One Trip Across." But he did not understand that the kind of thing John Dos Passos tried to accomplish with his "Camera Eye" is not done by slinging mud at real people. Even if he had understood, his beliefs about human fate were at odds with social realism anyway.

Even so, *To Have and Have Not* works better than most of its critics would concede, a fact that the entire Max Eastman carnival tended to hide.[5] If the novel finally fails, however, it does so not because the strategy of fictional substructures designed to reflect on the main action is itself faulty. Indeed, Hemingway may have been responding to the critical success of *The Sound and the Fury* when he attempted to unify story lines by the use of narrative analogy and parallelism. In earlier fiction, all the way back to Fielding, embedded stories were used as fictional rhetoric to affect the reader's responses to the main action. Eliot, and other Victorian novelists, found ways to accommodate divergent narrative lines. On the contrary, Hemingway's commitment was always to the single action, although *In Our Time* attempts the unity of separate stories. His entire view of fictional reality depended on the loneliness of the individual, even when he tried, in *Sun,* to represent the tragedy of an entire group: Jake, like Nick, fishes alone. Moreover, when fictional rhetoric—comparison, contrast, amplifications, and so forth—was needed in a story, Hemingway usually preferred to invent a character, like Cohn or Rinaldi, to assist the author in his task of getting the story told while seeming to the reader to be just another smoothly integrated part of the overall action. This is the source of the seamlessness of his stories, a lesson he learned from a number of the great novelists, but especially from Conrad. It is a measure of Hemingway's vexation in the mid-1930s that he returned to a fictional technique, the embedded "exemplary story," for which Jane Austen long before had found a superior alternative.

So the decision to tie the seamier side of Key West society to Harry's solitary tale need not be a mistake, were it not for the fact that Harry's story does not need such "coloring." If Hemingway conceived of Morgan's tragic decline primarily in terms of social causation, he should simply have let the main action stand alone, as he did in his next novel. All of the rest, primarily the story of Richard Gordon, issues from Hemingway's desire not to get his story told or, curiously, even to comment on American society—he does that with values subordinated to Harry's story—but rather to punish it for being what it is. The result is a radical split between Harry's solitary fate and the society Hemingway portrays to give it meaning. Harry's dying words, "No man alone now. . . . a man alone ain't got no bloody fucking chance" (225), do not affirm solidarity with the working class. That is Marxist wishful thinking which a later Marxist like Macherey, who knows the intimate relationship between the formal and the ideological, would never indulge. Harry summarizes what is thematically active throughout the novel: no matter how bad life may be, it is worse in the United States in the 1930s. Even *this* man, bigger than life, who has always operated best alone, who believes that "anything is better alone" (105), has no chance. The rest of the novel, as Harry lies dying, is thematically relevant in that it demonstrates—in the hopelessness of the veterans, the malevolence or incompetence of the authorities, and the drunken impotence of even the best of the country's intellectuals—that Harry is right; alone is best, even though alone is also doomed. There is, however, a big difference between narrative relevance and necessity, especially when the merely relevant sections are clearly based on personal attack. The shift from tragic mimesis to personal satire is too drastic for even the most gymnastic readers' imaginations.

Hemingway suggested, when he wrote to Ivan Kashkin in 1935, that the story depends on a view of tragedy at variance with his other novels: "I go to Spain and write a damn good story about necessity which maybe you did not see called *One Trip Across*" (*Selected Letters*, 418). If by "necessity" he means what compels Harry to take on more and more dangerous tasks, leading to his death, then this is a new kind of tragedy for Hemingway. Jake's story portrays misery as a constant in experience; Frederic's extends the fate to those who find themselves in situations of choice, which turns out to be a mirage. Harry is just an ordinary fisherman minding his own business, reluctant even to break the law until something happens to make him conclude that he "can't choose now" (28). Indeed, Hemingway chooses for his antihero a man of reduced stature, as if he has concluded that the social forces that will bring him down are not profound enough to destroy a greater man. It is in the limitation of his choice that Harry's acts have their tragic validity. It is also where Hemingway most tellingly comments on his society, for the shift from a tragedy of fortuity to one of social compulsion is equivalent to the move from Paris and Switzerland to Key West—as if only in America could such a mechanistic fate play itself out.

The care with which Hemingway arranges the steps of Harry's downfall and the issues implied at each step deserve close attention. In addition, the tightly constructed "main story" contrasts, in its manner of telling as well as in its subject, with the subplot in such a way as to reflect back again on the reader, especially the one who fails to read the story in the same way Richard Gordon fails to "read" Marie Morgan. The tragic plot of the story is of a man, as able to take care of himself and his family as anyone, running into a series of situations in which his merest efforts to get by are so difficult that they endanger his life. The clear choice is always between agreeing to commit dangerous, illegal acts and accepting some sort of handout from the state, a situation of quotidian necessity no other Hemingway hero faces—appropriately, since the "trap" into which Jake and Frederic fall has nothing to do with daily bread. Harry's fortunes spiral steadily downward until, as an important and easily overlooked thematic modification of the story, his tragedy shifts away from a purely economic basis and he takes on a job that seems inevitably fatal from the start.

Hemingway's largest intention, then, is to join the ideology of his earlier tragedies with social causation. For example, although Harry's decline is primarily economic, it is never only a matter of money but always also involves his pride in his solitary ability to make his way. In this regard, the story is a thumbing of the nose at those critics who insist Hemingway join the Movement: combining his view of tragedy as part of the fabric of existence with an action largely socially determined suggests that collective exertion is double delusive. First, it won't work, in part because the terms of "success" in the world are almost always solitary. Even the best of loves ends in anguish for the partner left behind, as Hemingway points out in *Death in the Afternoon* and *A Farewell to Arms,* and as Marie Morgan stands as a reminder, by the end of the novel joining Frederic as one of the bereft. In addition, the values of "the group" seldom appeal to those obsessed with the peculiarly American virtue of self-reliance, such as Harry and Marie, who disdain the state-supported herd. If the ideology strikes some readers as simpleminded and "hairy chested," it is nevertheless perfectly in accord with Hemingway's earliest presented views.

For while Hemingway's "American action" traces necessity in part to the arbitrary limiting of an intrusive society, it also makes clear that luck, the outcome of the particular draw, makes all the difference. Hemingway has it both ways. In the brilliant and brutal beginning of the book, Harry refuses to take the three young Cuban revolutionaries across to Florida because he fears losing his boat to the authorities. When the three are gunned down as they leave the café, Harry says that the "whole thing made me feel pretty bad" (8), which makes little sense until one understands that if he had agreed to help them the previous night, when they first asked him, they would probably all have been at sea that morning, safely on their way to the Keys. He allows the repressive laws of two countries to cow him. He could save them and he doesn't—and they are nice boys, despite being "plenty nervous" (6). What they ask is little more than what Frederic and Catherine do so innocently—in a different world, of course—which is to flee a country where their lives risk being forfeit. Harry feels bad because his refusal to brave the ire of Cuban and American authorities—the same sort of men who want to shoot Frederic at Caporetto—keeps him from doing something that under other circumstances he would never decline: "I would have liked to have done them the favor" (3).

It is only after Mr. Johnson runs off without paying Harry's charter fee, or for the rod and reel he has lost through what is clearly, in Hemingway's mind, typical rich American stupidity, that Harry can no longer afford the luxury of staying within the law. With only a few cents in his pocket, he looks for a way to gain a stake to last through the summer. He agrees to take on the Chinese refugees, an ongoing illegal and brutal confidence game in which the innocent pay to be transported to a new life and are drowned or shot instead. Mr. Sing, whom Harry deals with, has been carrying on the trade for two years, having replaced someone murdered in the course of the ugly business. Harry's understated comment on Mr. Sing cannot hide, from anyone but a reader who wants only to see Harry's brutality and not the brutality of his world, that Sing is a monster: "Some Chink. . . . Some business. . . . Wonderful. . . . Wonderful" (37–38); "it would take a hell of a man to butcher a bunch of Chinks like that" (57). Because Sing has threatened to turn Harry in to the consulate if he takes Sing's money and just drops the Chinese off back in Cuba, Harry sees little to do but kill the man, if he wants the money. As he says to Eddy (who, like the reader, does not fully understand why Harry strangles Sing), he does so to "keep from killing twelve other Chinks" (55). He also clearly does so to rid the world of Mr. Sing.

It is Harry's brutality—or Hemingway's in describing it—in killing Sing that appalls most readers: "I got him forward onto his knees and had both thumbs well in behind his talk-box and I bent the whole thing back until she cracked. Don't think you can't hear it crack, either" (53–54). In this, perhaps Harry's and the novel's most cold-blooded moment, is the special quality of this plot, what sets it off from Hemingway's other books and ensures its condemnation in most reviews. Here, he does not want sympathy for Harry, who is decidedly an "other." Nick, Jake, Frederic, and Robert could all carry on civilized conversations with Grace Hemingway in her Oak Park music room, with nothing more indecorous than an occasional aside about irony and pity. Harry would call her a "bitch" and demolish the screen door on his way out. His ruthlessness and ready violence are intended to be not admirable but awesome. They allow him to survive, if anyone can, in this brutal world, but also ensure his demise. While there is no explaining away Harry's amorality and willingness to kill—they are bloodcurdling—if *he* can't survive this society, who can? Hemingway wants the reader to recognize just what is involved in Mr. Sing's "business," how many innocents he has killed or had killed. There is a certain amount of justice in having the very man he hires put an end to his murderousness. In addition, while Harry's ruthlessness is unsoftened by sentimentality, Hemingway shows in Harry's deliberations about whether he must kill the "rummy" Eddy that he is not without feeling. It is, of course, the minimal humanity allowed by Harry's brutal surroundings. Even so, it is clear that although Eddy's presence on the boat, unauthorized on the crew list—or so Harry thinks for a while—is a clear danger to him, he is especially reluctant to kill him. When Harry finds out that the pitiful drunk has gotten himself on the crew list and there is no problem in carrying him back to Key West, he is clearly relieved.

Harry borders on the repugnant because he is so often in the midst of situations in which any action involves unpleasant consequences, a powerful personal metaphor for many people in 1935. To survive, much less to thrive, Harry must act. He cannot afford to watch life as Jake does, or allow himself the fatal luxury of gentle remonstrance when face-to-face with brutality, as Albert does. As Cuban robber-revolutionaries rush aboard the boat, Albert stands up to them. "Wait a minute," he says to Harry, "Don't start her. These are the bank robbers." The reward for his heroism is a volley of machine-gun bullets. If Harry's character is never very effectively "softened," Albert's fate makes it clear that if staying alive is the goal, Harry's way is better.

More important, at the thematic heart of the novel is the implication that both societies, Cuban and American, are themselves the source of the greatest brutality. It is the Cuban government that keeps 100,000 Chinese in the country to perform menial labor and refuses to allow Chinese women entrance, for fear they'll have children. It is the Cuban government, in the person of its secret police, that has sent the two assassins to kill the three young revolutionaries and that threatens Harry so that he really has no choice but to take on Mr. Sing. It is the American government that has—in fact, not fiction—sent hundreds of veterans (of the war Hemingway saw firsthand) to the Florida Keys in hurricane season. Hemingway reported to Max Perkins what the scene looked like after a brutal hurricane came through in early September 1935: "We were the first in to Camp Five of the veterans who were working on the Highway construction. Out of 187 only 8 survived." As it turned out, nearly a thousand of the helpless men drowned. Hemingway thought he knew who was to blame: "The veterans in those camps were practically murdered. The Florida East Coast [Railroad] had a train ready for nearly twenty four hours to take them off the Keys. . . . Washington wired Miami Weather Bureau which is said to have replied there was no danger and it would be a useless expense. The train . . . never got within thirty miles of the two lower camps. The people in charge of the veterans and the weather bureau can split the responsibility between them" (*Selected Letters*, 421).

Even though many critics refuse to distinguish the kind of killing that Harry did from Roberto's murder of Albert, it is clear that Hemingway does. Roberto does not kill out of necessity but because he likes it; he is mad for power, like the government official who reports Harry and costs him his boat and, indirectly, his life. Roberto needlessly murders the kind, harmless Albert. Harry kills the odious Mr. Sing because he must if he is to save the other twenty. If this is a subtle moral distinction—and it isn't—it is not an impossible one, although it seems to be for one critic, Cyril Connolly, who finds the book morally "odious" and then demonstrates that he didn't read it: "When a winter visitor doesn't pay Morgan for fishing lessons he makes up for it by breaking the man's neck" (Meyers, 228). From its first chapter this novel depends upon even more precise moral inferences than *Sun* or *Farewell*, and critics like Connolly show that they fail the test, as does Philip Rahv, who calls Harry, correctly, "the most violent character one has ever encountered in Hemingway" and then misses the boat with "his sole method of coping with life is to kill everyone who blocks the fulfillment of his needs" (Meyers, 241). Thinking of Harry Morgan as trying to "cope" or searching for "fulfillment" takes us completely out of Hemingway's world. One does not have to be naïvely nostalgic to believe that part of Hemingway's problem with his critics was that they were not nearly so formally, or ideologically, perceptive as Eliot's were two generations before.

If Harry's story makes thematically active the view of society as brutal and requiring a similar brutality to survive it, it also, in Harry's last adventure, returns to a more personal kind of motivation that removes Harry's final fate from the arena of the social. In assisting the bank-robbing revolutionaries to escape, Harry still acts from necessity. "I could stay right here," he meditates, "and there wouldn't be anything. . . . I'd be out of it. But what the hell would they eat on? Where's the money coming from to keep Marie and the girls? I've got no boat, no cash, I got no education. What can a one-armed man work at? All I've got is my *cojones* to peddle" (147). He is in this fix because of "Cuban government bastards" and

"U.S. ones" and has "no choice in it" (148). Even so, the last chance Hemingway gives Harry is a desperate one. Harry knows that they will probably try to kill him. He is outnumbered and they are practiced killers, especially Roberto. Can he even keep any of the money they give him to help them escape? Or does he expect to get a reward, or keep the bank money? What the reader sees is a Harry Morgan who knows the desperateness of the situation and still goes ahead with a certain degree of grim pleasure. This is, after all, the supreme challenge. "Once they put it up," he thinks, "once you're playing for it. Once you got a chance. Instead of just watching it all go to hell. With no boat to make a living with" (107). While the note of necessity enters with that last sentence, it is clear that Harry likes risking his life, likes depending on his own talents and toughness to save himself. Later, almost ready to go into action, he even speaks "cheerfully" (144).

Hemingway, that is, is incapable of writing a tragedy based only on economic necessity. Without somehow converting Harry's needs into something volitional—an eagerness, almost, to "play for it"—he does not have a tragedy, only a man driven to his doom; which is, of course, part of the story too. Harry accepts the challenge and dies, horribly, and largely as a result of bad luck. One of the robbers Harry puts three bullets into survives and shoots Harry in the stomach: "One thing to spoil it. One thing to go wrong. . . . Who'd have thought I hadn't gotten him" (173). Harry's fate rests finally, as do Jake's and Frederic's, on universal causes, the tendency of life to go wrong in precisely the worst imaginable way, of hips too narrow for childbirth, of wars to wound us in places that don't show but render us unfit for life.

As in "Macomber," however, the universality of the central story is undermined by (unnecessary) attempts to give it a significance at variance with its basic ideology. While Hemingway often talked as if he believed action speaks for itself, he knew it does so only when the right author writes at his best for the right reader—at the right time. This is not one of those occasions, or at least he doesn't think so. The Richard Gordon sequence, and all the other narrative "analogies," parallel and contrasting, positive and negative, that Hemingway uses to comment on Harry's story, have blurred functions. Gordon's sexual inadequacy, for example, contrasts obviously with Harry's virility, and the complexity of difficult choices facing Harry makes Gordon's life seem morally barren, just as Gordon's makes Harry's seem rich. Yet Gordon's other failings, like his falsified writing, comment only distantly on Harry's genuine feeling and directness. It is almost as if Hemingway cannot make up his mind what his story means. Gordon's lack of understanding and readiness to misjudge—as when he sees Marie Morgan on the street and imagines a life for her the opposite of her real life—seem to point directly to the imperceptive reader (since again, no one else is watching). Rather than a generalizing element, at least part of the purpose of Gordon's story is to castigate those who do not properly infer the nobility of Harry and Marie from the evidence Hemingway provides. If this is part of Hemingway's intention, then the responses of critics like Connolly and Rahv confirm his purpose.

The novel's social substructures often indicate an even more explicit distrust for the reader. The same kind of overtness that mars "Macomber" is found here: "Down the street Richard Gordon was on his way to the Bradley's big winter home. He was hoping Mrs. Bradley would be alone. She would be. Mrs. Bradley collected writers as well as their books but Richard Gordon did not know this yet" (150). Even worse, after the description of Gordon's imagined, comically erroneous life for Marie Morgan, whom he has seen on the street and intends to put into his novel about a strike in a textile mill, is the comment, "The woman he had seen was Harry Morgan's wife, Marie, on her way home from the sheriff's office" (177). Worse still is the narrator's comment in chapter 24, Hemingway's chronicle of forms of modern deviance and despair, after Henry Carpenter's desperate life story, his inability to live on two hundred dollars a month: "The money on which it was not worth while for him to live was one hundred and seventy dollars more a month than the fisherman Albert Tracy had been supporting his family on at the time of his death three days before" (233).

To Have and Have Not implies an author who has lost sight of the nature of his own success. Hemingway overwrites. He writes to punish his enemies, and his thrusts at real people like Dos Passos fail to achieve fictive generality because he does not give them the clear narrative functions they have in the earlier novels. He fails to make clear the connections between his main action and episodes designed as generalizing rhetoric; or, put another way, he relies too much on the implicatory power of proximity. Even so, the novel comes together, after a fashion, as Harry lies dying. Is it Hemingway's intention to suggest to his critics this fundamental contrast of incompatible subject matters: Harry and his world? A man seemingly destined to be destroyed, Harry represents many of the things Hemingway feels are beyond admirable, are simply necessary. All of the clamor for Hemingway to write a social novel has resulted here in an asocial hero set loose, seemingly to be destroyed by the most trivial of societies but really meeting his fate on his own terms, ones that effectively cancel the social structures meant to generalize Harry's story.

The novel is virtually a challenge to the reader to decide among a series of less-than-desirable alternatives, Harry or Richard Gordon, drunken self-pity or doomed assertion. Another level of choices involves how stories are told, and here Hemingway sets the terms probably without realizing he is doing so. Shall the reader opt for the unembellished starkness of Harry's tragedy, in which the truth must be fought for, just as Harry fights to get by; or the leisurely social chronicle of the Dorothys and Henrys we get in chapter 24, stories that caress the reader's indolence? Hemingway's fiction never backs away from presenting readers with matters defined as better or worse. While he projects a public image of experiential certainty, the terms in which books like *To Have and Have Not* present moral choice serve both to reflect their readers' disunity and to magnify it. Dorothy's choice of sexuality at the end of chapter 24—she masturbates with her sleeping lover next to her—constitutes for Hemingway an active contrast to Marie Morgan's loss of sexuality with Harry's death. One suspects that many readers in 1937 did not "go along" with Hemingway in his moral ranking of sexual pleasures and that this contrast was as lost on them as it is on many readers today.

To Have and Have Not is Hemingway's first attempt to combine his universalist tragedy with social action, but it fails. Perhaps stories could no longer "stand alone" as they did in the 1920s; with the world coming apart once again in 1939, they now needed social and political "frames." What Hemingway misunderstood in the 1930s is that one does not "reflect" society in the novel, one *constructs* it. All fictional societies are themselves fictions, ideological ones. The way to accomplish his end is to subordinate the social material to the main action, as he does in his next novel, *For Whom the Bell Tolls*. Robert Jordan's story is, like Jake's and Frederic's, based on a view of life as inherently tragic. Even so, Hemingway now knows fictive generality not necessarily to be incompatible with social and historical density, and here he provides the context that gives his story the wider meaning he missed in *To Have and Have Not*. He uses reminiscences of characters like Pilar to tell their stories to Jordon, revealing the *why* of the republican cause. He sends Andre on his nightmarish sojourn among the mad generals. He "rediscovers" his impersonal narrator, whose perceptions are most often filtered through one or another character.

What continues from Harry's story to Robert Jordan's story is the sense, as the reader nears the conclusion, of characters doomed by their worlds; the stupidity, the waste of all but the effort of the solitary warrior, who will inevitably die because something just didn't go quite right. Hemingway leaves behind the American society he hates so much but discovers that even his beloved Spain is fragmented and doomed. In his later works he turns to nostalgia for a Paris that no longer exists and forces his heroes to places like Bimini, where the hand of "government" reaches feebly.

Like the other authors I have discussed, Hemingway found a surprise when the urgency of innovation came upon him. In the space between his older ways of writing and the fictional yearnings for lost paradises he finally fled to, he learned that he "belonged" to a society he could not portray.

6

Fiction

and Ideology

An objection to the preceding analyses might be that they hold forth a naïve or at best incomplete view of "ideology." Certainly I do not align my readings with precisely those assumptions and methods most often successfully employed in investigations of ideology—namely, one of the many available Marxist frameworks. It should be obvious that my readings stop far short of investigating the texts' "historical reality," as Pierre Macherey calls it, the structural contradictions of belief that, for Marxist critics, characterize ideology everywhere and always. I could, for example, have employed more usefully the work of Fredric Jameson, perhaps the preeminent critic of narrative ideology writing today. He divides the study of literary ideology into three distinct but interrelated "semantic horizons": the "narrowly political or historical"; the "ideologeme," the "smallest intelligible unit of the essentially antagonistic collective discourses of social classes"; and the separate "sign systems, which are themselves traces or anticipations of modes of production" (1981:76). From this point of view, my readings do not seem even to do justice to the narrowest of ideological concerns, much less to engage the larger sign systems glimpsed through the textual screen of ideology. In short, I have chosen not to heed Michael Springer's advice to combine Macherey's dialectical view of history with R. S. Crane's poetics. This "refusal" needs to be explained.

I have assumed that urgent innovation comes about as a result, though by no means through the agency of "mechanical causality," of strong authorial belief. That I am not much concerned with the source or cause of authorial ideology will be for some readers my most serious omission. I see my true subject as what happens to narrative structure once an author "discovers" it to be inadequate to express a newly conceived reality. Even so, the circumscription of an inquiry is no reason to ignore the validity of the assumptions on which it is based. In looking closely at urgent innovation, I became convinced that questions of the origin and value of ideas were too complex to be traced to a common ground, something like the means of production. No overarching explanation of narrative thought is possible without severe distortion or the kind of over-simplification, involving the use of homology, that would have prevented precisely the kind of readings I wanted to execute. I know of no way to demonstrate this assertion except in practice, as I have tried to do here.

What I can do, however, by means of contrasting my own enterprise with some others in the current debate over ideology, is isolate the present contribution and how it differs, mainly from "structural Marxism" but also from some other possibilities, and examine how those differences affect the "products" of interpretation. My own assumption in dealing with these different claims about ideology is that no single way of viewing the workings of belief in narrative ever exhausts the useful possibilities. It should become clear, however, that although my analyses share with structural Marxists certain assumptions about the ubiquity of narrative ideology, and even methods for dealing with it, I have very different, indeed radically incommensurable, views on the nature and role of the author in the expression of ideas.

One central question in the study of ideology, for example, is its origin. I have assumed that narrative belief comes from authors, although not "simply," not unmediated and unvexed. There is a sense in which almost no fabulist "invents" ideology; it is a reformulation of earlier problems and solutions, or the reader could not

contradictions" (1990:79). He takes seriously what *is* said as well as what isn't, what the structure engages as well as what it repels.[2] In some of his most recent work, for example, he describes a general situation of innovation, involving modernism, to which I have no difficulty subscribing, one in which "social 'determinants' . . . present a radically altered situation . . . to which a fresh and unprecedented aesthetic response is demanded, generally by way of formal, structural, and linguistic invention" (1990:50). His insistence on the ideological nature of narrative has been widely influential; less so has been what I think is equally important, the implication that one must be a skillful formalist to understand ideology.

So, while Jameson's specifically Marxist assumptions regarding the fundamental causal nature of the means of production are ones I do not share, a view of the structural nature of narrative ideology not incompatible with his informs this study. Unlike the Marxists, however, I assume that narrative ideology is individual and idiosyncratic, "nonscientific" in that its appearance is not predictable in either form or content; it is *as much* a response to "the midst" as to the dictates of social structure, which it will reflect in unstable ways. I am relatively unvexed by the unscientific nature of my nontheory, for I am primarily interested in matters of narrative art, in which questions seldom yield more than *probable* results. My procedure, in other words, has usually been the opposite of that followed by critics—Marxist, feminist, or deconstructionist—who emphasize the normative priority of "the absent," the missing term in a dialectic of difference. Without denying that narrative ideology partakes of the necessities of history—it must, after all, have a subject, a portion of "the real"—I find much more powerful explanations of both form and ideology in the *structure of a writing career*. Even if beliefs issue ultimately from the means of production, from the contradictions of any epoch, they still undergo transformations that depend on individual experience and volition.[3] These changes, however, cannot compare in complexity with what happens when ideas begin to serve the needs of narrative representation. It is my view of the complex conditions of narrative belief—and structure—as much as any hermeneutic assumptions that draws me to what might be called a "historical individualist" position. Ideology in fiction always partakes of the commonplace;

it always "feels" a little used and old-fashioned—but only in abstraction. It is *story* that makes ideology exciting; it is story that is finally the "artist's 'gift'" that Macherey identifies.

Yet, as I have tried to show in each instance of a striving author, the relationship between story and ideology, at least in urgent innovations, is never merely additive. Story transforms ideology, makes it new, not so much so that it may be "interrogated" as so it may escape the commonplace. The great advance in the treatment of fictive ideology made over the thematizing of some New Critics consists of our insistence on the historical specificity of ideology, that belief not be abstracted and homogenized into just another example of "appearance and reality." Hypotheses about the source of Austen's change of mind about the individual's ability to effect her own happiness—not a trivial if perhaps an unanswerable question—risk missing the way Austen made a mundane question, a "theme," important: her ability to dramatize, not the "historical structure," as Macherey suggests (although she may do that *too*), but a created person living the theme. It is not R. S. Crane's aversion to ideas that defines them, for him, as subservient to mimetic structure; it is rather his appreciation of their contribution and vividness as fully subordinated elements in such structures achieving the "appropriate" as poetic wholes: "to use the resources of rhetoric in order to achieve nuances of character and emotion and to adapt the speeches in a particularized way to what is going on, as well as to the universal issues involved in the action" (1953:74).

The ideological features I identify in the innovative situation do not, therefore, presuppose a poetics or genre of new forms, any more than the ideas themselves require a belief in Crane's "universal issues." Urgent innovations are tentative experiments, undetermined except by the pressure of new and uncomfortable belief and the expressive needs of an emerging structure, its contours perhaps still blurred. This is not to argue that the new text is autonomous, for it comes at least in part from the complex edifice of the author's career—even, sometimes, from other careers. In this sense of the lure of new paradigms, Jameson's model of invention is apt: "the hold of Dickensian paradigms over Gissing is not the result of some charismatic power of a temperamental or an artistic sort, but rather testimony for the fact that these paradigms offered objective 'solutions' (or imaginary resolutions) to equally objective ideological problems confronted by the younger writer." Frequently, as Jameson goes on to point out, the new solution creates its own "fresh problems . . . for which a new and distinctive solution . . . must be invented" (1981:186). The innovative "presence" of the text is always an elongated one.

In addition to the fact that I find more persuasive answers to ideological questions in biographical sources and poetic methods, the methodological consequences of applying the principle of the "absent cause" disturb me. Whether "worked up" or "worked down," the systematic application of standards of difference results in an author always (already) having failed the critic's test before beginning to write. The implication that an author's choice of subject edges out the more accurate or correct one demotes representation to an act of self-deluded mystification instead of, as I have tried to suggest in each of my analyses, a painful attempt to "cure" one's beliefs and one's fiction. The negative use of difference to show how the author's choice of what to represent indicates some serious deficiency of perception or even ethical understanding is just as damaging to authors but more difficult to argue against. If one is convinced, as I sometimes am, that Defoe revealed his "true" beliefs when he represented Roxana's sexuality, the pressure of the process can still be described without assuming a stance of ethical superiority. Indeed, to imply that an author who wrote in 1723 or 1724 somehow failed because he revealed fears of female sexuality is to commit an act of retrospective, egocentric hegemony. These "arguments by omission" are, in addition, inevitably conjectural and political—the first because there is seldom only one plausible explanation for why an idea appears, or does not appear, in a text; the second because one ordinarily analyzes an author's omissions in order to show how incorrect he or she is. Yet no relationship in aesthetics is more potentially treacherous or destructive of the critic's merest hopes for probable results than the truce that exists between idea and image. One serious problem in ideological criticism today is the proscribing of fictional subjects and even the authors who venture them, or playing the role, in Myra Jehlen's words, of "adversary of the work" (5), a role made possible only when what the text "knows" (Macherey, 64) comes to be less important than what it can be shown to have hidden.

Finally, what I wish to suggest in the remainder of this chapter is that the issue of ideology is so vexed that a general, abstract answer is never adequate to its appearance. Each case is distinct, which is not the same thing as saying that, having taken the uniqueness of narrative ideology seriously and explored it, formally and biographically, we might not then begin to have something to say about the conditions of meaning in stories.

Innovation and Ideology

As we saw with Defoe's attempts to define the world of a tragic action, the beliefs needed for the plot may not always be the same ones the author has carefully thought out, the ones he or she could comfortably expose to public scrutiny. An encyclopedia of misreading could be drafted just from those critics who have merely assumed that because ideas have a clear function in the action they therefore must somehow represent authorial intention, or at least meaning ascribable to the "author function." Of course, actions have their own "intentions," sometimes coercive, always slippery. Austen, whose ideological consistency Stuart Tave has admirably demonstrated (1973), nevertheless designed narrative structures that are capable of being read as contradictory. In *Sense and Sensibility*, Austen's representation of the dangers of the heartstrong head, Marianne's infatuation with nature is a common source of Elinor's and the reader's amusement. When Marianne's autumnal "transporting sensations" result in a heartfelt lament over the unmourned fate of fallen foliage, she provokes Elinor's droll, "It is not everyone . . . who has your passion for dead leaves" (73). The point—at least the one the story seems to make—is not that effusions over nature are inherently fatuous. Austen may or may not have thought so, at different times and about different people. Marianne is ludicrous because she attributes qualities, like pathos or love, to things and people that do not possess them. Fanny Price and Mary Crawford, in *Mansfield Park*, seem at first to be playing a similar duet. Fanny launches her paean to the "beautiful . . . welcome . . . wonderful . . . evergreen!" to which Mary replies by comparing herself with the famous but unsylvan Doge who professed wonder at finding himself amidst the shrubbery at Versailles. Here it is the interlocutor of the nature fanatic who comes off second best in Austen's unending, painstaking, and formally functional efforts to sort between better and worse in character, for Mary's jaded response signals her unsuitability for Edmund. He is no addlepated romantic, but he can share Fanny's enthusiasm if Mary cannot. While the indirections of the action may not exert pressure on an author to falsify views, they may elicit only a semblance of ideology. The mixed purposes that sometimes constitute an act of innovation further complicate the search for meaning.

The comic action, in Austen's hands, cannot even get itself told without these "rankings" of belief, some of which are authorially indifferent, or not "functional," to use Phelan's term. A more serious use of narrative ideas is always involved with anything but the lightest of comedy. The ideological question that may not be ignored is the fate of goodness in the world. Unlike the tricky topos just explored, this one goes to the heart of comic structure. To achieve the full satisfaction for the reader implied by the "ideal" structure of comedies of fulfillment, the author must meditate an unavoidable question of ethical causality: What will be the relationship between what the character destined for happiness has done, thought, and felt, and his or her fate? There is no poetics of comedy to help here, nor will rhetoric come to the rescue. Every comic author, even one who inherits an established belief in a rigid moral and cosmological order, must construct the ethics of comedy anew.

A simple example, in romantic comedy, is the pairing of the lovers at the end signaling closure. There are a number of possible relationships, which any reader can work out for any comic character previously defined as "deserving." Reward seems to be a constant, a minimal material constraint that may not be avoided without departing the genre—which is, of course, just what many authors choose to do. On the other hand, goodness, or any other moral quality, may play no part in the outcome. The task is not really this easy, however, since the representation of the "because" or the "no part" is never an abstract but always a specific problem, one easily missed by a critic who believes ideology is a simple matter—about which more later. Jane Austen's novels seem to be a series of attempts to work out a large number of the possible relationships among virtue, exertion, and reward, with the "conclusion" occurring amongst a general well-being. Is Lizzy Bennet rewarded with marriage to Darcy because she has finally realized her mistakes about his character? Yes and no, but the celebratory note on which her story concludes is just as much a result of Darcy's refusal to drop his suit because Lizzy has told him he is the last man on earth she would ever marry.

The poetics of serious comic fiction, then, almost force a consideration of the place of goodness in the world. I have come close to suggesting that just about any relationship between virtue and reward will work in the comic action, but writers are not that free. A genre that presupposes an attractive hero or heroine and a happy ending has at its bottom a favored ideology: goodness ought to count for something, in comedy and in the world. Some writers, such as Fielding, have been able to ignore the premises of the form, almost, as it were, to tincture their invented comic world with the despair of the wider one. Even Fielding, however, did everything possible to make the reader desire his good characters' good fortunes.

Expressive Form

Expressivity—the degree to which narrative choices, including those involving technique, tell us something about the author's meaning—is at the heart of the matter, if, indeed, we grant fictional worlds the ability to express anything. It seems that there is a price to pay for the distinction Phelan and I want to maintain between beliefs that are functional in the telling of a story and others that are merely incidental. Don't we run the risk of begging the question, of simply assuming functionality is equivalent to meaning—the "author's" or the "text's"? For example, to study the complete works of any particular author is often to discover discrepancies in belief. Ordinarily, a reader assumes that the author has changed his or her mind. Often, evidence is available in letters, essays, poems, or other confessional documents. Even so, the action demands so many different kinds of operations involving belief—as anyone who has ever tried to write one knows—that it often seems as difficult to determine which ideas represent the author in the action as it is in pseudofactual works like Defoe's. Perhaps, despite Phelan's efforts, and my own, to reintroduce thematic specificity to fictional narrative, Crane is well advised after all to see ideas in mimetic fiction as the mostly neutral building blocks of the storyteller's art. If some ideas are indeed authorial, Crane still runs less risk of distortion in considering them primarily mimetic functions, expressive only in their establishment of the "universal," than does the critic who assumes that all ideas in a fiction are endorsed.

Even so, I assume throughout this volume that expressivity is at the heart of some kinds of narrative innovation. In doing so—not only so that I may conveniently posit reasons for innovations but also because, like Jameson, I see narrative as inherently ideological—I do not mean to gloss over the sometimes insoluble problem of whether an ideological structure represents authorial belief or not, or, more fundamentally, whether narrative is *ever* ideologically meaningful in any stable sense. Since ideology is at the heart of so many contemporary criticisms, the relationship between story and belief must not, as is so often the case, be simply assumed.

A second pitfall must be avoided. Too many theories equate difficulty and uncertainty of result with impossibility, but nothing could be more illogical or more destructive of any progress in understanding. In the humanities, questions often do not admit of serene certainty, but radical skepticism is not perforce the only alternative, just as, if a science or even a poetics of narrative ideology is not possible, the only remaining alternative is not perforce an atomistic chronicle.

Both the difficulties and successes of ideological criticism are illustrated by recent feminist readings of a number of novels. Indeed, like Marxism, feminist criticisms provide an admirable site for testing assertions about narrative meaning, because many feminists insist upon ascribing meaning to some version of the "author." What is striking, however, is the degree to which so many of these critics so often feel unconstrained by the theoretical difficulties of their ascriptions.

Roxana *and Foe*

Paula Backscheider, one of the most knowledgeable of recent Defoeans, treats the "genesis" of *Roxana,* which she finds a part of the already established (by 1724) tradition of novels for women. She believes that "Defoe intended *The Fortunate Mistress* to be a 'woman's novel,'" but one which no one could read for "more than a few pages . . . without realizing that this is a novel by a man" (211, 220). Defoe assigns to Roxana fears that Bachscheider finds characteristically "male," but when she comes to deal with Roxana's sexuality, she argues that Roxana "pays men in sex sometimes because she had rather part with her body than her money" (222), a conclusion with which I have no argument but which seems curiously "ungendered." Backscheider's view of Defoe's attitudes toward Roxana seems quite benign: "Defoe makes Roxana such an arresting character partly by having her embody the most basic, archetypal fears men have of women" (225). This is as close as she comes to suggesting that Defoe not only portrayed but also felt the threat; but it is not really very close.

For my purposes, what matters here has nothing to do with Backscheider's argument, although it is very useful. What is important is the unspoken assumption that it does not *matter* what Defoe believed, but only what he represented. Even Phelan, who has found a way to identify values activated in the narrative representation, stops short of suggesting that the themes Austen made "functional" in *Pride and Prejudice* she also *believed in.* Indeed, I think the act of making a belief functional is equivalent to belief, although I wouldn't want to have to prove it. On the other hand, as I have argued repeatedly, narratives may represent ideological structures toward which the author feels only indifference, elements of thought "for the sake of the story"—although this is always going to be a contested point for each narrative and belief. Urgent innovations, however, come about because authors *do* feel strongly that a new structure must be found to convey the new truth; new novels are desperately "needed." A series of "unprovable" hypotheses, a column of "ifs," threaten at this point: *if* Defoe sought in *Roxana* a new kind of novelistic structure, and if he needed it to express a new insight, and if, in his role as didactic author, he thought his readers needed a kind of story that would teach better than the old ones, then his own attitude toward his subject indubitably "matters."

At a distant remove from Backscheider, in terms of her attitudes toward the nature of expressivity in *Roxana*, is Robyn Wiegman, whose analysis of *Roxana* as a "gendered site" is invaluable to an understanding of Defoe's possible attitudes toward his character. Wiegman assumes that the "sexual division" that "maps the terrain of the story in essence before the story begins" is the result of "an authorial decision" (33). Here we seem to be in the presence of a serious concern for Defoe's intention, but this turns out not to be the case. Wiegman approves of the argument that "conventions of narrative do not merely illustrate cultural ideology but . . . constitute it: narrative is ideology" (48–49). Therefore, the "engendering of cultural formations" Wiegman finds in *Roxana* turns out not to be ultimately Defoe's responsibility at all, rendering her use of the phrase "authorial decision" somewhat problematic. Ideology is, for Wiegman, "the very basis of narrative representation" (33), but not a matter of choice. We are back with Macherey. Wiegman may or may not be right about the source of gendering in *Roxana*. I have certainly tried to show that, like many authors in the throes of urgent innovation, Defoe "accidentally" revealed his attitudes about women as a result of an intention to write a new kind of structure. Even so, it is a long way from my position to Wiegman's and Teresa de Lauretis's, the critic she cites to make her case about the inevitability of Defoe's initial act of gendering.

One would not want to posit, of course, that just because Wiegman and de Lauretis are dealing with a social and political force that cannot be demonstrated in any matter-of-fact manner that the gendering tendency they see in narrative is a chimera; nor that it is doubtful that narrative, which is among other things a *manner* of story telling, has "conventions" apart from specific authorial practice. Even so, the effect is to remove Defoe, and all other authors, from active participation in his own innovation, even from responsibility for his attitudes toward feminine sexuality. If, with Althusser and Macherey, one assumes that the most important thing about ideology is that it is always a kind of screen, the product of an absent cause, then the historical complexity of Defoe's task in inventing an expressive novelistic form will be less important than the mode of production that acts as the ultimate cause of the new structure. Evidence is available, however, that Defoe's gendering was the result of his own highly idiosyncratic views of women, which may or may not be expressive of the sexual "climate" of his times, but which are given equally idiosyncratic form in *Roxana.*

Carol Houlihan Flynn points out, for example, that although Defoe believed in "justice" between husband and wife, there is an ominous connection in *The Family Instructor* between examples of stubborn female behavior and providential "accidents"; "Lacking the simple faith of the old and feeble, or the young and idiotic, [Defoe's narrator's] less willing subjects are brought to the patriarchal good through 'accidents,' providentially plotted, that result in maiming, illness, fever, and madness. Once chastened, they usually become necessarily abject, ready to assume their duties with all the ardor appropriate to affective domestic structures" (74–75). Like Wiegman, Flynn is interested in understanding how the gendered basis of *Roxana* affects the famous (non)closure of the novel. The difference between their conclusions stands as a model of how "abstract" and "concrete," or "dialectical" and "biographical," criticisms of innovations part company. For Wiegman, the ending of the novel, which involves Roxana "in the symbolic destruction of her only avenue of forgiveness"—that is, her daughter Susan—"disrupts the conventions of the female body in representational paradigms" (42). For Flynn, "Roxana . . . tragically collides with the moral and economic system in a disaster that clarifies the irony of Moll's triumph and invalidates the code of behavior Defoe sets out in his tracts" (76).

I do not mean to suggest that Flynn's interpretation of the novel is somehow superior to Wiegman's, especially not merely because Flynn supports her case with evidence of Defoe's gendered attitudes from other works. As with so many disagreements today that seem to be about interpretation, what is really involved here is a valorized choice of *subjects:* Wiegman values conventions, Flynn values historically situated authors. Both oversimplify as a result of their choices. Indeed, when Flynn quotes the "he" of *The Family Instructor,* clearly equating the speaker of the didactic tract with the historical Defoe, I am uneasy enough to emend "he" to "Defoe's narrator." The automatic assumption that the narrators of "nonfiction" prose must be closer to the speaking author is not warranted, and therefore neither is Flynn's sarcasm—a barometer of how, even though she takes authors seriously, she has turned Defoe into "foe." The "Defoe" of his tracts may feel freer to speak his views directly, but he is just as much a creation, just as much a function of a rhetorical purpose, as the "Editor" of Moll's and Roxana's "memoirs." So, while Flynn's attempt to assemble evidence of Defoe's attitudes toward women from other sources is not only admirable but also necessary, it is full of its own kind of dangers, calling to mind Edward Said's recent warning that "the one thing that intellectuals *cannot* do without is the full intellectual process" (20). However, if one wishes, as I do, to reemphasize the role of volition—and its occasional failures—in narrative innovation, Flynn's subject and procedure here and in her recent book on the body in Swift and Defoe (1990) seem better adapted than Wiegman's to yielding results that may be judged more or less accurate estimates of Defoe's intentions and accomplishments.

Form, Ideology, and Decanonization

In one of the small ironies of narrative innovation, it sometimes happens that the ideological conditions that contribute to the new structure's creation change and the innovation falls into disrepute—for ideological reasons on the side of reception. In this last section I consider the example of an innovative novel, once widely read and studied as expressing something important about the early 1960s, which now seems in the process of being decanonized: Ken Kesey's *One Flew Over the Cuckoo's Nest*. Kesey, in the late 1950s, found a way to tell a tragic story that reverses the ordinary relationship between personal responsibility and fate, and the ordinary expectations usually associated with that pattern. Tragedy often shows us someone who commits act after act that, because of some flaw, or ignorance, or the malignity of the cosmos, damns him or her. Kesey's novel shows us a man who is doomed because he is influenced to become *better* than he was before he entered the mental hospital. For the story to work, as tragedy, Kesey must devise some powerful means of making the reader want McMurphy to do what clearly will lead to his destruction.

One thing Kesey does is to suggest how much is at stake. The plot of the novel therefore almost demands that some characters cruelly but indirectly emasculate the male patients on the ward, since the pressure on McMurphy must be of a sort that will make him act, but only after long hesitation, only after he has finally recognized the rottenness behind the façade of concern. Female oppressors are obviously a better choice for such a role, since they, more than men, would plausibly work to control through indirect rather than physical means. Yet, since physical abuse is a part of the horror of the ward, some characters must be represented as hating the patients "abstractly," enough to hurt them, and Kesey uses African Americans, who can economically be given plausible reasons for hating. They have the added virtue of seeming, in how they too are oppressed by the Big Nurse, to lend weight to Kesey's clearly thematized argument against institutional American conformity and control. The more formidably hateful the oppressors are, the better they serve as worthy adversaries for McMurphy's admirable but doomed attempts to free the men. If a reader accepts this formal hypothesis, the Big Nurse, Billy's mother, Harding's wife, and the rest of the women, and the black attendants, seem perfectly appropriate choices; and the character, briefly presented, of the kind and caring female nurse on the Disturbed Ward is adequate evidence that Kesey is no misogynist. I discuss elsewhere in greater detail the formal requirements of the special kind of tragic experience Kesey offers (1979), but here a different question arises: What in the ideological necessities and implications of this action has brought it from its once secure, admired position in the canon to face current charges of ethical disreputability? The answers to this question constitute virtually a paradigm of the way some varieties of ideological criticism perform a too-common and formidable act, exclusion.

First of all, Kesey's task is virtually the opposite of what came, in high modernism, to be the desired way to write a novel. Formally, McMurphy's story must be very tight, almost lockstep in its progression; indeed, if one is willing to commit the fallacy of imitative form, the plot of *Cuckoo's Nest* suggests a belief in causality very unlike the works of novelists like Joyce, Ford, and Woolf. Second, its characters are divided between the good and the bad, with little attempt to suggest how they got that way. Such features, however, should lead to no more than a split between the novel's detractors and its admirers, not to a determined effort to banish Kesey from the classroom. The current animosity is the result of the novel's division on the basis of race and gender. The good guys are just that, while the oppressors are women and blacks. There are sound formal reasons for doing this, but they clearly do not matter to many readers. The assumption seems to be that in the very act of setting up his novel so that the struggle is maintained between a freedom-loving, sexually active "good ole boy" and a dictatorial, repressed "bitch"—who is only one among many such emasculators in the novel—Kesey has committed a narrative impropriety. The objections are raised even though without that gendered contest, Kesey could not have realized the novel's special and innovative affective structure.

One effect, in other words, of the critique of presence is to make us much more aware of the world from which each novelist slices his or her piece. Following from that desirable sensitivity, however, and perhaps not inevitably, is a growing tendency to dismiss fiction not deemed ideologically "copious" enough or, in the case of questions of gender, race, or class, either inadequately generous (if a contemporary writer) or insufficiently anticipatory (if a "pre-postmodernist" writer). In chapter 2 I engage in a version of this kind of criticism by identifying Defoe's only partially examined beliefs about female sexuality. While it seems to me perfectly legitimate to engage in a critique of values that are "thematized," *made functional*—as is Roxana's sexual license in Defoe's novel—it is a very different thing to object to the representation of a material structure because, elsewhere, a particular undesirable point of view is associated with it. Kesey, then, is the victim in this case of critics taking the ideologically accidental—his representation of a gendered conflict—as essential. There is nothing in Kesey's choosing to show us a man fighting against a woman that implies anything more than that he believes such a conflict might plausibly occur, although *how* he represents that battle tells us volumes. Logically, to object to the representation of a clearly plausible antipathy between a man and a woman, one would have to suggest that literature should never represent such scenes, or that the gendered basis of the division is itself a structure in need of deconstruction and, finally, abandonment. Such is not usually the basis for criticizing Kesey. Narrative ideology is understandable only by virtue of the closest attention, not only to how material action is treated but also to the way in which values may *appear* in a novel but not add up to its *message*.

If the critics who dismiss Kesey were as skillful formalists as, say, Phelan is, they would see that at many points in the novel the fully functional *nongendered* theme is that the world is replete with people who will take one's freedom away if they aren't resisted. As McMurphy says, "No, that nurse ain't some kinda monster chicken . . . what she is is a ball-cutter. I've seen a thousand of 'em, *old and young, men and women.* Seen 'em all over the country and in the homes—*people* who try to make you weak so they can get you to toe the line, to follow their rules, to live like they want you to." The example McMurphy then gives is a "guy" (58; my emphasis). It is possible to object to Kesey's active theme here, to see it as a kind of cliché (although what is hackneyed or jejune to one reader may be liberating to another), but Kesey is clearly not guilty of misogyny on the basis of ideas that are *functional* in the novel.

Kesey's is a theme that receives treatment time and time again because it is important to many of us. When the "story" takes gendered form, as it does in *The Color Purple* and a recent film, *Thelma and Louise,* the reaction is fairly predictable: someone will object to the *fact* of gendered representation without bothering to discover the ideology that dictates its treatment. Such a priori, "determined" reactions should remind us of what Jameson criticizes in the work of Lucien Goldmann, in which facile homologies among "class situations, world views, and artistic forms" are made to account for complex literary phenomena (1981:44–45). Perhaps the world has enough such schemes for now, and criticism might more profitably engage in *employing* some of the frameworks and methods developed by Macherey, Jameson, Crane, and other original thinkers to do more than blaze another subsequently unexplored trail. Universities are full of English professors who never got very good at dealing with formal structure but now are content to declare the death of "formalism."

The relationship between ideology and fictional form, in innovations especially but also in the great mass of fictions we read to experience and learn from, is so complicated that no abstract, a priori set of beliefs is ever adequate to explicate even the simplest structure of represented belief. It is the great advance of Althusserian Marxism over previous versions that, as Michael Sprinker recently put it, "all the various 'levels' or 'instances' within a social formation can be seen to be both determined and determining." Curiously, such a development might, in Sprinker's view, open the way to a kind of unlikely wedding of R. S. Crane's "autonomous science of poetics," seemingly in fundamental antipathy to Marxism, and the "Althusserian/Marxist science of history" (205). It is not, of course, a project without the dangers attendant upon all acts of critical eclecticism, dangers Crane himself warns of in *The Languages of Criticism and the Structure of Poetry* (1953). It is an intriguing idea, to resurrect a dead poetics—for some today, itself a dead science—and make it speak to us about the means of production, precisely at a time when criticism itself has become a prominent commodity. I shall maintain my skepticism until I can determine whether such an amalgamation can preserve what, for me, is the most interesting side of urgent innovation, its unpredictability.

Notes

1 An Essay on Innovation

1. I choose the term "innovation" because it seems to fit the phenomenon of discrete, (possibly) separable events better than "novelty," "originality," or "creativity." This study is therefore an investigation not of a general quality or human "power" but rather of occurrences that are, at least in their uniqueness, unrepeatable. This is not, moreover, an attempt "to formulate a general theory of the nature of innovation" or to "analyze the conditions for," much less "the immediate social consequences of, the appearance of novel ideas," although I have learned much from H. G. Barnett's painstaking, sophisticated *Innovation: The Basis of Cultural Change*.

2. Every writer who has ever dealt with the origins of a text has, in one way or another, made an excursion into innovation. I have found particularly useful the following, represented in the Bibliography: Bloom, Corti, Croce, Howe, Kenshur, Kermode, Macherey, Mukarovsky, Rothenberg, and the essays in the collection edited by I. Hassan and S. Hassan. Also helpful have been: Robert A. Prentky, *Creativity and Psychopathology* (New York, 1980); Hans Robert Jauss, *Aesthetic Experience and Literary Hermeneutics*, trans. Michael Shaw (Minneapolis, 1982); Milton C. Nahm, *The Artist as Creator: An Essay of Human Freedom* (Baltimore, 1956); and Thomas McFarland, *Originality & Imagination* (Baltimore and London, 1985).

3. See Benedetto Croce, *Guide to Aesthetics,* especially chapter 1, "What Is Art"; and, for one alternative, Crane 1971.

4. Vaticination being risky, one must still suspect that the recent events in Eastern Europe and the Soviet Union call into the question ideas of social, political, and economic "necessity," at least in any simple or "vulgar" form. Perhaps they also invite, in the persons of Gorbachev and Lech Wałesa, a new investigation of the roles of individuals and ideas in historical change. I do not mean to suggest that individuals are free of influence. For example, as Umberto Eco says, "In every century the way that artistic forms are structured reflects the way in which science or contemporary culture views reality" (quoted in Kenshur, 28). I do not find this truism particularly helpful in explaining innovation, except in how it might alert us to another influence authors might ironize or negate, "the contemporary."

5. Since I argue that Defoe's *Roxana* uneasily reveals certain antifeminist clichés, it may seem contradictory to leave him out of this qualification. I do so out of respect for Defoe's astounding accomplishment at the beginning of the tradition of the novel. Then too, while I do not find Defoe's anxieties about female sexuality any less unattractive than Hemingway's more unfixed anger, they somehow seem so because of his obvious respect for Roxana.

2 Defoe's *Roxana:* Structure and Belief

1. The model of the action has changed as it has been adapted by a number of critics. For a useful and concise definition of the form and its variations, see Rader 1973:32–34, 67, n. 3.

2. Sacks (1964) believed that, to the extent that they were coherent, novels could not be actions and satires, or actions and apologues, or exhibit the properties of any two *coherent,* distinct forms. The novels I deal with here are all actions that begin to be something else, or, in the case of *Roxana,* aspire toward unity as actions after beginning as an older, "additive" form.

3. The relationship between thematic significance and the action form, about which Crane and Sacks disagreed, has been fruitfully explored by Phelan (1987). It will be obvious to my deconstructionist readers that I am ignoring the implications of the relationship between signifier and signified that would guarantee the incoherence of all narrative. I take the matter up in chapter 4, in regard to Cynthia Chase's reading (1978) of *Daniel Deronda,* and more directly in my final chapter.

4. I deal with thematic critics of Defoe in *Defoe and the Uses of Narrative,* especially 7–12.

5. Robert D. Hume's essay on *Roxana* (1970) remains one of the best treatments (for others, see Boardman 1983:169, n. 6). A recognition of the novel's chronological shift is crucial to an understanding of the causal basis of the concluding action. Some critics continue to misread what Defoe tried to make clear. Maximillian E. Novak, for example, rewriting an earlier essay, asserts that "we never learn how Roxana is eventually brought to final misery, how the external greatness of her life as a Countess comes to match her internal sufferings" (1983:119). Roxana, of course, tells the reader precisely "how" when she goes "back to another Scene" (265) to recount the threat posed by her daughter and how Amy murdered her. Innovations often escape critics—apart from those who are merely incompetent—who decide too firmly what an author "must" be doing based only on past practice.

6. It is irrelevant to the structure of *Roxana* whether readers "choose" to ignore the novel's formal demands. Textual signals, or any substructure, may always be bypassed in favor of strategies of reading that "unwrite" the text (see Lerner).

7. Innovations often raise the vexed question of the appropriate "match" of text and critical method. All disciplines that deal with "texts," no matter how they may be defined, need to be more aware of the implications of adopting existing frameworks to new kinds of phenomena that may not accommodate them.

3 Comic Fiction and Ideological Instability: Goldsmith and Austen

1. See Rader 1984 for an important analysis of the consequences of the moral "burden" of eighteenth-century fiction.

2. This is an interesting example of Goldsmith's conscious perception of his problems with the Vicar's dual role. In chapter 3, Goldsmith needs to signal the reader that Burchell is not who he seems. Burchell, ostensibly telling the story of Mr. Thornhill (really himself), in the first edition stumbles as he is winding up: "I now found that—but I forget what I was going to observe." After revision this became, "I now found that—that—I forget what I was going to observe" (30). Goldsmith wants the reader to have a bit more "recognition time" for Burchell's slip, so that his identity and potential role as deus ex machina will be apparent while the Vicar remains still plausibly mired in ignorance.

3. See Morgan for a useful summary of the ways in which the novel might be seen as "new" (168–69).

4. The temptation is especially great when one wishes to "salvage" an

admirable structure which happens to be caused by, or at least expresses, beliefs now deemed deficient. See Boardman 1979.

5. See Bradbury for a useful summary of complaints about the novel, including its "mechanical or haphazard" progression, the "moral stasis" of Anne's character, and its plot as a mere "succession of delaying events" (383). In my view, these are all traces of a new, comprehensive intention.

6. Walter Anderson's essay is part of a book on Austen that has not yet been published, and I have therefore summarized his argument in my text. His is the single best elucidation of the formal questions the novel raises, and my argument, while not in basic agreement with his, owes a great deal to his analysis.

7. Maaja Stewart called my attention to the probable reason for Sir Thomas's voyage.

8. Whether a novel is "finished" or not is always problematic, as Richardson's "notes" to *Clarissa* ought to caution us. Goldsmith stated that had he "made" *The Vicar* "ever so perfect or correct," he would "not have had a shilling more" (Friedman, 8). The book's "inconsistencies," however, "cannot be taken as satisfactory evidence that Goldsmith failed to revise after the novel was finished, for in his extensive stylistic revisions for the second edition he left them unchanged" (Friedman, 8). Austen's (successful, I think) revisions of the ending of *Persuasion* do not tell us much about the state of the rest of the manuscript.

9. Another possibility, which I find less convincing, is that Austen made a fundamental error in point of view, and not, as Anderson says, in confusing Anne's knowledge with what the reader needs to know. If Anne's consciousness is what caught Austen's imagination, why not use the first person and filter everything through her? The answer, I think, is that she wanted precisely the duality she achieved: it expresses her own despair at the possibility of achieving knowledge about even simple matters, much less about happiness, while representing at the same time how "easy" such knowing ought to be, how right on one's fingertips it seems at times.

10. See Sieferman (293–95) for a discussion of the revised ending's better "answer" to Anne's question, "How was the truth to reach him?"

4 Eliot, the Reader, and Parable

1. Personal communication.

2. Some recent critics, like Cynthia Chase, have found Deronda central to the book's concerns—as how could he fail to be? I deal with Chase's deconstructive reading later in this chapter.

3. See Beaty 1960.

4. See Rader 1989 on the "loose baggy monsters" of Victorian fiction for a reading of *Middlemarch* on which much of my own analysis is based.

5. Eliot wrote to Blackwood: "Mr. Collins has my gratitude for feeling some regard towards Mr. Casaubon. . . . When I was at Oxford in May, two ladies came up to me after dinner: one said, 'How could you let Dorothea marry *that* Casaubon?'" (*Letters,* 5:441).

6. Peter K. Garrett has attempted to explain the "dialogical form" of *Deronda.* His analysis lacks any means for even suggesting why Eliot would want *these* two plots in dialogical relationship (see 167–79).

7. Eliot does not, of course, deal with the issue directly. What she does make clear is that Daniel's mother could have accomplished almost anything she wanted, including preventing Daniel from being circumcised, especially since his father died when he was still a small child. The account is in chapter 51 of the novel. Chase's main enterprise is to deconstruct the concept of causality in the novel. What she ends up demonstrating is that Eliot wasn't as worried about details as Chase is.

8. In this novel even the typical novelistic strategy of using the admiration of one character as testimony to the goodness of another is complicated by questions of gender. Given Sir Hugo's lukewarm affection for his daughters, his paternal affection for Daniel serves as a less-certain validation of Deronda's worth than, say, Parson Adam's "certification" of Joseph's innate goodness. It is difficult to say whether this ambiguity is a function of Eliot's positive intention or a consequence of the book's mixed form.

5 Innovation as Pugilism: Hemingway and the Reader after *A Farewell to Arms*

1. It is more than interesting, given the times and much of the criticism of Hemingway's "irrelevance" in the 1930s, that the hypothetical symphonic auditor's irrelevant "response" involves economics.

2. This is not to say that a represented society plays always and only a negligible part in Joyce—it is prominent on every page as a dead weight on the lives of each Dubliner—only that it need not be prominent, as it is in Fielding, Austen, Twain, Fitzgerald, and many others.

3. At the end of March 1936, Henry Payne Burton, editor of *Cosmopolitan,* came to Key West. He offered "7500 for anything the length of One Trip Across . . . down to 3,000 for the shortest ones" (*Selected Letters,* 441). Burton ended up interested in two stories: "A Budding Friendship" and "The Happy Ending." They were published later that

year as "The Snows of Kilimanjaro" and "The Short Happy Life of Francis Macomber." Hemingway mused to Gingrich: "if I sell A Budding Friendship to Cosmo they couldn't publish it before July or Aug. Then if they bought The Happy Ending that would carry into Sept. . . . the guy was down here asking for them" (*Selected Letters*, 444).

4. See his 1938 preface to *The First Forty-nine Stories*, in which he leads off his list of the stories he "liked the best" with "Macomber."

5. As Raeburn has pointed out, "The scrap with Eastman gave several reviewers" of the novel "a pretext for lecturing Hemingway on his 'well known admiration for the hairy-chested man'" (97).

6 Fiction and Ideology

1. Myra Jehlen provides a useful historical summary of the shifts in the Marxist definition of ideology, especially from "false consciousness into . . . consciousness per se," or, in Adorno's formulation, which Jehlen quotes, "Today . . . ideology means society as appearance" (7).

2. Terry Eagleton (1976) seems closer to Macherey than to Jameson: "to explain the literary work in terms of the ideological structure of which it is a part, yet which transforms it in its art . . . means grasping the literary work as a *formal* structure" (19).

3. In one interpretation of Eagleton, ideology is so in the saddle that daily life is lived not only in the midst of Machereyan deception but also social servitude. Payne and Habib, in their introduction to Eagleton's *The Significance of Theory:* "I dress in a certain way . . . I teach, write articles, go to committee meetings; I attend conferences and deliver papers. All of these activities bind me to the social orders I am serving . . . by supplying me with a reasonably satisfying and unified image of myself. . . . All of my social actions, all that I read and all that I write constitute the inescapable web of this ideology, which is in truth the Other but which I come to believe is myself" (3–4). As is often the case with such pronouncements, the reader is left wondering whether Eagleton and his interpreters are deceived like the rest of us, and if they are, what is to be made of the assertion of ideological blindness. Or is this a special instance of Macherey's distinction between the blindness of art (and life in the midst) and the "scientific analysis" available to the Marxist theorist?

Bibliography

Abrams, M. H. *Doing Things with Texts: Essays in Criticism and Critical Theory.* New York and London, 1989.

Althusser, Louis. *Philosophy and the Spontaneous Philosophy of the Scientists.* London and New York, 1990.

Aristotle. *Poetics.* Trans. Ingram Bywater. In *An Introduction to Aristotle.* Ed. Richard McKeon. New York, 1947.

Arnheim, Rudolf. *Art and Visual Perception: A Psychology of the Eye.* Berkeley and Los Angeles, 1954.

Auerbach, Nina. "O Brave New World: Evolution and Revolution in *Persuasion.*" *ELH* 39 (March 1972):112–28.

Austen, Jane. *Emma.* Ed. Ronald Blythe. Harmondsworth, Middlesex, 1966.

———. *Mansfield Park.* Ed. James Kinsley and John Lucas. Oxford, 1980.

———. *Persuasion.* Ed. R. W. Chapman. New York, 1958.

———. *Pride and Prejudice.* Ed. James Kinsley and Frank W. Bradbrook. Oxford, 1970.

———. *Sense and Sensibility.* New York, 1961.

Austen-Leigh, J. E. *A Memoir of Jane Austen.* With *Persuasion.* Ed. D. W. Harding. Harmondsworth, Middlesex, 1965.

Backscheider, Paula R. "The Genesis of *Roxana.*" *The Eighteenth Century* 27 (Fall 1986):211–229.

Baker, Carlos. *Ernest Hemingway: A Life Story.* New York, 1969.

———. *Hemingway, The Writer as Artist.* 4th ed. Princeton, 1972.

Barnett, H. G. *Innovation: The Basis of Cultural Change.* New York, 1953.

Beaty, Jerome. *"Middlemarch" from Notebook to Novel.* Urbana, 1960.

Beck, Warren. "The Shorter Happy Life of Mrs. Macomber." *Modern Fiction Studies* 1 (November 1955):28–37.

Bell, Ian. *Defoe's Fiction.* London, 1985.

Bender, John. "Prison Reform and the Sentence of Narration in *The Vicar of Wakefield.*" In *The New Eighteenth Century: Theory, Politics, English Literature.* Ed. Felicity Nussbaum and Laura Brown. New York and London, 1987.

Bloom, Harold. *The Anxiety of Influence.* New York, 1973.

———, ed. Introduction to *Charles Dickens's "Hard Times": Modern Critical Interpretations.* New York, 1987.

———, ed. *Modern Critical Views: Ernest Hemingway.* New York, 1985.

Boardman, Michael M. *Defoe and the Uses of Narrative.* New Brunswick, N.J. 1983.

———. "Defoe's Political Rhetoric and the Problem of Irony." *Tulane Studies in English* 22 (1977):87–102.

———. "Fictional Coherence and Disruption." In *Narrative Poetics.* Ed. James Phelan. Vol. 5 of *Papers in Comparative Studies* (1986–87):79–91.

———. "*One Flew Over the Cuckoo's Nest:* Rhetoric and Vision." *Journal of Narrative Technique* 9 (1979):171–83.

Booth, Wayne C. *The Rhetoric of Fiction.* Chicago, 1961.

Boswell, James. *Life of Johnson.* Ed. G. B. Hill and L. F. Powell. 6 vols. Oxford, 1934–50.

Bradbury, Malcolm. "*Persuasion* Again." *Essays in Criticism* 18 (October 1968):383–96.

Brown, Laura. *English Dramatic Form, 1660–1760: An Essay in Generic History.* New Haven, 1981.

Butler, Judith. *Gender Trouble: Feminism and the Subversion of Identity.* New York, 1990.

Carlisle, Janice. *The Sense of an Audience: Dickens, Thackeray, and George Eliot at Mid-Century.* Athens, Ga., 1981.

Carpenter, Mary Wilson. *George Eliot and the Landscape of Time.* Chapel Hill and London, 1986.

Carroll, David, ed. *George Eliot: The Critical Heritage.* New York, 1971.

———. "The Unity of *Daniel Deronda.*" *Essays in Criticism* 9 (1959):369–80.

Chapman, R. W., ed. *Jane Austen's Letters to Her Sister Cassandra and Others.* 2d ed. London, 1952.

Chase, Cynthia. "The Decomposition of the Elephants: Double-Reading *Daniel Deronda.*" *PMLA* 93 (March 1978):215–27.

Christensen, Jerome. "From Rhetoric to Corporate Populism: A Romantic Critique of the Academy in an Age of High Gossip." *Critical Inquiry* 16 (Winter 1990):438–65.

Coetzee, J. M. *Foe.* London, 1986.

Corti, Maria. *An Introduction to Literary Semiotics.* Trans. Margherita Bogat and Allen Mandelbaum. Bloomington and London, 1978.

Crane, R. S. "The Concept of Plot and the Plot of *Tom Jones*." In *Critics and Criticism.* Chicago and London, 1952.

——. *Critical and Historical Principles of Literary History.* Chicago, 1971.

——. "Ernest Hemingway: 'The Short Happy Life of Francis Macomber.'" In *The Idea of the Humanities.* Vol. 2. Chicago and London, 1967.

——. "Jane Austen: *Persuasion*." In *The Idea of the Humanities.* Vol. 2. Chicago and London, 1967.

——. *The Languages of Criticism and the Structure of Poetry.* Toronto, 1953.

Croce, Benedetto. *Guide to Aesthetics* (*Breviario di estetica* [1913]). Trans. Patrick Romanell. Indianapolis, 1965.

Daleski, H. M. *Unities: Studies in the English Novel.* Athens, Ga., 1985.

Daniels, Elizabeth A. "A Meridithian Glance at Gwendolen Harleth." In *George Eliot: A Centenary Tribute.* Ed. Gordon S. Haight and Rosemary T. VanArsdel. London, 1982.

David, Diedre. *Fictions of Resolution in Three Victorian Novels.* New York, 1981.

Defoe, Daniel. *Moll Flanders.* Ed. G. A. Starr. London, 1971.

——. *Robinson Crusoe.* Ed. J. Donald Crowley. London, 1972.

——. *Roxana.* Ed. Jane Jack. London, 1969.

Doyle, Mary Ellen. *The Sympathetic Response: George Eliot's Fictional Rhetoric.* Rutherford, N.J., and London, 1981.

Durant, David. "Roxana's Fictions." *Studies in the Novel* 13 (Fall 1981). In *Modern Critical Views: Daniel Defoe.* Ed. Harold Bloom. New York, 1987.

Eagleton, Terry. *Marxism and Literary Criticism.* Berkeley, 1976.

Eliot, George [Mary Anne Evans]. *Daniel Deronda.* Ed. Graham Handley. Oxford, 1984.

——. *The George Eliot Letters.* Ed. Gordon S. Haight. 9 vols. New Haven and London, 1954–78.

——. *Middlemarch.* Ed. David Carroll. Oxford, 1986.

Eliot, T. S. "Tradition and the Individual Talent." In *Criticism: The Major Statements.* Ed. Charles Kaplan, 474–82. New York, 1975.

Ellis, Bret Easton. *Less Than Zero.* New York, 1985.

Feingold, Richard. *Moralized Song: The Character of Augustan Lyricism.* New Brunswick, N.J., 1989.

Ferguson, Oliver. "Goldsmith as Ironist." *Studies in Philology* 81 (1984): 212–28.

Feyerabend, Paul. "Creativity: A Dangerous Myth." *Critical Inquiry* 13 (Summer 1987):700–711.

Fitzgerald, F. Scott. *The Great Gatsby.* New York, 1925.

———. *Tender is the Night.* New York, 1933.

Flynn, Carol Houlihan. *The Body in Swift and Defoe.* Cambridge, 1990.

———. "Defoe's Idea of Conduct: Ideological Fictions and Fictional Reality." In *The Ideology of Conduct: Essays on Literature and the History of Sexuality.* Ed. Nancy Armstrong and Leonard Tannenhouse. New York and London, 1987.

Friedman, Arthur. Introduction to *The Vicar of Wakefield* (1974). Quoted in Sheldon Sacks. "Novelists as Storytellers." *Modern Philology* 73 (May 1976):S106, n. 30.

Garrett, Peter K. *The Victorian Multiplot Novel.* New Haven and London, 1980.

Goldsmith, Oliver. *The Vicar of Wakefield.* Vol. 4 of *The Collected Works of Oliver Goldsmith.* Ed. Arthur Friedman. Oxford, 1966.

Gottfried, Leon. "Structure and Genre in *Daniel Deronda.*" In *The English Novel in the Nineteenth Century: Essays on the Literary Mediation of Values.* Ed. George Goodin. Urbana, 1972.

Haight, Gordon S. *George Eliot: A Biography.* New York and Oxford, 1968.

Halperin, John. *The Life of Jane Austen.* Baltimore, 1984.

Hartman, Geoffrey H. "The New Wilderness: Critics as Connoisseurs of Chaos." In *Innovation/Renovation: New Perspectives on the Humanities.* Ed. Ihab Hassan and Sally Hassan. Madison, Wisc., 1983.

Healey, George Harris. *The Letters of Daniel Defoe.* Oxford, 1955.

Hemingway, Ernest. *Death in the Afternoon.* New York, 1932.

———. *A Farewell to Arms.* New York, 1929.

———. *For Whom the Bell Tolls.* New York, 1940.

———. *In Our Time.* New York, 1925.

———. *Selected Letters.* Ed. Carlos Baker. New York, 1981.

———. *The Short Stories of Ernest Hemingway.* New York, 1938.

———. *The Snows of Kilimanjaro and Other Stories.* New York, 1936.

———. *The Sun Also Rises.* New York, 1926.

Hemingway, Leicester. *My Brother, Ernest Hemingway.* Cleveland and New York, 1962.

Holland, Robert B. "Macomber and the Critics." *Studies in Short Fiction* 5 (1968):171–78.

Hopkins, Robert H. *The True Genius of Oliver Goldsmith.* Baltimore, 1969.

Hotchner, A. E. *Ernest Hemingway: A Personal Memoir.* New York, 1966.

Howe, Irving. Introduction to *Daniel Deronda.* New York, 1979.

Hume, David. *Four Dissertations* (1757). Reprint. New York, 1970.

Hume, Robert D. "The Conclusion of Defoe's *Roxana:* Fiasco or Tour de Force?" *Eighteenth-Century Studies* 3 (1970):475–90.

Jameson, Fredric. "Modernism and Imperialism." In *Nationalism, Colonialism, and Literature.* Minneapolis, 1990.

———. *The Political Unconscious: Narrative as a Socially Symbolic Act.* Ithaca, N.Y., 1981.

Jehlen, Myra. "Introduction: Beyond Transcendence." *Ideology and Classic American Literature.* Ed. Sacvan Bercovitch and Myra Jehlen. New York, 1986.

Johnson, Samuel. "Preface to Shakespeare." In *Johnson on Shakespeare.* Ed. Arthur Sherbo. Vol. 7 of *The Yale Edition of the Works of Samuel Johnson.* New Haven and London, 1968.

Kaufmann, David. *George Eliot and Judaism: An Attempt to Appreciate "Daniel Deronda".* Trans. J. W. Ferrier (1877). Reprint. New York, 1970.

Kay, Carol. *Political Constructions: Defoe, Richardson, and Sterne in Relation to Hobbes, Hume, and Burke.* Ithaca, N.Y., and London, 1988.

Kenshur, Oscar. *Open Form and the Shape of Ideas.* Lewisburg, Pa., 1986.

Kermode, Frank. *The Genesis of Secrecy: On the Interpretation of Narrative.* Cambridge, Mass., and London, 1979.

Kesey, Ken. *One Flew Over the Cuckoo's Nest.* New York, 1962.

Koelb, Clayton. "The Story in the Image: Rhetoric and Narrative Invention." *Modern Fiction Studies* (Autumn 1987):509–21.

Leavis, F. R. Introduction to *Daniel Deronda.* New York, 1961.

Lerner, Laurence. "Unwriting Literature." *New Literary History* 22 (Summer 1991):795–815.

Lewis, D. B. Wyndham. *The World of Goya.* London, 1968.

Lynn, Kenneth. *Hemingway.* New York, 1987.

Macherey, Pierre. *A Theory of Literary Production.* Trans. Geoffrey Wall. London, 1978.

McKeon, Michael. *The Origins of the English Novel, 1660–1740.* Baltimore and London, 1987.

Meyers, Jeffrey, ed. *Hemingway: The Critical Heritage.* London, 1982.

Miller, James E., Jr., ed. *Theory of Fiction: Henry James.* Lincoln, Neb., 1972.

Molan, Ann. "Persuasion in *Persuasion.*" *Critical Review* (Australia, 1982). In *Jane Austen: Modern Critical Views.* Ed. Harold Bloom. New York, 1986.

Moore, John Robert. *Daniel Defoe: Citizen of the Modern World.* Chicago, 1858.

Morgan, Susan. *In the Meantime: Character and Perception in the Novels of Jane Austen.* Chicago, 1980.

Mukarovsky, Jan. *Aesthetic Function, Norm and Value as Social Facts.* Trans. Mark E. Suino. Ann Arbor, 1979.

New, Melvin. "Surviving the Seventies: Sterne, Collins, and Their Recent Critics." *The Eighteenth Century: Theory and Interpretation* 25 (Winter 1984):3–24.

Novak, Maximillian E. *Realism, Myth, and History in Defoe's Fiction.* Lincoln, Neb., and London, 1983.

Oldsey, Bernard. *Hemingway's Hidden Craft: The Writing of "A Farewell to Arms".* University Park, Pa., and London, 1979.

Payne, Michael, and M. A. R. Habib. Introduction to *The Significance of Theory,* by Terry Eagleton. Oxford, 1990.

Phelan, James. "Character, Progression, and the Mimetic-Didactic Distinction." *Modern Philology* 84 (February 1987):282–99.

Plimpton, George. "An Interview with Ernest Hemingway." In *Modern Critical Views: Ernest Hemingway.* Ed. Harold Bloom. New York, 1985.

Probyn, Clive T. *English Fiction of the Eighteenth Century, 1700–1789.* London and New York, 1987.

Rader, Ralph. "A Comparative Anatomy of Three Baggy Monsters." *Journal of Narrative Technique* 19 (Winter 1989):49–69.

———. "Defoe, Richardson, Joyce, and the Concept of Form in the Novel." In *Autobiography, Biography, and the Novel.* Los Angeles, 1973.

———. "The Dramatic Monologue and Related Lyric Forms." *Critical Inquiry* 3 (Fall 1976):131–51.

———. "From Richardson to Austen: 'Johnson's Rule' and the Development of the Eighteenth Century Novel of Moral Action." In *Johnson and His Age.* Ed. James Engell. Cambridge, Mass., 1984.

Raeburn, John. *Fame Became of Him: Hemingway as a Public Writer.* Bloomington, 1984.

Richetti, John. *Daniel Defoe.* Boston, 1987.

———. "The Novel and Society: The Case of Daniel Defoe." In *The Idea of the Novel in the Eighteenth Century.* Ed. Robert W. Uphaus, 47–66. East Lansing, Mich., 1988.

Richter, David H. *Fable's End.* Chicago, 1974.

Rothenberg, Albert. *The Emerging Goddess: The Creative Process in Art, Science, and Other Fields.* London and Chicago, 1979.

Sacks, Sheldon. "Clarissa and the Tragic Traditions." In *Irrationalism in the Eighteenth Century.* Ed. Harold E. Pagliaro. Cleveland, 1972.

———. *Fiction and the Shape of Belief.* Berkeley and Los Angeles, 1964.

———. "Novelists as Storytellers." *Modern Philology* 73 (May 1976):S97–S109.

Said, Edward. "The Politics of Knowledge." *Raritan* 11 (Summer 1991):17–31.

Saunders, David, and Ian Hunter. "Lessons from the 'Literary': How to Historicise Authorship." *Critical Inquiry* 17 (Spring 1991):479–509.

Showalter, English, Jr. *The Evolution of the French Novel, 1641–1782.* Princeton, 1972.

Sieferman, Sylvia. "*Persuasion:* The Motive for Metaphor." *Studies in the Novel* 11 (Fall 1979):283–301.

Spilka, Mark. "Warren Beck Revisited." *Modern Fiction Studies* 22 (1976):245–55.

Sprinker, Michael. "What Is Living and What Is Dead in Chicago Criticism." *Boundary 2* 13 (Winter–Spring 1985):189–212.

Starr, G. A. *Defoe and Spiritual Autobiography.* Princeton, 1965.

Stewart, Philip R. *Imitation and Illusion in the French Memoir-Novel, 1700–1750.* New Haven and London, 1969.

Tave, Stuart M. *The Amiable Humorist.* Chicago, 1960.

———. *Some Words of Jane Austen.* Chicago, 1973.

Todorov, Tzvetan. *The Conquest of America.* New York, 1984.

Watt, Ian. *The Rise of the Novel.* Berkeley, 1957.

Wess, Robert. "The Probable and the Marvelous in *Tom Jones. Modern Philology* 68 (August 1970):32–45.

Wiegman, Robyn. "Economies of the Body: Gendered Sites in *Robinson Crusoe* and *Roxana.*" *Criticism* 31 (Winter 1989):33–51.

Wilson, Philip E. "Affective Coherence, a Principle of Abated Action, and Meredith's *Modern Love.*" *Modern Philology* 72 (November 1974):151–71.

Wilson, Robert N. *The Writer as Social Seer.* Chapel Hill, 1979.

Woolf, Virginia. "Jane Austen." In *The Common Reader.* New York, 1925.

Index

About the Author

Michael M. Boardman is Associate Professor of English at Tulane University. He is the author of *Defoe and the Uses of Narrative.*